MEALS without SQUEALS

Child Care Feeding Guide and Cookbook
Third Edition

Christine Berman, M.P.H., R.D.
Jacki Fromer

A NOTE TO PARENTS
THIS BOOK applies as much to your own parenting and child care as it does to professional child care programs. As a bonus, you will learn about important issues facing child care providers as they plan nutrition programs. With this knowledge you can confidently interact with those who care for your children — helping them provide the good nutrition all children deserve.

Bull Publishing Company
Boulder, Colorado

Meals Without Squeals: Child Care Feeding Guide and Cookbook, THIRD EDITION
Christine Berman MPH, RD and Jacki Fromer

Bull Publishing Company
P. O. Box 1377
Boulder, Co. 80306
Phone (800) 676-2855
Fax (303) 545-6354
www.bullpub.com

ISBN 13: 978-1-933503-00-4
ISBN 10:-1-933503-00-9

Manufactured in the United States of America

Distributed in the United States by:
Publishers Group West, 1700 Fourth Street, Berkeley, CA 94710

Publisher: James Bull
Production: Dianne Nelson, Shadow Canyon Graphics
Cover Design: Lightbourne Images

Library of Congress Cataloging-in-Publication Data
Berman, Christine.
     Meals without squeals : child care feeding guide and cookbook /
  Christine Berman and Jacki Fromer.—3rd ed.
        p.   cm.
     Includes bibliographical references and indexes.
     ISBN 13: 978-1-933503-00-4
     ISBN 10: 1-933503-00-4
     1. Children—Nutrition.   2. Cookery.   I. Fromer. Jacki.
  II. Title.
  T
X361.C5B47   2006
64
9¢.3—dc21   97–29116
                    CIP

Contents

• •

PART TWO / YOUR FEEDING PROGRAM   59

Preface

• •

It has been nine years since the last edition of *Meals Without Squeals*, and much has happened in the wild, wonderful field of nutrition in the interim. There's more information available on the relationship between food and health than ever, both in the print media and on the internet. Some of this information is dependable and some falls more into the category of urban legend, but what's clear is that confusion reigns. The results of scientific studies are not always presented to laypersons in a context that's helpful, and the speed with which food manufacturers fill the shelves of our supermarkets with products meeting our perceived needs is nothing short of mind-boggling.

My goal in writing this revised edition of *Meals Without Squeals* is to offer you solid and practical advice about feeding children—advice that's based not just on reviews of research articles and official recommendations but also many years of experience in the business of feeding other people's children. There are so many food controversies swirling around—milk or no milk? Soy or no soy? High carb or low carb?—that I realized I couldn't possibly do most of them justice. A former classmate of mine, Dr. Marion Nestle, has written a book that may answer some of these questions. The name of the book is *What to Eat: An Aisle-by-Aisle Guide to Savory Food Choices and Good Eating* (North Point, 2006). Unfortunately, it's due to be released after this book goes to press, so I wasn't able to draw on her expertise in making recommendations to you. Go out and buy the book, then follow her lead—I trust her impeccably. She has written some other books I've found most illuminating, and I list them in the Resources section in the back of this book.

Let's consider a few of the significant changes in the way we look at food that have occurred in the past nine years:

The Government Released New Dietary Guidelines and MyPyramid— the "Interactive Food Guidance System." The U.S. Department of Health and Human Services (HHS) and Department of Agriculture (USDA) issued new Dietary Guidelines in 2005 that addressed more specifically than ever what a confused and increasingly overweight population needs to know about healthful eating. The new guidelines convey 9 major messages (I'll fill you in later in the book), with 23 key recommendations and 18 recommendations aimed at specific population groups. They emphasize more strongly the need to control calorie intake and be physically active in order to maintain a healthy body weight. Although the guidelines departed from previous versions by not directly addressing sugar consumption, they introduced the concept of "discretionary calories"—those calories from fat or sugar that we may be able to consume, depending upon how active we've been and whether we've made careful choices among our needed food groups. As a nutritionist, I was pleased to see more emphasis on consuming whole grains and an acknowledgement that not all fats are "bad"—though some (*trans*-fats) are.

Later the same year the USDA rolled out MyPyramid, the graphic representation of these recommendations, with guidance that at this point is most useful for consumers with internet access. There are criticisms of the Dietary Guidelines and MyPyramid that are probably valid, for example, that lobbying and politics had too much influence on their content and weakened it. But rather than focusing excessively on what's wrong with them, I can't help but feel that if people actually followed through with the recommendations instead of ignoring them or becoming discouraged and reverting to old habits, they'd be better off.

Childhood Obesity Has Been Declared an Epidemic. Ten percent of preschoolers and 16 percent of older children are now overweight, and many more are considered "at risk" for being overweight. In the past 30 years, obesity among preschoolers and adolescents has doubled; for children aged 6 – 11 it has tripled. It has been estimated that for children born in 2000, the risk of developing type 2 (adult-onset) diabetes is 30% for boys and 40% for girls at some point in their lives. African American, Latino, and Native American children who are obese and have a family history of type 2 diabetes are especially at risk. These statistics are frightening. How can we stand by and not do something about it? Type 2 diabetes is almost entirely preventable by not being overweight and being physically active.

To be sure, the rising rates of obesity have much to do with big forces at work in our society—perhaps more accurately, globally—that complicate balancing calorie intake with energy output. Family structure has changed, resulting in fewer family meals, more consumption of convenience foods and foods eaten in restaurants—thus less control over ingredients and larger portion sizes, less time to supervise children's active play, and more use of television and other electronic media. Children have less access to safe play spaces than previously. Schools are strapped financially and time-wise, and they struggle to provide healthful foods, nutrition education, and adequate opportunities for exercise. Food manufacturers aggressively market products that are high in calories and low in nutritional value. To consider all that's going on is, admittedly, daunting. But it is clear that those of us who care for children have the responsibility to find out what we can do, both collectively and in our own small ways, to help the situation—and then do it!

There Is Growing Awareness That Our Eating Habits Are Affecting, and That the Safety of Our Foods Is Affected By, the Environment. Our oceans are overfished, there's mercury in the very seafood that contains nutrients we need more of, and the demand for cheap food has degraded our environment, stripping our topsoil and polluting once pristine waters with runoff from agricultural chemicals and animal manure. The food on your average supermarket shelf may or may not contain genetically modified organisms or residues of hormones, antibiotics, or pesticides. No wonder consumers are concerned and often suspicious. And no wonder the organic segment of the food industry is growing by leaps and bounds! It's fair to say that most of us want to know what's in our food, and that we'd prefer to think that the chicken whose thigh we're eating was raised in a humane way, or that the lettuce in our salad was grown in conditions that caused no harm to the environment—or to the workers who cultivated it. After all, we do realize that this "environment" is what sustains our lives and that of future generations—and that the health of the environment and our health are inextricably linked—don't we?

The cheapest food is not necessarily the best deal, then, when we consider the health, social, and environmental implications. It's not always easy in this society to think and act for the long term, but we must. Our food dollars vote for the kind of world we want to live in and that we want our children and grandchildren to live in. Let's vote wisely.

Even with all of the recent developments in the field of nutrition, the basic dietary advice in the older editions of *Meals Without Squeals* still holds true. Eat more vegetables, fruit, and whole grains. Eat foods as close to the way Nature provides them as possible. Follow the "Division of Responsibility" (see pg....) when feeding children. Take very good care to prepare foods safely. Enjoy what you're eating and convey this enjoyment to the children in your care!

Thanks to my dear friend David Haskell—"Gardener Dave" as he's known to the children he gardens with—over the past year I have experienced growing significant amounts of my own food for the first time in 30 years. It has given me renewed appreciation for the incomparable taste of food eaten within seconds of harvest, as well as a sense of wonder at what seeds can do, given sunlight, water, and some minerals in their soil. There were moments out there among the green bean tepees and cucumber vines when I felt like "everything I need to know could be learned in this garden." Now, that may not quite be true, but there's so much to gain from growing one's own food, for adults and youngsters alike, that I strongly urge you to dig in! Unfortunately, it's outside the scope of this book to delve deeply into the subject, but there are many marvelous resources available, and I've listed some of them for you in the Resources section.

In preparing this new edition, I've altered some of the recipes to reflect changes in ingredients available since the first edition. I've deleted some recipes that don't make sense to include anymore and added others that do. You'll find a few more tools to help you organize your nutrition program and many more suggested resources. The essential content of our old volume *Teaching Children About Food* has been incorporated into this book in order to help you connect your feeding program with nutrition education. I hope it helps—feeding children well is incredibly important, and I commend your interest in doing it.

C.B.
March 2006

Acknowledgments

• •

Special thanks to Carol Larson for generosity of time and computer expertise in spite of an incredibly busy schedule, Reed Fromer and Peter White for guidance in editing and organizing, and David Fromer for those invaluable, enthusiastic pep talks.

With loving appreciation . . .

. . . to our family members for their assistance, encouragement, confidence, suggestions, patience, and love: David, Reed, and Rachel Fromer; Mitch Berman; Wynter and Mai Grant; Carol, Brad, Matthew, and Sierra Larson; Ann Spake; Jon Fromer; and Barbara and Art Storeide.

. . . to our dear friends and associates for their ideas, critiques, generosity, enthusiasm, moral support, friendship, and recipes: Barbara Abrams, DR.P.H., R.D.; Rita Abrams; Charlotte Albert; Pat Ayotte; Katy Baer, M.P.H., R.D.; Nina Baker; Judy Bartlett; Linda Bartshire; Elaine Belle; Georgia Berry; Ruth Bramell; Marek Cepietz; the staff at Community Action Marin, especially Gail Theller, Brent Triolo, Gamaliel Lopez, Mayte Lopez, and Enorina Vasquez; Doris Disbrow, DR.P.H., R.D.; Doris Fredericks, M.ED., R.D.; Elazar Freidman; Susan Gilmore of North Bay Children's Center; Diana Goodrow, Robin Goodrow, and Vanilla; Gail Hartman; Geri Henchy, M.P.H., R.D.; Bev Hoffman; Paula James; Sally Jones; Steven Kipperman; Mallory and Kevin Kopple; DeLona Kurtz; Sharon and Chiya Landry; Belinda Laucke; the staff of Marin Head Start, especially Kay Wernert and Jan Yarish; Elizabeth McGrady; Anne Milkie; Hannah Moore; Eileen Nelson; Marion Nestle, PH.D., MPH; Lisa O'Maley; Katie O'Neill, M.P.H., R.D.; Lloyd Partch; Bayla Penman; Karen Jeffrey Pertschuk, M.P.H., R.D.; Johanne Quinlan; Helen

Rossini; Zak Sabry, PH.D.; Ellyn Satter, R.D., A.C.S.W.; Max Shapiro; Jackie Shonerd; Steve Susskind; Mary Syracuse; The Earth Store; Barbara Taylor; Steve Thompson; Kate Warin; Rona Weintraub; Peter White; Barbara Zeavin; Jill Zwicky; and the Marin Child Care Council staff members: Emilie Albertoli, Lynne Arceneaux, Terry DeMartini, Teresa Leibert, Mary Moore, Susan Sanders, and Hilda Castillo Wilson. Extra-big thanks to the "garden guru," David Haskell.

. . . to the wonderful people at Bull Publishing Company for the opportunity to bring our project to fruition, and to those at Shadow Canyon Graphics for their expert and kind guidance.

. . . in loving memory and admiration of Florence Raskin, Katherine Fromer, Necia "Ida" Fromer, and Arthur Storeide.

. . . and for the continuing inspiration we receive from child care providers and teachers who are dedicated to the well-being of children.

How to Use This Book

. . . .

Meals Without Squeals is not the sort of book you must read cover to cover, like a novel. We wanted you to have a good place to find easily accessible answers to your questions about food and children, so we addressed very specific topics in one- or two-page sections.

We suggest that you start by reading the first chapter, "What You Should Know About Feeding Children," because that will introduce you to our philosophy and give you an overview of the important issues that come up when you are feeding children. Next, review the table of contents to find the topics that appear to be most useful to you. Briefly, here's what you will find in *Meals Without Squeals*:

Chapter One: What You Should Know About Feeding Children . . .
Your role in good nutrition for children and why it's so important.

Chapter Two: Feeding and Growth . . .
How to handle the feeding issues that arise as children pass through different stages of development.

Chapter Three: Planning How and What to Feed Children . . .
How to plan menus that incorporate the latest guidelines for healthful eating and how to set up mealtimes that everyone can enjoy, including you.

Chapter Four: The Recipes . . .
Dozens of easy, economical, and healthful recipes for foods children love.

Chapter Five: Sample Menus Using Our Recipes . . .

Chapter Six: Running a Ship-Shape Kitchen . . .
Tips for cutting food costs, choosing ingredients, keeping your kitchen clean and safe, and more.

Chapter Seven: Environmental Concerns . . .
How to run a feeding program that's earth-friendly.

Chapter Eight: A Basic Scheme for Nutrition Education . . .
How to integrate teaching children about food into your feeding programs.

Appendix A: Special Topics . . .
Information about subjects that often come up when you're dealing with children—for example, food allergies, dental health, or sugar.

Appendix B: Nutrition Basics . . .
A *very* short course in nutrition.

Appendix C: References . . .

Appendix D: Resources . . .
Where to go for supplies or more information.

To our children
Wynter and Mai
Reed and Rachel

PART ONE

Feeding and Children

CHAPTER ONE

What You Should Know About Feeding Children

Why a Child Feeding Guide?

Many factors determine whether we'll enjoy long and healthy lives. Some we don't have much control over, like our heredity and our environment. Others we can do something about, such as developing good eating habits, exercising regularly, managing stress, and not smoking, drinking to excess, or using drugs. Children are in a particularly vulnerable position regarding these lifestyle factors. They depend on adults to provide what they need in order to grow and be healthy, and they look to adults as role models in shaping their behaviors. We think that everyone who works with children, be they parents or caregivers, should be aware of the important connection between nutrition and children's health:

- Children need to consume the right amounts and kinds of nutrients in order to grow well; to avoid being overweight, having tooth decay, and other problems; and to have good resistance to illness.

- Children who aren't well nourished tend to have more problems in school. They are likely to be tired, inattentive, less curious, and less independent than their well-fed peers. They may also be irritable and less sociable, and in general have more behavior problems.

- During childhood, eating patterns and attitudes develop that may affect health later on. More than two-thirds of the deaths in the United States are caused by diseases that can be related to eating habits: heart disease, some cancers, hypertension, and diabetes.

- The way feeding is handled affects a child's perceptions of what to expect from the world—whether he will see it as a friendly and nurturing place or as a cold and frustrating one.

We have noticed that there is a lot of confusion among parents and caregivers about what to feed children, how to feed children, and how to teach children what they need to know in order to be healthy and happy adults. We wrote this book to make practical information about nutrition available to anyone involved in the care of children.

The Role of the Caregiver in Children's Nutrition

It's 6 P.M. on Wednesday evening. Father has just arrived home from the office. Mother is in the kitchen putting finishing touches on the evening meal. The cinnamony smell of fresh-baked apple pie permeates the air. Andy and Beth have just finished setting the table. Everyone washes up and sits down to a leisurely family meal. The phone does not ring, for everyone knows it's suppertime. The TV will not be turned on until the table has been cleared.

Sound familiar? Of course not! This scene is likely to be viewed on reruns of a 1960 family sitcom, but it's not so typical in the real-life household of today.

In our changing society, the responsibility for seeing that children are well-fed is more and more shifting from mother-in-her-traditional-role-as-homemaker to other caregivers. And in a society where 10 percent of preschoolers and 16 percent of older children are overweight and many more are at risk of becoming overweight, and where fewer than 25% of children eat the recommended 5 servings of fruits and vegetables in a day, the stakes are high. Whether meals and snacks are made on-site or brought from home, providers of child care have the opportunity, and the responsibility, to make a positive contribution to the nutritional well-being of children and to offer guidance to parents. Here is what you need to do:

- Create an environment where children feel good about food and eating.

- Help children learn to enjoy and value a variety of healthful foods.

- If you do serve meals and snacks, make sure they're consistent with the Dietary Guidelines for Americans (discussed later in this book).

- Be attentive to children with special feeding needs and with different cultural preferences.

- Protect children from such hazards as choking on food, food poisoning, and kitchen accidents.

- Establish feeding policies that reflect the beliefs and desires of the parents.

- Provide safe spaces and ample opportunity for children to be physically active.

- Provide information to parents interested in improving the eating habits of their families.

- Keep parents informed about their children's eating behaviors and alert them to nutrition-related problems that may require professional consultation.

Feeding other people's children can be intimidating, gratifying, fun, and frustrating, all at the same time. If you're new to it, it's only fair right now to give you some observations gleaned from many years of experience. Perhaps they'll fortify you for what lies ahead:

- It is well-nigh impossible to please every child in your group with everything on the menu on a given day. Don't take it personally.

- When you are trying to make changes to your menus to incorporate more healthful foods, there may be resistance from children and staff, and even a bit of pressure from parents who are worried that their children aren't eating enough. By all means listen and evaluate whether you're moving too quickly or perhaps had a recipe "flop." But if you really want to make a difference in these children's lives, you need to be confident and courageous—and persistent.

- There will most likely be food waste, especially with children who are experiencing a food for the first time. It depends on the group of course, but so many children are eating a diet comprised mostly of convenience foods, which are tasty in part because they are so high in sugar, salt, and/or fat, that it may take a while to train their palates to enjoy fresh, unprocessed foods. If it really bothers you, compost all of the leftovers you can (more on that later).

- Feeding can be messy, especially with younger children who are still developing their fine motor skills. It's important not to let this bother you too much, because some kids really need to dive right into the sensory exploration of their food in order to accept it, and they also need the fine motor practice.

- Feeding children in group settings can actually be enormously beneficial in teaching children to accept new foods. You don't even have to do the teaching; the other children do it! We've encountered lots of parents who've had the experience of seeing their children chow down foods at the lunch table in child care or preschool that they would never, ever eat at home.

Getting Serious About Our Epidemic of Overweight in Children

Read any fashion magazine, watch any movie, and you can see that our society is obsessed with thinness. And in the midst of this obsession, more and more children (and adults) are becoming overweight, or more precisely, obese. (Obesity is excessive body fat, versus overweight, in which the excessive weight could be coming from heavy bones, large muscles, or too much fat. We will use the terms somewhat interchangeably, because heavy children have certain problems regardless of where their weight comes from.)

In the past 30 years, obesity among preschoolers and adolescents has doubled; for children ages 6–11 it has tripled. The trends are truly frightening. It has been estimated that for children born in 2000, the risk of developing type 2 (adult-onset) diabetes is 30% for boys and 40% for girls at some point in their lives. However, diabetes isn't waiting until adulthood to show up; adolescents and teens are now commonly diagnosed with it, and cases are even occurring in children as young as 4 years. African American, Latino, and Native American children who are obese and have a family history of type 2 diabetes are especially at risk.

The health problems associated with obesity in adults are numerous and serious. These include:

- high blood pressure

- respiratory diseases

- gallstones

- orthopedic conditions

- diabetes

- high blood cholesterol

- coronary heart disease

- angina pectoris

- congestive heart failure

- stroke

- gout

- osteoarthritis

- sleep apnea

- complications of pregnancy

- poor female reproductive health

- bladder control problems

During childhood, it's generally believed that obesity causes more social and psychological problems than physical ones. Heavy children are likely to be viewed as unlikable or lacking in self-control. They may suffer a poor self-image and sense of failure, and they will undoubtedly feel pressure to lose weight by dieting. Obese children are also subject to developing high blood pressure, breathing problems like asthma and sleep apnea, liver problems, problems with hip development or bone growth in legs, gallstones, early puberty, and polycystic ovarian syndrome.

Whether these children will be obese as adults generally relates to how long they've been obese, how obese they are, and whether or not they are obese as adolescents, but in truth we have no way of knowing whether a particular child will be obese when she reaches adulthood. Why are some people obese? The basic reason is that they have taken in more calories than their bodies can use, so the leftovers are stored as fat. But contrary to popular belief, all obese people don't necessarily eat more than thinner ones. There are no simple explanations for why some people gain excess fat and others don't, but here are some of the possible reasons:

- heredity

- lack of physical activity and excessive time spent watching television

- the composition of the diet—overconsumption of high-calorie foods like sodas and snack foods, underconsumption of high-fiber foods like fruits, vegetables, and whole grains

- slower metabolism, which is largely inborn but may be influenced by such factors as repeated attempts at weight loss or the number of daily meals

- overeating, which may be the result of:
  – eating too fast
  – being out of touch with true feelings of hunger and satisfaction
  – eating in response to stress, boredom, or traumatic events
  – skipping meals

Preventing obesity is much simpler than treating it. If those of us who work with children are going to make any impact on the rising tide of obesity in this country, we need to commit ourselves to creating an environment—in the home, in childcare and schools, and in the community at large, where making healthful eating choices and being physically active is normal, easy, and enjoyable. That requires taking a long hard look at the way we "do business" and fine-tuning every detail to be more health-positive. In childcare settings it looks like this:

- Support mothers in breastfeeding exclusively for the first 4 to 6 months of life and continuing to breastfeed, while feeding other foods, at least through the first year.

- Provide foods that follow the Dietary Guidelines for Americans 2005 and MyPyramid, and especially, make it your mission to help children learn to enjoy fresh fruits and vegetables!

- Limit high-fat and highly sweetened foods (especially high-fructose corn syrup).

- Serve water and skim or low-fat milk (for children 2 and up) instead of fruit juice.

- Cultivate eating environments where children develop positive attitudes about eating and learn to self-regulate, that is, to listen to their bodies' messages about whether they're full or still hungry.

- Never use food as a reward or withhold food as a punishment.

- Structure at least 1 hour of active play into each day . . . even when it's raining!

- Limit television or other screen media time to no more than 2 hours of quality programming per day. Even better: no screen time.

- Help children learn to make healthy eating choices.

- Support families in developing healthy eating and physical activity habits.

When a Child is Already Overweight

Unfortunately, concerned adults sometimes use tactics with overweight children that cause more serious problems than the weight itself. Putting pressure on children about their weight can lead to:

- obsessions about food, dieting, and body image

- lowered self-esteem and an overwhelming sense of failure on the child's part

- damage to the adult-child relationship in the midst of battles over food choices, food quantities, and exercise

The most common mistake that parents and some physicians make is putting children on diets or being overly restrictive with their eating. For one thing, as mentioned earlier, not all overweight children are big eaters. Limiting their calories may interfere with normal growth and development. Furthermore, children who aren't allowed to eat until they feel satisfied, or to eat the foods that they enjoy, may feel deprived and singled out, and they tend to become obsessed with eating. And when adults exert too much control over what children eat, the children never learn to manage eating for themselves.

What You Can Do to Help the Overweight Child

- **Foster a Positive Self-Image**
  Let him know he's lovable and has something valuable to contribute, no matter how his body turns out.

- **Encourage Lots of Physical Activity**
  Provide plenty of opportunities for active play and set limits on sedentary activities like watching television, for everyone, not just the overweight child.

- **Promote Healthful Eating Habits**
  Serve healthful foods at regular times and let the child make his own decisions regarding eating.

- **Attend to Emotional Health**
  If the child has unmet emotional needs or is dealing with trauma, make sure he gets the help he requires.

- **Be a Good Role Model**
  Eat healthfully without falling into the "dieting trap," stay active, and value yourself.

Overweight children are victims of other strong-arm tactics as well. One mother told us of the humiliation her daughter felt when her upper-arm fatfold measurements were read aloud to her sixth-grade class. And this very conscientious young student received a failing grade in her gym class because she couldn't quite run a mile. Can you imagine how this girl might feel about her body and exercise when she grows up . . . thanks to these early experiences? Forcing the exercise issue can be just as counterproductive as restricting food intake.

Helping an overweight child, as with preventing a child from becoming overweight, involves setting up the best situation you can for nurturing, feeding, and active play and trusting the child to make her own decisions within that structure.

How You Feed Is As Important As *What* You Feed

You will find that we spend as much time talking about the "hows" of feeding as we do the "whats." This is because we believe that a lot of unhappiness related to food can be prevented by helping children develop a healthy relationship with food, right from the start.

Look at your own feelings about food. Do you feel like you must finish everything on your plate even if you're full already? Do you feel vague pangs of guilt about getting great enjoyment out of eating? Do you find yourself dreading having to eat? These feelings started somewhere, and for most people their origins are in childhood.

Food figures prominently in our lives from day one on, so it's important to feel positive about it and to use it appropriately. Additionally, conflicts over food can do great damage to your relationship with a child, and that's the last thing you want!

Ellyn Satter, in her wonderful books *Child of Mine* and *How to Get Your Kid to Eat . . . But Not Too Much*, describes the "division of responsibility in feeding"* that is central to establishing healthy feelings toward eating. Engrave this on your brain right now! It is one of the most important feeding concepts you will ever learn.

- **Parents** (and caregivers) are responsible for what is presented to eat and the manner in which it is presented.

- **Children** are responsible for how much and even whether they eat.

The idea that you don't have to force-feed a finicky eater or restrain a heavy eater may be shocking at first, but it works.

Now, don't get the idea that we're advocating letting children eat *whatever* they want. Contrary to an old belief, children will not intuitively eat what is good for them, given the choice between a plate of gooey doughnuts and a raw vegetable platter. (The idea that they might was a mis-interpretation of some experiments a woman named Clara Davis performed in the 1930s. She confined several orphaned children to a hospital ward for long periods of time and found that they all grew beautifully when allowed to eat as much as they wanted of the foods offered to them, even when they didn't appear to be consuming a "balanced diet." The hitch is, the foods the children were offered were all natural, nutrient-dense foods like plain meats, organ meats, eggs, milk, whole grains, vegetables, fruit, and bone marrow—no heavily sweetened cereals, cookies, or soda pop. Even Miss Davis emphasized the importance of offering nutritious, natural foods to children.)

Of course, you will want to take into consideration the food preferences of your children when planning your menus, but it will be up to you to

---

* Source: Satter, Ellyn. *How to Get Your Kid to Eat . . . But Not Too much*. Boulder, Colo.: Bull Publishing, 1988.

determine exactly what the choices will be and when they will be offered. The idea is to set it up so that no matter what a child eats from your offerings, he can't go wrong. Then you've done your job, and you can let the children take it from there. Depending on their age or level of development, you may have to help children with their eating. We'll talk about age-specific issues in their appropriate sections later on.

What Every Child Should Learn About Food and Eating

- When he is hungry, that need will be met.

- His own food preferences will be respected.

- Eating is an enjoyable activity.

- There are ways to deal with uncomfortable feelings, besides eating.

- Our food choices affect our well-being.

- People in different cultures, and families within those cultures, have different ways of eating and different ways of celebrating special occasions with food.

- Food is made available through the efforts of many members of the community.

- To eat, we use up resources, and we create waste that needs to be dealt with responsibly.

The first four concepts are crucial in the development of a child's emotional relationship with food, and the last four in his physical and social relationship with food. Review them often—together they make up the framework for all of the discussions of child feeding and nutrition education in this book.

Children will learn these very important concepts from *you*. How you handle feeding them, how they see you relate to food and eating, the exposure you give them to the world's diversity of food habits, how you dispose of food packaging—all will send clear messages to impressionable young minds.

Children learn that their hunger needs will be met when:

- You feed infants "on demand."
- You set up regular meal and snack times for the older children.
- You help their families find resources for food if they're having problems with it.

Children learn their food preferences will be respected when:

- You let them choose what and how much to eat of what you've offered.
- You ask them what they'd like when you're planning your menus.

Children learn that eating is enjoyable when:

- You make sure that the mealtime environment is pleasant.
- You enforce a code of respectful behavior at the table.
- You make an effort to serve foods they enjoy.
- They see you enjoying eating.

Children learn to deal with feelings in other ways besides overeating when:

- You encourage them to verbalize their feelings.
- You resist the temptation to comfort them with cookies or candy.
- They don't see you running to the cookie jar when you're upset.

Children learn that our food choices affect our well-being when:

- They see you eating with the intention of providing proper nourishment for your body, and you describe to them the benefits of good nutrition.

Children learn to appreciate the foodways of other cultures when:

- You plan meals that have cultural diversity.

- You ask parents to contribute recipes from their own heritage or have potluck dinners with each family contributing a dish that relates to their background.

- You have books and posters that show how people in other cultures eat.

Children learn about the people who provide food for them when:

- They go on field trips to markets, farms, dairies, and bakeries.

- They spend time in home, child care, or school kitchens.

Children learn to be responsible consumers when:

- They see you making an effort to cut down on waste (food or packaging).

- They participate in gardening and get a feel for the energy that's expended to produce food.

- They help with recycling projects.

When Concern About Children's Eating Goes Awry

Many caregivers and parents ask what they should do when an overweight child wants second helpings—or thirds—at lunch. Likewise, adults may be shocked to see their "sugar free" children stuff themselves when they encounter plattersful of sugary treats at parties.

It's not easy to artfully walk the line between offering the foods you know are good for children—in the amounts you feel are appropriate—and being overly restrictive. The problem with being too restrictive is that it often backfires. For example, research has shown that children whose parents most limit their consumption of certain foods will eat more of those very same foods in a laboratory setting when their parents aren't there.

What's the solution? First, it's crucial to remember that as the adult, one of your tasks in the feeding relationship is to decide what foods will be offered to the children in your care. You can determine whatever limits make the most sense to you, but it's wise to plan for a little flexibility as well. There is no good reason why a healthy, active child can't have ice cream or cookies or cake every now and then, and to offer them occasionally may help remove the attraction of the "forbidden fruit." Just be careful that "now and then" stays that way; for example, a small ice-cream cone on Sunday afternoons or healthier versions of cookies for snack once or twice a month (in large classrooms where sugar consumption could go through the roof due to frequent birthday celebrations, perhaps a monthly party with cookies, cupcakes, or cake would work best).

We know that portion sizes are an issue, especially in our "supersized" food culture. Very young children are generally pretty capable of regulating their food intake, especially if the adults around them haven't interfered with them too much. Older children may have more trouble due to being "trained" to be out of touch with their bodies' hunger cues or because of the mindless eating that can go along with watching television or hanging out with friends. Overweight children should be treated no differently at the meal table than children of normal weight. All children should be offered a variety of healthful foods and be free to choose what and how much they want to eat, being considerate of the needs of their fellow diners, of course. Meanwhile, there are some "tricks of the trade" borrowed from the food service industry that can help you gently guide portion sizes, without being too interfering.

How to Control Portion Sizes, Without Being Controlling

- Prepare smaller amounts of the foods children should eat less of—those higher in fat or sugar. There's no point in fretting over an overweight child taking thirds of pizza or macaroni and cheese if you've put enough on the table to feed an army.

- Prepare larger amounts of the foods you'd like the children to eat more of, especially fresh fruits and vegetables. When the more highly desirable foods (usually the meat-based or higher fat ones) are gone, you can smile and say, "But look! We have lots of yummy broccoli trees left! What are you waiting for, dinosaurs?"

- Serve foods that should be eaten in small amounts with small utensils and serving pieces. If you give a child a pitcher full of maple syrup, you can expect to see a big puddle of syrup with a pancake in the middle. If you give the child a squeeze bottle with a small hole, he will lose interest before he gets too much syrup. Restaurant supply stores—which are frequently open to the public—and stores like the Container Store often have a vast array of possibilities for serving pieces. Look for shakers with small holes and squeeze bottles that allow you to cut the opening to the desired size. Demitasse spoons are fun, too!

- Avoid overdoing "liquid calories" in the form of juice or other sweetened beverages by offering milk at breakfast, lunch, and the occasional snack, and water at other times.

Establishing a Nutrition Philosophy Statement and Related Policies for Your Setting

We urge you to spend some time considering what you feel about the importance of nutrition for children and what your commitment to it will be in your program. You may want to do this in a group, with interested parents or staffpersons. When you are done, you should have a nutrition philosophy statement unique and relevant to your setting. Here's an example of what one might look like:

> We believe that good nutrition is a basic right of every child. Our nutrition policies reflect our commitment to ensure that the children's nutritional needs are met in a positive, nurturing manner with respect for individual needs and preferences of the children and their families.

Once you have settled on a nutrition philosophy, you have a guide that will help you determine how you will handle food and nutrition issues. Next, you will find it very useful to have some written policies as well. These policies will ensure that parents and/or staff members know what to expect, or what their responsibilities are, in certain situations related to nutrition. There are many such situations, including:

- Standards for menus and the types of foods that will be served (meal patterns, organic foods, foods without added sugars).

- Meal schedules and routines (who will eat with the children, what will be done about reluctant or slow eaters, expected mealtime behavior).

- Creating a nurturing environment regarding food and body image (division of responsibility in feeding, body acceptance).

- Infant feeding (how breastfeeding will be supported, transport and storage of breast milk, who will provide formula, how feeding will be done and by whom, introduction of new foods).

- Allergies and special meal requests (how substitutions will be handled, whether families will be responsible for providing special foods, written feeding and emergency plans).

- Foods brought from home (if and what is allowed, food safety guidelines).

- Celebrations (what kinds of foods will be allowed at holiday or birthday celebrations).

- Nutrition education for the children, families, and staff (healthy foods used in cooking activities, content for staff training).

- Daily goals for physical activity.

A sample policy is included at the end of this section that may be helpful as a template in writing up your own.

How Parents Can Be Involved in Child Care or School Nutrition Programs: A Baker's Dozen

Everyone benefits when parents are able to contribute some of their time and ideas to the nutrition component in a child care or school setting. What can they do? Well, here are a few ideas:

- Help to establish or update statements of philosophy or policies.

- Participate in planning the menus (within established guidelines).

- Take turns cooking lunch.

- Contribute recipes for foods their children particularly like.

- Act as chaperones for nutrition-related field trips.

- Work with groups of children on cooking projects.

- Make materials for nutrition learning activities.

- Collect appropriate food packages and other props to be used in role-playing activities.

- Be the supervising adults at meal tables.

- Put together bulletin boards or newsletters for other parents with feeding tips, recipes, and other items of nutrition interest.

- Organize and carry out tasks in your children's gardens or recycling and composting program.

- Engage the children in physical activity—long walks, yoga, dancing, bicycle "obstacle" courses.

- Confer with caregivers or teachers about feeding problems.

Steps to Take Before You Start Feeding Other People's Children

To be successful in promoting good nutrition among the children in your care requires that you plan ahead. We strongly suggest that before you begin to care for other people's children, you:

- Learn about the basic nutritional needs of children in the age groups you will be serving.

- Decide which meals, if any, you are going to provide.

- Decide what your policies will be about which foods, if any, parents are to provide; about what will be done in the case of children with allergies or other special feeding needs; and about what will be served at birthday parties or other celebrations.

- Call your local Child and Adult Care Food Program (CACFP) sponsor and investigate signing up for the program.

- Practice planning menus that meet meal pattern guidelines required by the CACFP or licensing authorities, even if you aren't required to do so by a program or regulatory agency. These are good guidelines for everyone!

- Investigate money-saving sources of food and kitchen supplies in your area. (You may get better prices by linking up with other child-care providers to purchase from wholesalers or in large quantities.)

- Make sure your kitchen meets standards for safety and sanitation if your local health department has special requirements; otherwise, review the section on food safety in this book, and use the "Checklist for a Kid-Ready Kitchen" and the "Food Safety and Sanitation Mini-Inspection."

- Check your feeding equipment to make sure it's safe and user friendly.

- Plan for gathering information about each child's special dietary needs, feeding problems, cultural food patterns, and holiday customs when he or she is enrolled. We have included a form in this book, or you may prefer to design one of your own.

- Develop a resource file and list of important phone numbers. (Appendix D in the back of this book may help.)

- Learn how to perform the Heimlich Maneuver.

- Plan how you will teach the children about nutrition. Look over your books and posters to make sure they give appropriate messages about food; put together a kit of equipment for cooking activities, including some children's cookbooks; find out what resources are available in your community for field trips (farmer's markets, bakeries, cheese factories, recycling centers, and so on); and ideally, plan a garden!

A Sample Feeding Policy

Policy Regarding Special Dietary Requests

Community Action Marin's Child and Adult Care Food Program and Central Kitchen will honor families' requests that certain foods not be served to a child for reasons of religious, cultural, or health belief, for example, vegetarianism.

If a child has a food allergy, intolerance, or medically necessary food restriction, the classroom staff must take precautions to ensure that the child does not eat the offending food. A note from the doctor or nurse practitioner must be on file attesting to the food restriction, and, if possible, suggesting substitute foods.

In all cases of food restriction, a Feeding Plan for Children with Special Nutrition Needs will be completed by the parent, caregiver, nutritionist, and if necessary, the child's health provider. This plan will spell out expected activities and who will be responsible for carrying them out. One copy of the plan will remain in the child's file and one copy will be given to the parent.

Unless it has been determined that the food service will not be able to adequately accommodate the child's needs, parents are requested not send special foods to school. Although elaborate meal preparation will not be possible, the food service will make every effort to supply acceptable substitute meals for the child. Teachers will support the child in developing responsibility for his or her food restrictions and make eating as enjoyable as possible. If a child simply does not like a certain food or group of foods, parents can be assured that classroom staff will never force children to eat foods they do not wish to eat.

Rationale:

Children with food restrictions need to be treated with respect and support; they must learn how to recognize foods they should not be eating and feel good about mealtimes in spite of the fact they may not get to eat what their friends eat. In the case of allergies, possibly dangerous reactions could occur if a child was exposed to a food to which he or she was allergic. Other children simply suffer poorer health because of reactions to foods. These problems must be avoided, and at the same time certain meal pattern requirements for the Child and Adult Care Food Program must be met, so substitute foods will be offered. The classroom staff, nutritionist, and food service will work together, with the family, to meet the needs of the child with food restrictions.

Feeding Plan for Childen
With Special Nutrition Needs

_____ **Child and Adult Care Food Program**

Child's Name _____   ❐ Food restriction:_____

Site: _____   ❐ Developmental delays

Date: _____   ❐ Other:_____

Background Information and Description of Tasks	Person(s) Responsible
Goals for child specifically related to dietary intake, self-feeding skills, or other:	
Describe necessary modifications in *types* of foods to be offered:	
Describe necessary modifications in *texture* of foods to be offered:	
Describe specialized feeding equipment or routines to be used:	
If parents will be bringing food from home, describe: (1) Expected contribution to food needs of child:	
(2) System to ensure that food is *safely* transported from home and stored in center:	

Signed:

_____   _____
Parent   Date   Caregiver or Center Director   Date

_____   _____
CACFP Nutritionist   Date   Health Provider (MD, RN, PT, OT, etc.)   Date

CHAPTER TWO

• •

Feeding and Growth

Feeding children well is both a science and an art. The science requires understanding the nutritional needs of children at each stage of their growth. This understanding is the basis of decisions you must make about what kinds of foods to offer, what equipment to buy, and what kinds of feeding structures to set up. The art of feeding children involves being sensitive to their responses to foods or your feeding methods and responding appropriately—maintaining a robust sense of humor, creating a spirit of adventure, and keeping respect and kindness ahead of everything else on your agenda. You will certainly enjoy feeding children more when you have refined the "art" of it, and the chances are they will eat better, too.

Growth and the Nutritional Needs of Infants

An infant generally will gain 1 ounce per day (about 2 pounds per month) during her first 5 months, and a half ounce per day (1 pound per month) during the remainder of her first year. By 4 to 5 months, a baby generally will double his birth weight, and by 1 year, he will triple it. The average baby grows in length by 50% during the first year (that means that an infant who was 20 inches long at birth will be 30 inches long at 1 year).

Largely because of this rapid growth, infants have a greater need for calories, for each pound of body weight, than adults do.

- Good nutrition is extremely important during this time, not just for general bodily growth, but for the infant's brain as well. The growth of the brain begins prior to birth, continues at a rapid pace into the child's second year, and is essentially complete by age 6. In some cases, but not always, the brain can recover from the effects of poor nutrition if a good diet and stimulating environment are provided later.

- In the first months of life, a baby can only swallow liquids and has an immature digestive system that cannot handle the same foods older children can. *Breast milk or iron-fortified formula provides for essentially all of an infant's nutritional needs during the first 4 to 6 months of life.*

- Infants have small stomach capacities and must eat more frequently than adults or older children. They should be fed "on demand," that is, when they indicate that they're hungry. You can expect some variability in eating patterns; a baby may be able to wait 4 hours for one feeding and then be hungry again 2 hours later.

- Babies usually go through what doctors call "hungry periods." A common time for one of these periods is between 14 and 28 days of age. Follow the baby's lead . . . if he's hungry more often than usual, feed him! He's probably getting ready for a growth spurt.

- Breast milk or formula generally provides enough water for a healthy young infant. Offer extra water *only* if directed to do so by the child's doctor. Once an infant starts eating solid foods, especially protein-rich foods like meats or egg yolks, she will need extra water to help her kidneys eliminate the waste products. Keep in mind that babies sometimes cry because of thirst, not just hunger.

    But never try to give an infant extra water by diluting her formula. And don't give a bottle of water as a pacifier; too much water can be as dangerous as too little.

- Iron deficiency is one of the biggest nutritional problems among young children (read about it in the section on anemia and iron deficiency, pages 000–000 in Appendix A, later in this book). The most critical time for making sure that a child has adequate iron intake is during the first year. The child will be building up a large blood supply in pace with her rapid growth. Children who do not consume adequate iron at this time are at greater risk for iron deficiency anemia during the toddler and pre-school years.

Different Ages, Different Stages . . . Infants

Stages of Infant Development	Related Nutritional Considerations
1. She is attached to her primary caregivers.	1. She needs stable care, and she may refuse to accept feeding from strangers.
2. She will be developing a sense of trust about the world.	2. She is dependent on caregivers for her nourishment. She should be fed when she's hungry and allowed to stop eating when she's full. Weaning (from breast or bottle) should be a gradual process.
3. She uses her mouth to explore her environment.	3. She needs to be protected from hazards associated with choking and from poisonous substances.
4. She will be starting to view herself as a separate person. She needs to feel a sense of control over her environment.	4. She should be allowed to set the pace in feeding. She may refuse food in an attempt to get some sort of response from her caregivers.

How Child Care Providers Can Support Breastfeeding Moms

Because breastfeeding offers an infant so many advantages—just the right balance of nutrients, immune factors, and a special relationship—it is the recommended method of feeding infants today. Many mothers face a challenge: they must return to work but would still like to be able to nurse their babies. There are several ways to manage breastfeeding and child care: an infant can be given breast milk in a bottle; or the mother can nurse the baby in the child care setting during breaks from work; or the baby can be fed formula while in child care and breastfed at home. Make a plan with each breastfeeding mother to let her know how you will support her breastfeeding for as long as possible.

If the mother will be nursing in the child care setting:

- Don't feed the baby for 1 to 1½ hours before her mother is due to arrive, so that she will be hungry enough to nurse and keep up her mother's milk supply. Of course, you and the mother will need to have a clear understanding that if for some reason she is late, you will feed the baby as necessary to prevent having a frantically hungry infant on your hands.

- Offer the mother a comfortable chair in a cozy place for nursing.

If you will be feeding the baby breast milk from a bottle, keep the milk safe:

- Ask the mother to transport the milk in a cooler or insulated bag with an ice pack.

- You can store breast milk in the refrigerator for 5 days or in the freezer for no more than 3-6 months after it has been expressed.

- Expressed milk should be stored in sterilized bottles or disposable plastic nursing bags and clearly marked with the infant's name and date expressed.

- Do not allow the milk to sit at room temperature; take it from the refrigerator or freezer right before you use it.

- Thaw the milk, if frozen, by running it under cool, then very warm, water. Shake gently to mix (breast milk separates during storage).

  Do not warm breast milk in a microwave oven! To do so may destroy some of its antiinfective properties.

- Once breast milk has thawed, do not refreeze it.

- Discard unused portions after one hour.

Formulas for the First Year

Young babies are only equipped to swallow, digest, and obtain proper nourishment from milk. Even after infants are adept at eating solid foods, milk continues to be an important source of nutrients. Breast milk is the ideal first food for infants, but not all mothers want to breastfeed or have favorable circumstances for doing so.

Throughout a large part of human history, animal milks have been used as substitutes for mother's milk. Cow's milk has been used most frequently, but goats, sheep, donkeys, horses, camels, pigs, deer, reindeer, and even dogs have provided milk for human babies! It has been only recently, however, that substitute milks, or formulas, have come close to duplicating the nutritive qualities of breast milk. Thanks to the wonders of modern technology, there are now three major types of commercially prepared formulas that meet the specific needs of infants:

Modified Cow's Milk Formulas

(Similac®, Enfamil®, Good Start®). Most babies who aren't breastfed get these formulas. The milk proteins have been altered to be more digestible, and vegetable oils provide the fat calories. Lactose is added to bring the carbohydrate levels up to that of human milk. Vitamins, minerals, and some other nutrients are added as well. These formulas are made with or without iron; iron-fortified formula is recommended.

Soy Formulas

(ProSobee®, Isomil®, Good Start Essentials Soy®). These formulas are sometimes used for infants with allergies to cow's milk or infants who are sensitive to lactose after a bout with diarrhea (the carbohydrate in these formulas comes from sucrose or corn syrup).

Hypoallergenic Formulas

(Nutramigen®, Alimentum®, Pregestimil®). Because some babies can tolerate neither cow's milk nor soy milk, another variety of formula is available. These protein hydrolysate ("predigested") formulas may not smell or taste very good, and they are expensive, but for some infants they are the only option.

Whole cow's milk is absolutely inappropriate as a food for young infants. It is too high in protein and soluble salts, and too low in iron and vitamin C. It also can cause small amounts of gastrointestinal bleeding. The American Academy of Pediatrics' latest position is that using breast milk or iron-fortified formula for the first 12 months of life, along with age-appropriate solid foods, best provides balanced nutrition for infants.

Reduced-fat (2%), low-fat (1%), and skim milk should not be given to children under the age of 2. They are proportionately too low in fat and too high in protein to provide adequate nourishment for babies. Infants also should not be given nondairy creamers or imitation milks. Soy milk, rice milk, oat milk, nut milks, and other milk substitutes, even when fortified with some vitamins and calcium, do not have the full range of nutrients necessary to make them acceptable substitutes for breast milk or formula.

Some commercial "weaning formulas" have appeared on the market recently. They give the impression that they are somehow advantageous for older babies, but in reality, they aren't. They aren't harmful, but don't feel pressured to buy them.

How to Prepare a Baby's Bottle

Select the Right Feeding

- You should give a baby only formula, breast milk, and water from a bottle. Juices, cereals, and other solid foods or sweetened liquids do not belong in bottles.

- If you are using formula, get the iron-fortified variety. Babies need the iron, and contrary to popular belief, these formulas are no more likely to cause tummy upset than the varieties without iron.

- If you will be using concentrated liquid or powdered formula, read the directions and measure carefully. It can be very dangerous for a baby to receive formula with too much or too little water in it.

- Check the expiration date on the container of formula, and reject cans that are bulging, badly dented, or rusty.

Make Sure Everything Is Clean

- Wash your hands before preparing bottles.

- For babies up to 3 months of age, boil the water you will be using to mix the formula for 5 minutes.

- Use clean bottles:
  - Wash the bottles, nipples, rings, and caps in hot, soapy water, using a brush to scrub all the nooks and crannies. Rinse in hot water, and boil the bottles, nipples, caps, and rings for 5 minutes. Or, after soaking to loosen dried-on formula, run them through the dishwasher.
  - If you will be preparing fresh bottles for each feeding, let the clean equipment air-dry, then store it covered in a clean place.

- Wipe the top of the formula can with a clean, damp towel before you open it.

- Add formula for one feeding to each bottle, put the clean nipple in (upside down and with a cap on top if you'll be storing the bottle), and screw the ring on.

- Store prepared bottles for no more than 24 hours in the refrigerator; an open can of formula should be covered and used within 48 hours.

Prepare the Bottle for Feeding Time

- Some babies will take a cold bottle; if you are going to warm the bottle, do it right before giving it to the baby.

- *Never heat a bottle in a microwave oven.* You can set the bottle in a bowl of warm water, hold it under warm running water from the faucet, or use a bottle-warming appliance.

- If you use a crockpot for warming bottles, make sure that the temperature of the water does not exceed 120°F. Leave the bottle in the water for no more than 5 minutes.

- Before feeding the bottle to a baby, shake the formula or milk gently to mix it, and sprinkle a little onto your wrist to test its temperature.

How to Give a Bottle to a Baby

Feeding a bottle to a baby may seem like a simple task. Don't you just warm it up, stick the nipple in the baby's mouth, and stop when the milk is gone?

Actually, bottlefeeding doesn't always go so smoothly. Some babies are willing to go along with whatever happens; others may fuss, spit up a lot, or drink very little and be hungry again in an hour. When you are feeding a baby, remember that it is important, even at this early stage, for the child to feel relaxed and happy about eating. He will need to do this in order to be able to eat what he needs, as well as to begin a comfortable lifelong relationship with food. It is very easy to think of feeding as the process of making a baby drink a certain number of ounces of formula at a certain time. But what a baby really needs is to have his hunger satisfied when he feels it, and to experience the security of your love at the same time.

- *Feed an infant when she is hungry,* not because the clock says to. Some babies have characteristic cries or wiggles that let you know they're ready to eat; others may be fussier in general, and it may be harder to figure out what these babies want. It's worth checking to see if a baby has a wet diaper, needs to be burped, or just wants company. Once you've explored these possibilities, if she's still fussing, try feeding her.

- Gently get the baby settled down and comfortable for feeding.

- *Always hold a baby when giving a bottle.*
  - Hold his head higher than the rest of his body, so the milk doesn't flow into his inner ear and cause an infection.
  - Tip the bottle so milk fills the nipple and air doesn't get in.

- Midway through the feeding, switch sides as a breastfeeding mother would.

- Wait for the baby to stop eating before you try to burp her. Then pat or rub her back gently while she rests on your shoulder or sits, supported with your other hand, on your lap.

- Avoid too many disruptions while you're feeding. Babies can get distracted or upset by a lot of burping, wiping, bouncing around, jiggling, and changing of positions.

- Pay attention to messages from the baby that he's full. He may:
  - Close his lips
  - Stop sucking
  - Spit out the nipple
  - Turn his head away
  - Cover his mouth with his hands
  - Cry
  - Bite the nipple

  Sometimes a baby will pause a bit (we all do, don't we?). Maybe he just needs a breather. Offer him the nipple again, but if he refuses it, he's probably had enough.

- Resist the temptation to make a baby finish the little bit of formula left in a bottle. Assume she knows her needs better than you do, and discard what's left. Rinse out the bottle with cool water to make cleaning easier later on.

When Should a Baby Start Eating Solid Foods?

Breast milk or iron-fortified formula (perhaps with vitamin or mineral supplementation prescribed by a doctor) gives an infant all of the nutrients he needs for the first 4 to 6 months of life.

Some parents and caregivers want babies to eat solid foods as soon as possible. They may believe (mistakenly) that solid foods help young babies sleep through the night, or they may want to prove that their children are truly "advanced." Other parents or caregivers may wait too long to introduce foods with new textures to babies. A time will come when a baby needs the nutrients and the challenges that solids provide; meanwhile, there are good reasons to wait until the infant is developmentally ready to accept them:

- Babies can choke on foods they can't swallow easily.

- Some foods are difficult for young infants to digest.

- Babies can develop food allergies when they're exposed to certain foods too early.

- When babies start eating solid foods, they cut back on breast milk or formula, which is their ideal source of nutrients for the first 4 to 6 months.

Suppose a baby is 5½ months old and you're wondering if it's time for her to try some infant cereal. How will you know she's ready? In general, she should be able to:

- Hold her neck steady and sit with support.

- Draw in her lower lip when a spoon is removed from her mouth.

- Keep food in her mouth and swallow it.

- Open her mouth when she sees food coming.

- Other signs that a baby may be ready for solids are that she has doubled her birth weight (and weighs 13 pounds or more) and that she is hungry after 8-10 breastfeedings or 32 ounces of formula in a day.

It is very important that parents and child care providers communicate with each other and agree on their approach to this transitional time. You need to discuss what is to be introduced as well as when to start. Many parents want to be the first to experience these developmental changes with their babies.

A Solid Food Itinerary for Baby's First Year

The solid foods that you offer a baby will give her three basic things: needed nutrients, exposure to new tastes, and the opportunity to develop her eating skills while dealing with new textures. Hopefully by the end of her first year, she will be feeding herself soft table food and drinking from a cup. During the transition from exclusive nipple feeding to a more adult eating pattern, she will become accustomed to a wide range of flavors and textures in a relatively short time. It's really quite an accomplishment!

We agree with child-feeding expert Ellyn Satter, who asserts that the best way to get through this time is to start solids late and move quickly into table foods. We recommend that you read *Child of Mine: Feeding with Love and Good Sense* for the finer details of feeding infants. Meanwhile, we've adapted recommendations from her book and from the recently published *Start Healthy Feeding Guidelines for Infants and Toddlers* (American Dietetic Association and Gerber Products Company). You may be surprised at some of the recommendations, because they fly in the face of advice that has been passed down to many of us over the years—advice that was never really grounded in good scientific research.

Age: About 6 months
Nutritional needs: Iron, zinc, vitamin C
Physical skills: Sits with support
Eating skills to develop: Swallowing smooth, semisolid foods
New foods: Iron-fortified infant cereal, pureed meats, pureed vegetables and fruits

Start with any single-ingredient iron-fortified infant cereal and mix it with breast milk, formula, or water. A tablespoon of cereal mixed with 4 tablespoons of liquid may be the right consistency to start, but experiment to see how the baby can best accept it. Feed the same variety of cereal for 2 to 4 days, observing for any reaction before moving on to the next variety.

Common reactions are hives, rashes, vomiting, diarrhea, coughing, or excessive gas.

We don't recommend that you give an infant regular oatmeal or other adult cereals, because they don't have enough available iron. And don't buy jars of fruit mixed with cereal; it's hard to tell how much cereal is in them. Please, never add sugar or other sweeteners to a baby's cereal. He doesn't know that cereal is supposed to taste sweet, and what he doesn't know will be good for him!

After the baby has become accustomed to eating pureed foods from a spoon, you can begin to introduce single-ingredient vegetables, fruits, and meats as well. Again, feed the same variety for 2 to 4 days in a row, watching for any adverse reactions, before moving on to the next variety. It doesn't really matter whether you introduce fruits or vegetables first. Be patient but persistent—it can take 10 to 15 tries before a baby will readily accept a new food.

While mashed, ripe bananas had often been recommended as a first fruit for babies, they aren't good sources of vitamin C. Be sure to try vegetables and fruits like sweet potatoes, squash, mangoes, apricots, peaches, spinach, carrots, purple plums, blueberries, strawberries, broccoli, cauliflower, green beans, peas, cantaloupe, kiwis, pears, and potatoes. These should be soft or soft-cooked and pureed in a blender or baby food grinder with the skins and seeds removed at first. Avoid canned vegetables, which are often high in sodium, and canned or frozen fruits with added sugar. Commercial baby fruits are fortified with vitamin C and may be a convenient option for you. The only problem with them is that they are so smooth and thin that they don't challenge a baby to learn about new textures. They also don't have the taste of fresh foods.

The idea with solid foods at this age is not to replace breast- or formula-feeding but to complement it and to give the infant some experience with tastes and textures. This will lay the foundation for the next steps.

Age: 6 to 8 months
Physical skills: Sits independently
Eating skills to develop: Swallowing thicker purees, raking food toward self with fist, transferring food from one hand to the other, drinking from cup held by feeder
New foods: Thicker pureed baby foods, soft mashed foods without lumps, 100% juice

As baby gets older, she'll be able to take on the challenge of thicker foods with more texture. You can also let her experience new flavor combinations by combining foods that you know she can tolerate.

Portion sizes will still be small at this stage, but by the end of the first year a baby should be eating about ¼ cup each of five different fruits and vegetables every day.

Age: 7 to 10 months
Physical skills: Crawls
Eating skills to develop: Mashing food using tongue and jaw, feeding self finger foods, holding small foods between thumb and forefinger, holding cup
New foods: Modified table foods—round or soft mashed foods with noticeable lumps, crunchy foods that dissolve such as baby crackers and dry cereals, grated cheese, yogurt, mashed dried beans, tofu, pasta

When an infant has mastered mashed fruits and vegetables, you can let him try to feed himself dry cereals such as Cheerios as a snack. By the time he is 8 months old, he'll be able to start eating some table foods and the real fun begins! Meat should be finely ground at first. Moistening it with gravy or some other liquid helps baby swallow it, as does mixing it with mashed potatoes or pasta in a casserole. Work up to an ounce of meat or the equivalent of a meat alternative every day.

Meat Equivalents

1 oz. beef, lamb, poultry
1 oz. cheese (¼ cup grated)
¼ cup cooked dried beans
¼ cup cottage cheese
¼ cup flaked fish (watch for bones)
2 oz. tofu (does not meet CACFP guidelines at this time)

For the remainder of the first year, the baby will be able to master increasingly coarse textures and enjoy complex flavor combinations. He'll be able to easily feed himself with his fingers and will no doubt demand to spoon-feed himself as well.

Babies can easily choke when they try to eat foods that are too advanced in texture for them. Be especially careful not to give babies foods that can form hard plugs in their throats, such as raw hard vegetable or fruit chunks, nuts, tough meats, hot dogs, or anything with bones or pits. Hard candies and snack chips are dangerous and have no place in their diet anyway.

In the past, people tended to shy away from giving infants foods that had herbs and spices in them, assuming that somehow the babies wouldn't like or couldn't digest them. This isn't necessarily true, however. In our experience, older infants love garlic and seasonings like curry—go ahead and let them enjoy what others are eating!

These foods should be avoided for all infants less than a year old:

Added salt and sugar (nutritional concern)
Honey, even in cooked goods (risk of infant botulism)

These foods should be avoided, until the time recommended by the child's physician, for children with a strong family history of allergies:

Egg whites
Wheat
Cow's milk
Soy foods
Peanuts and peanut butter
Tree nuts
Fish
Shellfish

How to Feed Solid Foods to a Baby

Don't discourage any method of getting food from plate to mouth. Enthusiasm is what matters. —Penelope Leach

We said earlier that how you feed is as important as what you feed. Both you and the baby will have an easier time if you keep the following guidelines in mind when feeding solid foods. Call on all your reserves of patience and humor, and realize that even when the baby ends up with more squash in his hair than in his mouth, he will think it's a terrific experience if you do!

- Feed a baby only when he's sitting up; if he can't sit up yet, he's not ready for solid foods.

- When you first offer solids (usually cereals), try them only at one meal a day to get the baby used to the idea of spoon feeding. Serve only a teaspoon or two of a new food at first. You can add more meals and bigger servings later.

- In the beginning, feed the baby a little breast milk or formula first, so he'll be patient but not stuffed. By the time he is 8 to 10 months old and eating table foods, you can skip the milk feeding before the meal entirely.

- Wash your hands and the baby's hands before feeding time.

- Try to keep the atmosphere as tranquil as possible. Sit facing the baby and be friendly but not too entertaining.

- Test the food first to make sure it isn't too hot.

- Offer the food on a small spoon and wait for the baby's mouth to open. Place a small amount of food between the baby's lips; he may force it out of his mouth, in which case it's okay to scoop it up and try again. However, if he doesn't seem to like it, respect his preference.

- Feed the baby at the pace at which he wants to eat.

- Some babies need a lot of exposure to certain foods before they like them. If a baby refuses a food, try it again some other time.

- Stop feeding the baby when he lets you know he's full. He may:
  - Close his mouth
  - Turn his head away
  - Spit out food
  - Cover his mouth with his hands
  - Play with utensils
  - Cry
  - Shake his head "no"
  - Hand you the bowl or cup

- When a baby grabs the spoon from you and tries to feed himself, or when he wants to eat (or explore) the food with his fingers, stay out of the way and enjoy the show!

- Keep the food safe:

  - Don't feed right out of a baby food jar (unless you're willing to throw out the leftovers).

  - Throw out what the baby hasn't eaten from her dish.

  - Store opened jars of baby food in the refrigerator for no longer than these recommended times:
    - strained fruits and vegetables: 2-3 days
    - strained meats and eggs: 1 day
    - homemade baby food: 1-2 days

How to Prevent Early Childhood Caries (Baby Bottle Tooth Decay)

We have met young children whose teeth were so rotten that it was painful for them to eat. They were suffering from early childhood caries (also known as "baby bottle tooth decay"). Cavities formed in their primary ("baby") teeth when these children were put to bed with bottles containing milk, formula, juice, or other sweetened liquids. Such children endure unnecessary discomfort and may require expensive dental work.

Early childhood caries can be prevented by:

- Using bottles to feed infants breast milk, formula, or water *only*.

- Offering bottles only at feeding times, not before naps or bedtime.

- Not dipping pacifiers in honey, maple syrup, or corn syrup.

- Putting a baby to bed with stuffed animals, lullabies, or back rubs, not bottles.

- Serving juice to a baby in a cup, not a bottle.

- Not allowing childen to walk around with a "sippy" cup all day long.

- Gently cleaning gums or erupting teeth after feeding; use a clean wash-cloth or gauze pad or soft baby toothbrush.

Weaning a Baby from Breast or Bottle

Weaning is ideally a *gradual* transition from milk feeding by nipple to a varied diet with milk drunk from a cup. We aren't going to argue here that one time is better than another for the completion of this process. Some parents are in no particular hurry to see their children off the breast or bottle, some children refuse to give up nipple feeding (and their parents have to endure remarks like "Is he planning to go off to college with that bottle?"), and some children lose interest in breast- or bottlefeeding as soon as they figure out how to drink from a cup.

We believe every family has to find their own best solution to this dilemma. If you are interested in pursuing the topic further, we suggest you read about it in Ellyn Satter's *Child of Mine: Feeding with Love and Good Sense.*

It is important that a child be well established on table foods by the age of 10 or 12 months. She won't receive adequate nutrition if milk remains the major component of her diet past this point. After the age of 1 (and through age 3), two cups of milk a day is plenty; she should be getting the rest of her calories from a variety of other foods selected from guidance such as the **Start Healthy Feeding Guidelines** (*see* resources section to obtain a copy) and **MyPyramid**.

Get the baby used to drinking liquids from a cup by offering small amounts of formula or water by cup when she's around 7 or 8 months old. She'll need your help at the time, of course, but with the right equipment (plastic cups with two handles are dandy) and lots of practice, in a couple of months she'll be able to drink milk at mealtime by herself. By then, if breastfeeding or a bottle is offered, it should be only at snacks or in the early morning or late evening. Eventually, as the child is eating more and more like the rest of the family or group, these milk feedings can be dropped, one at a time. Usually, the child will scarcely notice what's happened.

Remember, do not let a child of any age go to sleep with a bottle.

Growth and the Nutritional Needs of Toddlers

- Toddlers don't grow as rapidly as infants. For the next several years, they will be gaining about 3 inches and 4 to 6 pounds a year.

- By the end of the second year, a child's brain has reached 75% of its adult size.

- By the age of 2½ years, a child usually has all 20 "baby teeth." Even though these teeth don't have to last a lifetime, they are important for proper chewing. Young children need to learn how to care for their teeth, and they should be offered foods that don't promote cavities. Also, the nutrients taken in during the childhood years will affect the health of the permanent teeth.

- Iron deficiency and its late stage, anemia, can be problems among toddlers. Especially at risk are children who didn't get enough iron while they were infants, and those who drink too much milk and eat too few iron-rich foods.

- It is *normal* for toddlers to have erratic appetites or to go on "food jags." An example of a food jag is when a child wants nothing but macaroni and cheese for 2 weeks, then abruptly wants nothing to do with the stuff. Does this sound like anyone you know? Despite these problems, most toddlers manage to grow pretty well.

- Some children at this age are fond of eating nonfood items like dirt, paint chips, paper, and crayons. Dirt and paint chips can cause lead poisoning, so discourage them from eating these at least.

Different Ages, Different Stages . . . Toddlers

How a Toddler Is Developing	Related Nutritional Considerations
1. He has an expanding sense of self, as a separate person.	1. He loves to say "NO" and may refuse to eat even favorite foods as a way of establishing control.
2. He is becoming able to express himself verbally.	2. He can tell you when he's hungry and what he likes to eat.
3. He is involved in intensive exploration of the world around him and needs both the freedom to explore and the security of limits.	3. He may be more inerested in playing than in eating. He will play with his food as a way of learning about it. He needs limits in the form of established meals and snack times and expectations regarding behavior at the table.
4. He is refining his fine-motor control, but may be easily frustrated by setbacks.	4. He needs to be set up for success in self-feeding, with the right utensils and seating, and food that's easy to handle. If you are too fussy about tidiness at this point, you could delay the development of his feeding skills.
5. He is neophobic (afraid of anything new). Nature probably installed this tendency in toddlers to protect them!	5. He will almost certainly refuse to try a new food, at least once!
6. He has a short attention span.	6. He may not be able to sit through a long meal.

How to Survive Mealtime with Young Children (and Perhaps Even Enjoy It)

- Allow enough time for an unhurried meal.

- Let the children know in advance what kind of behavior you expect.

- Set aside quiet time before the meal, maybe reading a story or having them listen to some music.

- See that the children are comfortably seated and have the right equipment for eating.

- Respect the children's preferences when planning meals, but don't give in to "short-order cooking."

- Offer new foods in a matter-of-fact way along with some familiar foods, like bread.

- Allow the children to participate in food preparation.

- Don't allow them to fill up on juice or milk throughout the day.

- Help the children to *serve themselves* small portions, and be ready to help them with seconds later.

- Present food in a form that's easy for children to manage (*see* Modifying Foods for Children of Different Ages, page 72).

- Acknowledge desirable behavior and ignore undesirable behavior. Don't, however, praise or reward a child for eating or for trying new foods. Act as though you assume she is able to handle the situation, and she will (eventually).

- Do not make desserts the reward for eating the rest of the meal. Make them *nutritious* and offer them with the other foods. If they're eaten first, so what? Surprise! Fruit is *not* dessert, although many of us were raised to believe it is.

- Eat *with* the children and set a good example by eating a wide variety of foods and being open to trying new ones.

Young Children Eat Better When They Have the Right Equipment (for Feeding)

Picture yourself sitting in a chair that leaves your feet dangling 3 feet from the ground, at a table that reaches to your neck, trying to spear pieces of cauliflower with a fork that's 2 feet long. Would eating be enjoyable?

Well, eating with adult-size utensils at adult-size furniture feels like this to a young child. If children are going to be comfortable enough to sit through meals and successful enough at feeding themselves to feel good about it, they will need utensils they can handle and a thoughtfully set up environment. A bonus for you will be less mess to contend with.

- Chairs should have supports for children's feet or allow the children to have their feet on the floor.

- The table should be at a height that allows children to reach their food easily.

- Plates, bowls, glasses, cups, and flatware should be child-sized and made of unbreakable materials.

- Plates with curved sides are easier for younger children to work with. Glasses should have broad bases and be small enough to allow children to get their hands around them.

- Spoons should have short handles, blunt tips, and rounded bowls. Forks should have short handles and short, blunt tines. Knives should be small and have rounded tips. Disposable flatware isn't recommended except for picnics.

- Children can enjoy pouring their own beverages if you provide small (covered) pitchers with broad handles.

- When you're serving family-style meals, keep the serving spoons small enough for children to manage.

- Children with disabilities may require specialized eating equipment.

Growth and the Nutritional Needs of Preschoolers

- Preschoolers are growing at much the same rate they did as toddlers— approximately 3 inches and 4 to 6 pounds a year.

- The nutritional concerns for preschoolers are much the same as for toddlers. Iron deficiency anemia is still a problem, although it becomes less common as children get older. Overweight and tooth decay are significant health problems in this age group.

- Young preschoolers still display some of the eating behaviors that so worried their parents when they were toddlers: finickiness, erratic appetites, and dawdling at the table. By the time they're 4 or 5, though, most of these children will be eating pretty well and be good company at mealtimes.

Different Ages, Different Stages . . . Preschoolers

How a Preschooler Is Developing	Related Nutritional Considerations
1. Her ability to master skills more easily makes her eager to cooperate and try new experiences. She does need immediate reinforcement of her success to stay interested, however.	1. She will probably be more willing to try new foods. You can still expect some messiness while she eats, but she will be trying hard to imitate grown-up eating. She still needs to be set up for success, with the proper equipment and thoughtful food preparation.
2. She is becoming less attached to her primary caregiver and expands her relationships with peers, family members, and other adults.	2. She will be influenced by the food preferences of her peers and teachers or caregivers.
3. She is learing to feel positively or negatively about herself, depending on her interactions with others.	3. Her own food preferences should be respected. She needs to know that people care enough about her to attend to her basic needs (like food). She feels important when she helps out and will enjoy preparing food for herself and others.

George Won't Eat His Broccoli?
Melissa Won't Even Look at a Snow Pea?
Here, Try This . . .

- Let him grow it.

- Let her help you pick it out at the grocery store or farmers' market.

- Let him help you prepare it for eating (even quite young children can shell peas, pop beans, separate broccoli florets, and wash lettuce).

- Try serving it a different way— raw if you usually cook it, lightly steamed if you usually serve it raw, perhaps even pureed in a soup.

- Let him dip it.

- Put parmesan cheese on top.

- Give it a funny name.

- Serve it when she's hungry, not when she's filled up on other foods.

- Seat him next to a child who *loves* vegetables, and let peer pressure work its magic.

- Tell her she can have it for dessert, but only if she eats all of her cupcake (just kidding . . .).

- Eat it yourself, with obvious enjoyment.

- Don't assume he'll *never* like it. Some children take longer than others to feel comfortable with certain foods, so let it reappear occasionally.

- If a young child still won't eat vegetables, and you are concerned that her health will suffer, offer her fruits that are good sources of vitamins A and C (*see* lists, pages 92-93).

CALVIN & HOBBS COPYRIGHT 1985 UNIVERSAL PRESS SYNDICATE. Reprinted with permission. All rights reserved.

Growth and the Nutritional Needs of School-Age Children

- Up to about 7 or 8 years of age, children will be gaining their usual 3 inches per year in height and 4 to 6 pounds in weight. Then they'll slow down a bit, gaining about 2 inches a year, until they start their adolescent growth spurts (the spurt can happen as early as age 9 in girls).

- Between 6 years and puberty, boys are taller and heavier than girls. By the sixth grade, it's not unusual to find classrooms in which most of the girls are bigger than most of the boys (in high school, the boys regain their size advantage).

- It is *normal* for children to put on some weight before they experience their spurt in height. Tragically, many children, or their parents, become so concerned about this that dieting and weight obsession start at this young age.

- Feeding problems are uncommon among 6- to 12-year-olds, as children gradually become more accepting of what is served to them. However, as parents lose some of the control over what their children are eating, many children make poor food choices. One study found that school-age children were getting 25% of their calories from *sugar*!

Different Ages, Different Stages . . . School-Age Children

How School-Age Child Is Developing	Related Nutritional Considerations
1. He experiences mastery of physical skills and may become involved in organized sports.	1. He will probably have a hearty appetite.
2. He is increasingly influenced by peers and the school environment.	2. He may start to question his parents' (or caregiver's) credibility. Nutrition education activities may be part of the classroom curriculum.
3. He has more access to money and opportunities for shopping without parents.	3. He can buy foods on his own, some of which may not be acceptable to parents and caregivers.
4. He may have a hectic schedule as he becomes more involved in activities outside the home.	4. He may skip meals, especially breakfast.
5. He may spend large amounts of time watching television.	5. Watching television can contribute to obesity; advertising may encourage children to eat unhealthful foods.

Helping Older Children Make Better Eating Choices

Children become increasingly independent as they progress from kindergarten to junior high. They enjoy learning to make decisions for themselves, and eating behavior is one area over which they can exert some control. As money and opportunities become available, school-age children obtain access to foods their parents and schools or child care settings don't provide. And often the foods they choose to eat are not exactly nutritious!

These "junk" foods aren't going to go away, and so long as they're around, kids will want to eat them. So how can you support a child in thinking for himself, yet keep him from turning into a veritable candy-eating machine?

- Remember that it is still your job to determine what will be served to a child while he is in your home or child care setting, and at what time. It is still the child's job to decide whether to eat or how much to eat. You may not be able to control what a child eats when he's not with you, but at least you can be assured he's getting nutritious food when he is with you. And hopefully, he will enjoy a wide range of healthful foods.

- Include the children in your menu-planning process. Let them know what the guidelines have to be (such as servings from particular food groups or restrictions on sugar, fat, or salt). Explain to them the reasons for the guidelines. Then try to accommodate as many of their suggestions as possible. They will feel very important, and they'll be getting nutrition education at the same time.

- Involve the children in food preparation. As children get older they usually end up fixing more of their own meals and snacks. Teach them some simple but nutritious recipes (you can make your own laminated recipe cards with pictures); eventually, you'll be able to set out the ingredients and let them do all the work! By the way, it's as important for boys to learn to cook as it is for girls.

- Teach children to be informed consumers. Discuss how television advertising, prizes, and packaging can lead people to make unwise food choices. Have them read food labels. Make games of finding cereals with the least sugar or the lowest-fat crackers.

Child Feeding History

ALL CHILDREN	YES	NO	SPECIFICS
Is your child allergic to any foods, or are there foods he or she should not eat for any other reason?			
Does your child have any other special dietary needs?			
Does your child need assistance with eating?			
Does your child take any medications that may require consideration in timing or content of meals?			
Do you have any concerns about your child's eating habits?			
What are your child's favorite foods?			
INFANTS			
Is your child breast fed?			
Will you bring fresh or frozen breast milk to the site for feeding?			
Does your child drink infant formula?			
What is the usual amount of formula your child takes at one feeding?			
Does your child eat solid foods?			

Special instructions, holiday customs, cultural food patterns:

PART TWO

Your Feeding Program

. . . .

CHAPTER THREE

Planning How and What to Feed Children

Why Bother with a Feeding Program?

We believe that it's beneficial to everyone if a child's meals while in child care are provided by the caregiver. There are many reasons for this:

- Some of the mealtime disturbances that occur when a few children bring "junk" foods, or when food items are traded, can be avoided.

- Children will, in general, get more variety and nutrient balance in their meals. Bag lunches tend to be pretty much the same day after day, in part because they are limited to foods that travel well.

- You can make mealtimes valuable learning experiences when you introduce children to foods they might otherwise never encounter, or when you talk about foods that everyone is eating.

- Parents are usually extremely grateful to be spared the hassle of packing lunches.

Despite the advantages, however, you must look realistically at your situation—that is, the space, equipment, and time you have available—before you decide whether to offer a full meal program or snacks only. We don't want you to make yourself and everyone else miserable because you've taken on more than you can handle!

You may find that what works best for you is to offer snacks only, but in combination with a specific policy about acceptable bag lunch foods. (For example, some child care providers and schools have policies that forbid sodas, candy, or other sugary foods in lunches brought from home.) It is certainly possible to offer children a wide range of food experiences during snack times, when you're willing to move beyond crackers and juice (we'll show you how later on).

We also suggest that you look into signing up for the Child and Adult Care Food Program (CACFP)* if you haven't already. Qualified providers can get CACFP reimbursement for meals and snacks served in child care homes and centers, plus good training opportunities and support. We have followed the meal patterns and serving-size requirements of the program while developing the recipes for this book, to make it easier for you to meet their guidelines.

Scheduling Meals and Snacks

Young children need several opportunities to eat during the course of a day to ensure that their nutritional needs are met. Once past infancy, they begin to appreciate the structure of scheduled meals and snacks, but it's unrealistic to expect them to eat all they require for optimum growth in only 3 meals per day. Plan to feed children at least 2 snacks if you will be with them all day. Some research suggests that this is a healthier way for adults to eat, too. Try it . . . you might like it!

The health and safety guidelines of the American Academy of Pediatrics and American Public Health Association state that:

---

* Check the White Pages in your phone directory for "Child and Adult Care Food Program."

- Infants should be fed on demand.

- Children in child care for 8 hours or less per day should have at least 1 meal and 2 snacks or 2 meals and 1 snack.

- Children in child care for 9 hours or more should have at least 2 meals and 2 snacks or 3 meals and 1 snack daily.

- Children should be offered midmorning and midafternoon snacks.

- Unless children are asleep, they should be offered food at least every 3 hours.

    A few possible meal schedules are:

- Children in day care 7 A.M. to 5:30 P.M.

7:15	Breakfast
9:45	Midmorning snack
12:30	Lunch
3:30	Afternoon snack
5:00	Additional snack for children who will be eating dinner late

- Children in preschool 9:00 A.M. to 1:30 P.M.

10:00	Midmorning snack
12:30	Lunch

How to Serve Meals

There are several ways to set up a meal for children, and you may find that it's fun to vary your usual routine now and then. We don't recommend serving children meals already portioned out on plates if you can possibly help it, because it doesn't allow them to decide for themselves how much they want to eat. You may also find that a lot of food is wasted this way. There are better ways to serve meals, and we've outlined them next.

Family Style

Meal tables are set up with plates, flatware, and cups at each place, and the food is passed in small bowls, plates, or baskets from which the children help themselves. Beverages are served in small pitchers so the children can pour for themselves. This is the recommended method for serving most meals to children and can be used even with toddlers; very young children may need more assistance getting the food on their plates, however.

Buffet Style

Foods are placed in serving dishes on one table or counter, and children move along serving themselves from what's offered. Some teachers set up picture cards showing the food and its portion size (number of scoops, slices, etc.). This serving method is not recommended for very young children, but you may find it works well with older kids just as a change of pace, for snacks, or for special occasions. Be particularly careful that the children are capable of handling the food and utensils in a hygienic manner.

Picnics

You can serve these meals outside at picnic tables or on blankets, or even inside on a blanket if it's a cold or rainy day. Pack the food items in a basket or insulated chest, being especially careful to keep foods at safe temperatures if you are traveling farther than your back yard.

Whatever style you choose, remember that an adult should always eat with the children.

Mealtime 1-2-3's

- Start with a clean table.

- Designate a helper or two to assist in setting the table, with chores appropriate to each child's stage of development.

- Engage the other children in a transitional activity, such as listening to some mellow music or to a story.

- Turn off the television.

- Make sure everyone has washed hands, is comfortably seated, and has all the proper utensils.

- Allow the children to serve themselves small portions. Be ready to assist children who need help, and offer second helpings when appropriate.

- Model good food safety practices when passing and serving food, and be ready to respond when a child is about to contaminate food or has already done so. (You may need to provide new serving utensils or even replace the contaminated food.)

- Have enough serving bowls and platters so that children don't have to wait too long for food to be passed to them. One set for every 6 children is realistic.

- Give the children opportunities to practice skills such as peeling food with their fingers, spreading butter or jam, cutting soft foods with a table knife, and rolling their own burritos.

- Expect children to mop up their own spills, but don't make a fuss about it. (It's easier if you have a small sponge and container of sudsy water standing by.)

- Keep the conversation at the table light. Avoid nagging, criticism, and other unpleasantness, and don't allow fighting or rudeness.

- Please *do* talk about the foods being served (where they come from, what their sensory characteristics are, or why they are healthful to eat).

- Adults should eat meals and snacks with the children (the *same* meals and snacks, unless you have a medical or religious reason for avoiding certain foods, which should then be explained to the children).

- Respect children's food preferences, and resist the temptation to interfere by using such tactics as rewarding children for trying new foods or forcing them to clean their plates.

- Be ready to respond if a child starts choking.

- Allow children who finish early to leave the table and engage in some quiet activity like reading (after they've cleaned up their places, of course).

- Accept that because of variations in children's appetites and food preferences, some food will be wasted. Don't take it personally!

- At the end of the meal, discard food that has been on the plates, as well as food left in serving bowls on the table. Clean the table and wipe it down with a chlorine bleach solution (1 tablespoon bleach in 1 quart of water). Promptly refrigerate leftovers that have not been on the table.

- Finally, have the children clean their faces and hands and brush their teeth before moving on to the next activity.

Adults, your job is to:
- Make the meal pleasant
- Help the children participate in the meal
- Allow eating methods appropriate for the developmental levels of the children
- Enforce standards of behavior
- Model good manners and enjoyment in eating

How to Plan Menus

A well-planned menu is a time- and money-saving tool for you and a powerful nutrition education message to children and parents. A menu makes it much more likely that the children will get the best nourishment you can provide. Busy families, too, find that planning menus means fewer annoying trips to the store, better meals, and more time to enjoy each other! It seems intimidating at first, but we'll run you through it, step by step.

- Gather all of your tools together: menu form or pad of paper, pencil, cookbooks and recipes, a guide to seasonal fruits and vegetables, information on current prices of various food items, lists of foods high in vitamins A and C and iron, a calendar of holidays or special events, and the menu checklist. Make a list of foods you want to use soon because they are crowding your storage areas or nearing their expiration dates or maximum storage times. Menu forms (like the one on page 186) make it easy to remember to plan servings of all the required food groups.

- Decide the time period of your menu. Some cooks like to plan for a month at a time and then start over; some find that repeating "cycles" of 3 to 4 weeks work best. Families and small child care settings may prefer weekly menu planning.

- Think about the staff, equipment, time, and storage space you have available.

- Figure out how you want to approach planning the meals. You may want to plan breakfasts, lunches, and snacks for one entire day before moving on to the next day. Many people find it helpful to plan all of the main dishes for the time period, then all of the grain items, and so on. It's usually a good idea to plan snacks last, so that you can use them to fill in the nutritional gaps left by the breakfasts and lunches.

- As discussed earlier, you may need to plan adjustments in preparation methods, or even alternative items, in order to accommodate different age groups.

- Consider the time between snacks and meals when you plan snacks. If it will be 3 hours until the next meal, the snack should be more substantial (preferably with a protein-rich food included) than one that precedes a meal by an hour and a half. You want the children hungry at mealtime, but not frantically so.

- Use the menu checklist to see how you did.

- Check which ingredients you have on hand, then make up your shopping list or purchase orders.

Serving-Size Guidelines for Child Care

A convenient way to ensure that you're providing adequate amounts of nutrients to children is to plan meals that conform to the Child and Adult Care Food Program (CACFP) requirements.* **The CACFP guidelines call for a specified number of servings from the five major food groups: milk, meat or meat alternatives, breads and cereals, fruits, and vegetables.** We've printed them for your reference on pages 69-71.

To do the best possible job of planning meals for children, you should become familiar with the Dietary Guidelines for Americans (p. 74), MyPyramid (pages 76-78), and the good food sources of important nutrients (pages 92-95). (Note: The serving sizes for CACFP and MyPyramid do not correspond exactly, at least as of this writing.) You may also find it helpful to review Appendix B—Nutrition Basics.

---

* If you participate in the School Lunch Program, you will need to follow its guidelines.

Child and Adult Care Food Program
Infant Meal Pattern

	Birth through 3 months	Ages 4 through 7 months	Ages 8 through 11 months
Breakfast	• 4 to 6 fl oz. breast milk[1,2,3] or formula[1,4]	• 4 to 8 fl oz. breast milk[1,2,3] or formula[1,4] • 0 to 3 Tbsp. infant cereal[4,5]	• 6 to 8 fl oz. breast milk[1,2,3] or formula[1,4] • 2 to 4 Tbsp. infant cereal[4] • 1 to 4 Tbsp. fruit *and/or* vegetable
Lunch or Supper	• 4 to 6 fl oz. breast milk[1,2,3] or formula	• 4 to 8 fl oz. breast milk[1,2,3] or formula[1,4] • 0 to 3 Tbsp. infant cereal[4,5] • 0 to 3 Tbsp. fruit *and/or* vegetable[5]	• 6 to 8 fl oz. breast milk or formula[1,4] • 2 to 4 Tbsp. infant cereal[4] *and/or* 1 to 4 Tbsp. lean meat, fish, poultry, egg yolk, cooked dry beans or peas *or* 0.5 to 2 oz. cheese *or* 1 to 4 oz. (volume) cottage cheese *or* 1 to 4 oz. (weight) cheese food or cheese spread • 1 to 4 Tbsp. fruit *and/or* vegetable
AM or PM snack	• 4 to 6 fl oz. breast milk[1,2,3] or formula[1,4]	• 4 to 6 fl oz. breast milk[1,2,3] or formula[1,4]	• 2 to 4 fl oz. breast milk[1,2,3], formula[1,4], *or* fruit juice[6] • 0 to ½ slice of bread[5,7], *or* 0 to 2 crackers[5,7]

[1] Breast milk or formula, or portions of both, may be served; however, it is recommended that breast milk be served in place of formula from birth through 11 months.

[2] For some breastfed infants who regularly consume less than the minimum amount of breast milk per feeding, a serving of less than the minimum amount of breast milk may be offered, with additional breast milk offered if the infant is still hungry.

[3] Only the infant's mother can provide breast milk.

[4] Infant formula and dry infant cereal must be iron fortified.

[5] A serving of this component is required only when the infant is developmentally ready to accept it.

[6] Fruit juice must be full strength (100% juice) and offered from a cup, not a bottle, to prevent tooth decay.

[7] Must be made from whole grain or enriched meal or flour.

Child and Adult Care Food Program
Meal Pattern for Older Children

Food Components		
1–2 years	**3–5 years**	**6–12 years**

	1–2 years	3–5 years	6–12 years
Breakfast			
1. Milk, fluid	½ cup	¾ cup	1 cup
2. Vegetable, fruit, or full-strength juice	¼ cup	½ cup	½ cup
3. Bread and bread alternates (whole grain or enriched)			
Bread	½ slice	½ slice	1 slice
or cornbread, rolls, muffins, biscuits	½ serving	½ serving	1 serving
or cold dry cereal (volume or weight, whichever is less)	¼ cup	⅓ cup	¾ cup
	or ⅓ oz.	*or* ½ oz.	*or* 1 oz.
or cooked cereal, pasta, noodle products, or cereal grains	¼ cup	¼ cup	½ cup
Lunch or Supper			
1. Milk, fluid	½ cup	¾ cup	1 cup
2. Vegetable and/or fruit (two or more kinds)	¼ cup total	½ cup total	¾ cup total
3. Bread and bread alternates (whole grain or enriched):			
Bread	½ slice	½ slice	1 slice
or cornbread, rolls, muffins, biscuits	½ serving	½ serving	1 serving
or cooked cereal, pasta, noodle products, or cereal grains	¼ cup	¼ cup	½ cup
4. Meat or meat alternatives			
Lean meat, fish, poultry (edible portion as served)	1 oz.	1½ oz.	2 oz.
or cottage cheese, cheese food/ cheese spread substitute	¼ cup	⅜ cup	½ cup
	or 2 oz.	*or* 3 oz.	*or* 4 oz.
or egg (large)	½ egg	¾ egg	1 egg
or cooked dried beans or dried peas[1]	¼ cup	⅜ cup	½ cup
or peanut butter, reduced-fat peanut butter, soy nut butter, or other nut or seed butters	2 Tbsp.	3 Tbsp.	4 Tbsp.
or peanuts, soy nuts, tree nuts, roasted peas, or seeds[2]	½ oz.[2]	¾ oz.[2]	1 oz.[2]
or yogurt (plain or flavored, unsweetened or sweetened)	½ cup	¾ cup	1 cup
or an equivalent quantity of any combination of above meat/ meat alternatives			

(continued on next page)

Child and Adult Care Food Program
Meal Pattern for Older Children

	Food Components		
	1–2 years	3–5 years	6–12 years

A.M. OR P.M. Supplement
(select 2 of these 4 components)

	1–2 years	3–5 years	6–12 years
1. Milk, fluid	½ cup	½ cup	1 cup
2. Vegetable, fruit, or full-strength juice[3]	½ cup	½ cup	¾ cup
3. Bread and bread alternatives (whole-grain or enriched)			
bread	½ slice	½ slice	1 slice
or rolls, muffins, etc.	½ serving	½ serving	1 serving
or cold dry cereal (volume or weight, whichever is less)	¼ cup or ⅓ oz.	⅓ cup or ½ oz.	¾ cup or 1 oz.
or cooked cereal, pasta, noodle products, or cereal grains	¼ cup	¼ cup	½ cup
4. Lean meat, fish, or poultry (edible portion as served)	½ oz.	½ oz.	1 oz.
or cheese (natural or processed)	½ oz.	½ oz.	1 oz.
or cottage cheese, cheese food/ cheese spread substitute	⅛ cup or 1 oz.	⅛ cup or 1 oz.	¼ cup or 2 oz.
or egg (large)	½ egg	½ egg	½ egg
or yogurt (plain or flavored, unsweeteed or sweetened[4])	¼ cup	¼ cup	½ cup
or cooked dried beans or dried peas[1]	⅛ cup	⅛ cup	¼ cup
or peanut butter, reduced-fat peanut butter, soy nut butter, or other nut or seed butters	1 Tbsp.	1 Tbsp.	2 Tbsp.
or peanuts, soy nuts, tree nuts, roasted peas, or seeds	½ oz.	½ oz.	1 oz.
or an equivalent quantity of any combination of above meat/ meat alternatives			

1 Dried beans or dried peas may be used as a meat alternate or as a vegetable component, but *cannot* be counted as both components in the same meal.

2 No more than 50% of the requirement shall be met with nuts or seeds. Nuts or seeds shall be combined with another meat/meat alternate to fulfill the requirement. To determine combinations, 1 oz. of nuts or seeds is equal to 1 oz. of cooked lean meat, poultry, or fish. Roasted peas can count as a meat alternate or vegetable component but cannot be counted as both in the same meal.

3 Juice *cannot* be served when milk is served as the only other component.

4 If yogurt is used as the meat component in supplements, milk *cannot* be used to satisfy the second component requirement. Commercially added fruit or nuts in flavored yogurt cannot be used to satisfy the second component requirement in supplements.

Modifying Foods for Children of Different Ages

It may be necessary for you to adjust recipes, including those in this book, to make foods suitable for children at different levels of development. You may also need to modify the form of simple foods like apples or toast.

One reason for this is that the texture or shape of a certain food may make it difficult for a very young child to eat it. You want her to be able to get the food into her mouth, chew it, and swallow it without frustration, because, after all, she should feel successful and happy about her eating experiences. You also want her to get the benefit of its nutritional contribution, which she won't if she gives up on it.

Another important reason for modifying some of the foods you serve is that young children are much more likely to choke on foods that are generally safe for older children. Lastly, certain food ingredients are unsuitable for infants.

- Never feed honey to a child less than 1 year of age; this precaution is necessary to avoid the danger of infant botulism.

- Avoid adding salt and sugar to the foods you serve infants.

- Minimize choking hazards for children younger than 4 years of age. Refer to the chart on the next page.

- Depending on an infant's age and eating ability, you can puree, mash, or chop many of the same foods you are feeding to older children.

- Young children prefer meat that is very tender: cooking with moist heat and chopping or shredding the meat finely, or using ground poultry or beef, will make it easier for children to eat.

- Remember that toddlers and preschoolers enjoy "finger foods."

- Some young children prefer foods that are prepared simply and singly. They may balk at tuna salad sandwiches but eat plain flaked tuna and bread wedges eagerly, or they may enjoy plain steamed carrots and reject carrots mixed into a casserole.

Preparing Foods to Keep Children
Safe From Choking

Food Item	Child Under 1 Year	Children 1 to 4 Years
Baby carrots	Cook until *soft* and cut into quarters lengthwise so it is a skinny "stick."	Cook slightly (1-2 yrs.). Cut in half lengthwise (all).
Celery sticks	Don't serve.	Don't serve.
Grapes	Don't serve.	Don't serve.
Raw apples, peaches, pears, nectarines, or other firm fruit	Remove skin and pits or seeds. Grate or cut into skinny "sticks" or *thin* slices that the infant can pick up and hold.	Cut into sticks that look like a french fry or into *thin* slices.
Peanut butter	Serve only mashed with banana or applesauce, or as part of an ingredient in other foods (sauces, smoothies), and only after consultation with parents.	Mix with a jam or applesauce or mashed banana, or spread thinly on bread/cracker. *Never* serve on a spoon!
Nuts and seeds	Don't serve.	Chop finely.
Cheese sticks	Pull cheese into short shreds.	Cut/pull in half lengthwise and then let kids shred them.
Fish	Remove skin and all bones.	Remove skin and all bones.
Hot dogs	Don't serve.	Cut in quarters lengthwise.
Corn chips	Don't serve.	Only crush for salad topping.
General guide for *soft* table foods	Pieces no larger than ¼ inch	Pieces no larger than ½ inch (ages 1-2½ years).
Hard candies, popcorn	Don't serve.	Don't serve.
Marshmallows, raisins	Don't serve.	Chop into small pieces.

Following the Dietary Guidelines the Yummy Way

It's possible to eat the recommended number of servings from each food group and still be poorly nourished. This commonly happens when food choices are high in fat, sugar, or salt; when the foods are limited in their variety; or when foods have been stored or prepared in ways that cause losses of nutrients.

To address these concerns, several health organizations have made recommendations for healthful diets. One such set of recommendations is the *Dietary Guidelines for Americans 2005,* issued jointly by the U.S. Department of Health and Human Services and the Department of Agriculture. The previous version of the Dietary Guidelines had 7 recommendations; the most recent version has dozens, with 9 major messages targeted to the general public aged 2 and older. Further, the report gives key recommendations for specific population groups. The key recommendations for children are in italics here.

- Consume a variety of foods within and among the basic food groups while staying within energy needs.

- Control calorie intake to manage body weight.
  (Overweight children): Reduce the rate of body weight gain while allowing growth and development. Consult a healthcare provider before placing a child on a weight-reduction diet.

- Be physically active every day.
  Engage in at least 60 minutes of physical activity on most, preferably all, days of the week.

- Increase daily intake of fruits and vegetables, whole grains, and nonfat or low-fat milk and milk products.
  Consume whole-grain products often; at least half the grains should be whole grains. Children 2 to 8 years should consume 2 cups per day of fat-free or low-fat milk or equivalent milk products. Children 9 years of age and older should consume 3 cups per day of fat-free or low-fat milk or equivalent milk products.

- Choose fats wisely for good health.
  Keep total fat intake between 30 to 35 percent of calories for children 2 to 3 years of age and between 25 to 35 percent of calories for children and adolescents 4 to 18 years of age, with most fats coming from sources of polyunsaturated and monounsaturated fatty acids, such as fish, nuts, and vegetable oils.

- Choose carbohydrates wisely for good health.

- Choose and prepare foods with little salt.

- If you drink alcoholic beverages, do so in moderation.

- Keep food safe to eat.
  (Infants and young children): Do not eat or drink raw (unpasteurized) milk or any products made from unpasteurized milk, raw or undercooked meat and poultry, raw or undercooked fish or shellfish, unpasteurized juices, and raw sprouts.

The Dietary Guidelines are hefty reading and were published primarily for nutrition professionals to use in developing policies and educational efforts, but they can be downloaded from the internet at www.healthierus. gov/dietaryguidelines. There's also a consumer-friendly version, *Finding Your Way to a Healthier You*, that can be accessed at the same address. **MyPyramid** is the most recent tool for consumers to use in putting the Dietary Guidelines into practice, and it will be discussed later.

It's possible to follow the Dietary Guidelines and still have a lot of fun eating (and cooking). Some foods may need to show up on the menu less frequently or in smaller amounts, or some of your favorite recipes may need adjustments. Be patient, proceed with an attitude of experimentation, and realize that it make take a little while for jaded taste buds to adjust to the changes. Some day you may find that soups you ate for years taste much too salty. In the following pages, we'll show you how to put more variety into your menus; cut down on fat, sugar, and salt (sodium); and add more fiber and complex carbohydrates from fruits, vegetables, and whole grains.

Getting to Know MyPyramid

The first Food Guide Pyramid was introduced in 1992 to give consumers a visual representation of the Dietary Guidelines. It became widely recognized as a symbol of dietary guidance but didn't seem to work very well in helping people make healthful food choices. The most recent incarnation, **MyPyramid**, offers an individualized approach to formulating food and activity patterns that meet the Dietary Guidelines. It is available in print and interactive online form, and special versions are available for children—one is shown on page 78. The lack of food imagery in the pyramid graphic has resulted in some puzzlement among consumers and nutrition educators alike, but time will tell whether this "interactive food guidance system" can achieve the success in changing the food habits of Americans for the better, that its predecessor lacked.

As described by the USDA, the principal components of the pyramid symbol represent:

- **Activity** . . . the adult version of the pyramid shows a figure climbing steps, and the children's versions portray lots of children engaged in active play.

- **Moderation** . . . the bands representing food groups narrow at the top, representing the foods within the group—those containing more sugar or solid fats—that should be chosen less often.

- **Personalization** . . . the name says it all; this pyramid goes beyond the one-size-fits-all approach.

- **Proportionality** . . . the bands representing the 5 major food groups and oils are of different widths, suggesting how much food a person should choose from each group.

- **Variety** . . . the bands representing the food groups and oils are different in color, illustrating that foods from all groups are needed daily for good health.

- **Gradual improvement** . . . the slogan accompanying the new pyramid is "Steps to a Healthier You." It encourages individuals to take small steps to improve their diet and lifestyle every day.

To take full advantage of the features of the new pyramid, visit www.mypyramid.gov. You'll find lots of helpful tips, in-depth information on each food group, MyPyramid Plan—a personalized eating plan based on age, gender, and activity level, and MyPyramid Tracker—a tool that provides an analysis of eating and activity habits. The children's section could be very useful and fun as part of a nutrition education scheme for school-age children.

There are other food pyramids. One of the best is the Healthy Eating Pyramid from the Harvard School of Public Health. It may be interesting for you to see a well-considered, alternative approach to healthful diets: www.hsph.harvard.edu/nutritionsource.

MyPyramid, offering an individualized approach to formulating food and activity patterns that meet the Dietary Guidelines.

Variety Brings Your Menus to Life

Variety helps make your meals more interesting and more nutritious. Serving foods from the required components of the Child and Adult Care Food Program is a start, as is following the recommended serving guidelines of MyPyramid. It's still easy to get into ruts when planning menus, however. Sometimes you need to curl up with a few cookbooks or cooking magazines, stroll through the produce department at your local market, or even try out new ethnic restaurants for inspiration.

Vary Your "Main" Dishes

Look at your choices! You needn't serve chicken three times a week when you can choose from so many varieties of dried beans, lentils, nut butters, cheeses, eggs, fish and other seafood, turkey, beef, pork, and lamb. Balance meat days with vegetarian days. Or, try a main-dish salad.

Tired of Carrot and Celery Sticks?
Make a Vegetable Tray with These Instead

Tomatoes
Cucumbers
Sugar-snap peas
Green or red peppers
Jicama
Cauliflower
Turnips
Green beans
Fennel

Cabbage
Summer squashes
Broccoli
Radishes
Mushrooms
Edamame (green soybeans)
Blanched asparagus
Blanched snow peas

Think "Outside the Cold Cereal Box" for Breakfast!
Try These Other Ideas for Grains—Preferably Whole Grains

- Hot cereals (oatmeal, whole-wheat varieties or multigrain varieties)

- Corn tortillas with cheese and perhaps avocado or salsa

- Wheat tortillas with eggs, cheese, and chiles, or even spread with peanut butter or light whipped cream cheese and sprinkled with fruit before rolling up

- Muffins and quick breads

- Pancakes, waffles, and French toast—and rather than smothering them with butter and syrup, try toppings like a dollop of yogurt and then thinly sliced fruit, or peanut butter and bananas

- Sandwiches—turkey breast, grilled cheese, nut butter and honey or jam

- English muffin pizza

- *Swiss Breakfast* (p. 120)

- Leftover brown rice heated with milk or soy beverage, raisins or other dried fruit, slivered almonds, and cinnamon and perhaps nutmeg

Let's Ditch Some Saturated Fat, Trans-Fats, and Cholesterol and Emphasize the Better Fats

In the midst of years of confusion about the role of fats in promoting heart disease, certain cancers, and obesity, the message got lost that *some* fat in the diet is necessary for good health. Fats supply essential fatty acids and help in the absorption of fat-soluble vitamins. The type of fat you eat is important, however—eating too much saturated fat, trans-fat, and cholesterol can raise the levels of unhealthy blood lipids, which in turn may increase risk for heart disease. And because any dietary fats are high in calories, eating too much of any of them can make it harder to avoid gaining weight.

The Dietary Guidelines for Americans 2005 recommend that children 2 to 3 years of age get 30 to 35 percent of their calories from fat; for children 4 to 18 years of age a range of 25 to 35 percent calories from fat is recommended. Lowering saturated fat intake to less than 10 percent of calories and cholesterol to less than 300 milligrams per day is advised for everyone age 2 and up.

Trans-fats, which are formed in the process of making liquid fats into solids (like shortening and margarine), should be avoided—no amount of these fats are safe. The majority of the saturated fat in the American diet comes from cheese, beef, and milk, so those foods need to be selected carefully in order to obtain the least saturated fat.

Most fats should come from sources of monounsaturated and polyunsaturated fatty acids (fatty fish such as salmon, nuts and seeds, and liquid oils (olive, canola, high-oleic safflower, sunflower, corn, and soy). There is increasing evidence that we need to pay attention to getting enough **omega-3 fatty acids**, and consuming more of these foods, along with whole grains, fruits, and vegetables, and less meat will help.

When Shopping:

- Choose lean meats; these are generally the leaner cuts:
  - Beef: eye of round, top round steak, top round roast, sirloin steak, top loin steak, tenderloin steak, chuck arm pot roast
  - Pork: tenderloin, top loin roast, top loin chop, center loin chop, sirloin roast, loin rib chop, shoulder blade steak
  - Lamb: leg loin chop, arm chop, foreshanks
  - Veal: cutlet, blade or arm steak, rib roast, rib or loin chop

- Buy "select" grades of beef rather than "prime," which has more marbled fat.

- Buy ground meat that has the greatest percent lean to percent fat ratio.

- Select fish such as wild or canned salmon, skinless poultry, reduced-fat or non-fat cheeses, and, especially, dried beans, nuts, and seeds, as protein sources.

- Buy water-packed tuna, not oil-packed, and avoid all albacore (white) tuna.

- Buy low-fat (1%) or skim milk for everyone over age 2.

- Read labels on food packaging and opt for products low in saturated fat and cholesterol and with no trans-fats.

- Avoid prebreaded meat items.

- Buy plain frozen vegetables, not the varieties with sauces.

- Buy skim or low-fat (1%) milk for cooking. Evaporated skim milk is a good substitute for light cream.

- Limit your use of butter, cream, hard margarine, shortening, lard, coconut and palm oils, and foods containing them. Use olive or canola oil instead.

- Try yogurt as a substitute for mayonnaise or sour cream. Or use the reduced-fat versions of these foods.

When Cooking:

- Try combining small amounts of high-fat protein foods like ground beef or cheese with cooked dried beans (example: chili with beans).

- Broil, bake, roast, stew, or steam foods rather than frying them.

- Trim the fat from meat and take the skin off poultry. Drain cooked ground beef before adding to other ingredients (see below).

- Limit your use of whole eggs. Two egg whites can fill in for one whole egg in most recipes.

- Look for opportunities to incorporate nuts such as walnuts, almonds, pecans, and pistachios, and seeds such as pumpkin and sunflower seeds, into your recipes.

- Experiment with cutting the amount of added fat in your favorite recipes. It's amazing what you can do with a tablespoon or two of oil rather than a half-cup.

- Use non-stick or seasoned cast-iron skillets.

- Use non-stick spray to prevent foods from sticking to pans.

- Use olive or canola oil in place of butter or margarine where practical. Oil cannot be directly substituted for butter or shortening in baked goods without changing their texture. There are many recipes available for bakery items with a minimum of fat and saturated fat, however (try the quick bread recipes in this book that use "silken" tofu, which comes in a convenient aseptic package, along with a little oil, to substitute for butter). Look also in the resource section of this book for magazines and websites with "lighter" recipes.

When Serving Foods:

- Don't automatically add fat such as butter to breads, grains, and vegetables. Let children get used to the taste of foods without it. Many children enjoy salads more without dressing; that's a nice habit to get into!

- Serve high-fat foods in smaller portions and less often.

Remember: Do not restrict fat in the diets of children under the age of two!

Helpful Hint:
How to Remove More of the Fat from Ground Beef

Method #1
Cook the meat and drain off all the fat you can. Cover with cold water and refrigerate overnight. The next day, you can skim off the fat that has congealed, drain the meat, and use it in your recipe.

Method #2
Rinse the cooked meat with very hot water before using.

High-Fat Foods and Lower-Fat Alternatives

High-Fat Foods	Lower-Fat Alternatives
Whole milk	Nonfat or low-fat milk
Sour cream	Yogurt, light sour cream, *Mock Sour Cream* (p. 173)
Hard cheeses—cheddar, swiss, jack, American	Reduced-fat cheeses, low-fat cottage cheese
Cream soups (made with cream or cream sauce)	Clear soups or "cream" soups made with evaporated skim milk or vegetable purees
Mayonnaise	Yogurt, reduced-fat mayonnaise, mustard
Luncheon meats and sausages	Turkey and chicken breast, lean ham, lean roast beef
Oil-packed tuna	Water-packed tuna
Snack chips (potato, corn)	Toast points, *Pita Chips* (p. 127), pretzels, rice cakes
Gravies	Broth thickened with a little flour or cornstarch, tomato sauce, catsup
Ground beef	Ground turkey or chicken
Pizza with sausage	Pizza with vegetables or plain cheese
Vegetables frozen with butter sauce	Plain frozen vegetables
Pastries and cakes	Lower-fat muffins and quick breads
Doughnuts	Bagels, raisin bread
Croissants	English muffins
Ice cream	Nonfat frozen yogurt, sorbet
Fried foods	Baked, broiled, or steamed foods
French fried potatoes	*Oven-Fried Potato Sticks* (p. 145)
Fried fish	*Homemade Fish Sticks* (p. 158)
Chicken nuggets	*Chicken Fingers* (p. 164)
Buttered popcorn	Air-popped popcorn
Sugar cookies, sandwich cookies	Graham crackers, animal crackers

Next, Let's Get Rid of Some Sugar

A little bit of sugar can add palatability to some nutritious foods that wouldn't be so enjoyable otherwise. But a lot of sugar adds calories that few children and adults can afford. We're not saying never eat sugar—just use it judiciously.

- Watch out for "hidden sugar" in convenience foods. Read labels! Sugar = sucrose, glucose, dextrose, invert sugar, fructose, corn syrup, corn sweeteners, maple syrup, honey, molasses, raw sugar, turbinado sugar, Sucanat, brown sugar, malt syrup.

- Keep the sugar bowl and honey bear off the table.

- Serve fresh fruits, unsweetened frozen fruits, or fruits canned in natural juices or water.

- Serve 100% fruit juices, in very limited amounts, instead of fruit drinks. Read labels carefully!

- Choose breakfast cereals with less than 6 grams of sugar per serving.

- Sweeten cold or hot cereals with fruit, like bananas.

- Try cutting back the sugar (up to 50%) in your recipes.

- Serve muffins instead of cupcakes, graham crackers instead of cookies (or make your own cookies with less sugar).

- Use vanilla, cinnamon, nutmeg, or allspice to enhance sweet flavors.

- Add your own fruit to plain yogurt rather than buying the sweetened variety. Mash it first, and it won't seem so tart.

- When you do serve foods high in sugar, use small portions and serve them less often.

- Artificial sweeteners have been deemed "safe" for children, but our question is, why bother to use them? They haven't been proven to be that helpful in weight control and only add to the cocktail of new chemicals being introduced into our bodies.

Foods High in Sugar

Chocolate milk	Canned fruits in syrup
Milkshakes	Flavored gelatin desserts
Soft drinks	Candies
Fruit drinks/ades	Sweetened coconut
Jams, jellies	Flavored yogurts
Syrups, sweet sauce	Puddings
Ice cream, sherbet	Sweet pickle relish
Pies, pastries	Many children's cereals
Cakes, cookies	Sweet rolls, doughnuts

Kids Don't Need All That Salt, Either

Lowering salt (sodium chloride) intake is recommended to reduce the risk of developing high blood pressure. Although sodium is an essential mineral, most Americans consume much more than they need, most of it coming from processed foods. To keep sodium within reasonable limits, first, you should serve primarily unprocessed foods. Fresh foods don't need too much salt to have great flavor! Then be careful with the amount of salt you use in cooking and add at the table—a little goes a long way in enhancing flavor.

Foods High in Salt (aka Sodium)

Soy sauce	Bouillon
Gravies	MSG
Pickles	Olives
Sauerkraut	Commercial salad dressings
Bacon	Ham
Frankfurters	Bologna
Canned meats	Sausage
Corned beef	Processed cheeses
Salted nuts/nut butters	Salted crackers
Canned soups	Miso
Snack chips	Many prepared foods

- Don't add salt to pasta, rice, and vegetable cooking water.

- Leave the salt shaker and soy sauce bottle off the table.

- *Gradually* reduce the amount of salt in your recipes. *Never* add salt to baby foods.

- Use chicken or vegetable stock or water instead of bouillon.

- Use herbs, spices, and lemon juice to enhance the flavors of foods.

- Use unsalted nut butters and crackers with less salt.

- Serve high-sodium foods less often and in smaller quantities.

- Make homemade versions of foods you usually buy ready-to-serve or as mixes.

- Read labels! Check the nutrition information for the milligrams of sodium in a serving.

Now There's Room for More Fiber-Rich Carbohydrates

Carbohydrates are the important source of energy for our bodies. They're found in many forms, however—and we recommend that you concentrate on those closest to how nature offers them. That is, choose whole grains and fresh fruits and vegetables as often as possible.

- Look for *whole-grain* cereal products, breads, and tortillas.

- Serve lots of fruits and vegetables, *unpeeled.*

- Serve *raw* fruits and vegetables often.

- Serve (cooked) dried beans and peas often.

- Serve dried fruits like prunes, raisins, or dried apricots occasionally; they are sticky, however, so make sure children brush their teeth afterward.

- Make sure children drink plenty of water so the fiber can move through their intestines.

- Don't depend on bran products to add fiber to children's diets; they generally don't need them.

High-Fiber Foods

Whole-grain breads	Millet	Bananas
Whole-grain cereals	Nuts and seeds	Dried fruits
Oatmeal	Popcorn	Raw vegetables
Barley	Dried beans, lentils	Cooked vegetables
Brown rice	Fresh fruits with skins	with skins
Bulgur wheat	Berries	

Wonderful Whole Grains

Whole grains are rich in complex carbohydrates, B vitamins, iron, magnesium, and selenium. Refined grains are often enriched with at least some of these nutrients, and also with folic acid, but where whole grains really differ from their refined counterparts is in the fiber department. Whole grains also have beneficial phytochemicals in their outer layers. There is simply no good reason not to be eating more whole grains in place of refined grains. They're delicious, they're more nutritious—what more could we ask for?

The chart on the next page will help you distinguish whole grains from processed grains.

Is It Whole Grain?

"Whole grains or foods made from them contain all the essential parts and naturally occurring nutrients of the entire grain seed. If the grain has been processed (e.g., cracked, crushed, rolled, extruded, lightly pearled, and/or cooked), the food product should deliver approximately the same rich balance of nutrients that are found in the original grain seed."

Food	Yes	No	Maybe*
Whole wheat berries	✓		
Whole wheat flour	✓		
Whole wheat pastry flour	✓		
Enriched wheat flour		✓	
Cracked wheat	✓[1]		
Bulgur wheat	✓		
Wheat bran		✓[2]	
Couscous			✓
White rice		✓	
Brown rice	✓		
Wild rice	✓		
Triticale	✓		
Spelt			✓[3]
Kamut	✓		
Rye	✓		
Buckwheat	✓		
Whole barley	✓		
Pearled barley	✓[4]		
Cornmeal			✓
Degerminated cornmeal		✓	
Polenta		✓	
Corn flour		✓	
Popcorn	✓		
Millet	✓		
Oatmeal	✓		
Oat flour	✓		
Oat bran		✓[2]	
Amaranth	✓		
Quinoa	✓		
Teff	✓		
Sorghum	✓		

Source: Whole Grains Council
www.wholegrainscouncil.org

* Read the label!
1 Cracked wheat is whole grain, but many products containing it are mostly white flour; read the label carefully.
2 However helpful the fiber is, the bran is only the outside part of the grain.
3 Spelt may be found in the "white," refined form.
4 "Lightly pearled" barley loses so few of the benefits of the true whole grain, and is so much easier to cook, that we're counting it as a whole grain!

Foods Chock-Full of Vitamin A

Vitamin A is found in enormous quantities in fish liver oils and in animal livers in general. Milk products, eggs, butter, and margarine are also good sources of vitamin A. The most significant sources of vitamin A in our diets, however, are fruits and vegetables. Actually, they contain substances called *carotenes* (of which beta carotene is the best known), which the body can convert to vitamin A. Carotenes appear to be safe even when consumed in very large amounts in foods. So plan to serve some of these carotene-rich fruits and vegetables at least every other day!

Vegetables

Asparagus
Beet greens
Broccoli
Carrots
Chard
Chili peppers
Collard greens
Dandelion greens
Kale
Mixed vegetables (frozen)

Mustard greens
Peppers (sweet red)
Pumpkin
Romaine lettuce
Spinach
Squash, winter
Sweet potatoes
Tomatoes
Turnip greens

Fruits

Apricots
Cantaloupe
Cherries (red sour)
Mangoes
Nectarines

Papayas
Peaches (except canned)
Plums (canned purple)
Prunes

Foods Bursting with Vitamin C

Foods containing vitamin C should be included in meals every day. Because vitamin C can be destroyed by cooking and exposure to air, you must take special care with these foods. Serve fruits and vegetables raw or lightly cooked to get the most vitamin C from them.

Vegetables

Asparagus
Broccoli
Brussels sprouts
Cabbage
Cauliflower
Chili peppers
Collards
Cress, garden
Dandelion greens
Kale

Kohlrabi
Mustard greens
Okra
Peppers, red and green
Potatoes
Spinach
Sweet potatoes
Tomatoes
Turnip greens
Turnips

Fruits

Cantaloupe
Grapefruit
Grapefruit juice
Guavas
Honeydew melon
Kiwi
Lemons
Mangoes

Orange juice
Oranges
Papayas
Pineapple, raw
Raspberries
Strawberries
Tangelos
Tangerines

Good Sources of Iron

Iron is one nutrient that often comes up short in children's diets. The iron found in meats ("heme" iron) is absorbed much more efficiently than that from nonmeat sources ("nonheme" iron), but nonmeat foods can and do make important contributions to the iron intake of children. Nonheme iron is absorbed better if vitamin C-containing foods are eaten along with it. Include several sources of iron in your menus daily.

Meat and Meat Alternatives Group

Dried beans and peas
Eggs
Meats, especially liver
Peanut butter

Pumpkin and squash seeds
Sardines
Shellfish
Turkey

Vegetables

Asparagus (canned)
Beans (green, lima, canned)
Beet greens
Beets (canned)
Broccoli
Brussels sprouts
Chard
Collards
Kale
Mustard greens
Parsley

Parsnips
Peas
Spinach
Squash, winter
Sweet potatoes
Tomato juice
Tomato paste
Tomato puree
Tomatoes (canned)
Turnip greens

Fruits

Apples (dried)	Peaches (dried)
Apricots (canned or dried)	Prunes
Cherries (canned)	Raisins
Dates	Strawberries
Figs (dried)	Watermelon
Grapes (canned)	

Breads and Grain Products

Any enriched or whole-grain breads and cereals, especially fortified instant hot cereals.

That Crucial Calcium

There is no question about the importance of calcium for maintaining good health. There is considerable controversy as to the levels of calcium intake that are really necessary and whether dairy products specifically are important or even appropriate for a healthful diet. We are not going to even attempt to answer those questions in this book. Rather, we'll give the guidelines that a majority of scientists and nutritionists support, with a caveat that recommendations could change later as more research is done. And we'll suggest alternative sources of calcium for those who can't or don't want to eat dairy foods.

The Dietary Guidelines for Americans 2005 and MyPyramid recommend 2 servings of milk daily for children 2 to 8 years of age and 3 servings of milk for older children. The rationale is that diets with sufficient milk and milk products support building and maintaining a strong bone mass. There is some indication that dairy products help maintain a healthy body weight, as well. Milk and yogurt are good sources of potassium and vitamin D, both of which tend to be consumed in insufficient amounts by many Americans. While it is true that people in some cultures never eat milk or milk products, the usual American diet tends to rely on dairy foods as the primary source of calcium. Skim or low-fat milk or yogurt and reduced-fat cheeses are the best choices in this case.

Nonetheless, it's getting easier to find alternatives to dairy products for those who can't eat them or choose not to. Using low-fat (1%) milk as the standard against which the following foods are measured, we've compiled a guide to some non-dairy sources of calcium.

If you're using fortified soy, nut, or grain-based beverages as a milk substitute, be sure to (1) buy the brand that is fortified with calcium carbonate, which is better absorbed in this situation, and (2) shake very well before each use, because the calcium doesn't stay in solution as it does in milk—it sinks to the bottom. Also keep in mind that while the soy beverage may be close to milk in protein content, nut- and grain-based beverages are not. They may also not have the potassium and vitamin D content of milk.

Foods High in Calcium

Foods High in Calcium*	Amount Equivalent to One Cup of 1% Milk**
Fortified soy beverage	¾ cup
Atlantic sardines in oil	2¾ ounces
Tofu prepared with calcium sulfate	⅔ cup
Canned pink salmon, with bones	5 ounces
Collards, cooked from frozen	¾ cup
Blackstrap molasses	5 teaspoons
Calcium-fortified orange juice	1 cup
Green soybeans (edamame), cooked	1¼ cups
Turnip greens, cooked from frozen	1¼ cups
Instant fortified oatmeal	3 packets
White beans, canned	1½ cups
Kale, from frozen, cooked	1½ cups

* Source: Dietary Guidelines for Americans 2005. More information on non-dairy sources of calcium is available at www.healthierus.gov/dietaryguidelines.

** Absorption of calcium from foods may vary; data are not available for all at this time.

And a Few Things We Don't Want in Our Food

Consumers are told that the American food supply is the "safest in the world," yet many grow increasingly uncomfortable with the idea of "all those chemicals in our food." Some of these fears seem to be justified; others are not. After all, even "natural" foods are made up of chemicals; for that matter, so are our bodies. Not all "natural" chemicals are good for us, just as not all synthetic chemicals are bad. Most of us can accept that. What we resent are the invisible substances, which could cause cancer, birth defects, or other problems, that may be lurking in our food without having good reason for being there and without our having any say in the matter!

Pesticide Residues and the Case for Organic Foods

Much of the furor over contaminants in foods has involved pesticide residues. The "Alar scare" in 1989 brought the issue of pesticide residues in foods to public attention in a big way. Parents, especially, were concerned about the dangers their children might face while eating the very fruits and vegetables that were supposed to be good for them. Children may face greater risks from pesticides because:

- They eat more for their body weight of the foods likely to have high levels of contaminants (they eat more fruit and drink more apple juice, for example).

- They're more susceptible to the effects of toxins and cancer-causing substances, because their body cells are dividing rapidly, and their immune systems are immature. It should be noted, however, that this depends on the chemical being studied.

- They will be living longer than people who are adults now, so cancer will have a longer time to show up in their bodies.

The Food Quality Protection Act of 1996 required the collection of sufficient information on infants' and children's food consumption to accurately determine the risk of pesticide residues to their health. Government agencies and scientists are trying to resolve some other issues, as well, such as how much to rely on tests with animals when determining chemical safety.

While health experts disagree on the extent of the hazards posed by pesticide residues, they do agree that it's better to go ahead and eat fruits and vegetables than to avoid them out of fear. There are steps you can take to minimize your exposure to pesticides.

How to Minimize Your Exposure to Pesticides

- Buy produce that is grown organically or with Integrated Pest Management.

- The following fruits and vegetables are most likely to be contaminated with pesticide residues. Buy organic whenever possible:

Apples	Peaches
Bell peppers	Pears
Celery	Potatoes
Cherries	Red raspberries
Grapes (imported)	Spinach
Nectarines	Strawberries

- The following fruits and vegetables have the lowest levels of pesticide residues. If you need to prioritize which produce to buy organic, it's relatively safe to buy the conventional varieties of these:

Asparagus	Kiwi
Avocados	Mango
Bananas	Onions
Broccoli	Papaya
Cauliflower	Pineapples
Corn (sweet)	Peas (sweet)

- Wash all fruits and vegetables in water; use a scrub brush and rinse well.

- Peel produce that has been waxed; it's obvious when cucumbers have been waxed, but apples, bell peppers, citrus fruits, eggplants, tomatoes, sweet potatoes, and squash may be waxed as well. Stores should have a sign letting consumers know when produce has been waxed.

- Trim the fat from meat, poultry, and fish. These foods, as well as butter, lard, cheese, and whole milk, may contain more pesticide residues than produce! That's because pesticides tend to accumulate in fat.

- Peas and dried beans usually have very low levels of pesticide residues . . . serve them often! Besides, they're nutritious and inexpensive.

- Plant a garden and grow your own. Better yet, let the children do it.

Buying organic products cannot guarantee that a food will be free of any trace of pesticide residues, because there is the possibility of pesticides drifting from neighboring fields and of some chemicals still lingering in the soil on farms that have converted to organic agriculture. However, every dollar spent on organic foods is a vote for something larger—a system of agriculture that attends to the health of the soil, our water supply, our air, agricultural workers, and consumers. There are some recent studies indicating that organic produce may have higher levels of antioxidants, so there could be other health benefits as well.

Mercury and PCBs in Fish

Mercury gets into the fish that we eat when *they* eat organisms in water that has been polluted by rain or runoff containing mercury, often from power plants that burn fossil fuels (especially coal). Large fish that have been feeding on other fish throughout their longer lives have the greatest concentrations of mercury in their bodies. The problem with mercury is that it accumulates in the body and can damage the nervous system. This is particularly worrisome for women who are or may become pregnant, infants, and young children.

The obvious solution to the problem would be to eliminate industrial release of mercury into the environment, but that has been slow in coming. Because there are so many nutritional benefits associated with eating fish, health agencies are concerned about consumers avoiding fish altogether. They have issued advisories clarifying which fish are more likely to contain high levels of mercury and should be avoided, which fish have levels of

---

Fish and Seafood That Appear to Be Relatively Safe and at the Same Time Abundant

Anchovies	Sardines
Farmed catfish	Scallops (farmed)
Pacific cod	Shrimp (farmed)
Crab	Pacific sole
Atlantic flounder (summer only)	Squids
Pacific flounder	Striped bass (farmed)
Mussels	Tilapia
Oysters (farmed)	Trout (farmed)
Salmon	Tuna (canned light)

• From the California Academy of Sciences (www.calacademy.org) and the *Essential Eating Well Seafood Guide* (www.eatingwell.com). Both synthesized information from FDA seafood advisories and sustainable fishery data.

mercury in the middle range and should be eaten in limited amounts, and which are likely to have low levels of mercury and can be eaten freely. Unfortunately, many fish in the latter category are also severely overfished in their habitats, so environmental concerns come into play as well.

Although there are fish that contain much more mercury (king mackerel, swordfish, shark, and tilefish), intense consumer interest has focused on canned tuna. And well that it should—canned tuna is the most commonly eaten fish in the United States and also has large quantities of healthy omega-3 fatty acids. It's inexpensive and many children love it. What to do? First, avoid all white (albacore) canned tuna. It's a larger fish and therefore contains more mercury. Canned light tuna, which comes from smaller varieties of the fish, appears to be relatively safe when eaten in limited quantities—that is, the benefits of eating it outweigh the possible harm. The National Resources Defense Council posted a chart on its website from which the following table was adapted. You'll want to consider a child's likely consumption of tuna both at home and at school or in childcare when planning your menus:

Child's Weight in Pounds	Quantity of Chunk Light Tuna That Can Be Eaten Weekly
11	1 oz.
22	2.1 oz.
33	3 oz.
44	3.5 oz.
55	4.5 oz.
66	5.25 oz.
77	6 oz.
88	7 oz.
99	8.25 oz.

If only mercury was our only worry! Now that Americans are eating more salmon, researchers are sounding the alarm about toxins in that, too. Particularly worrisome are PCBs (polychlorinated biphenyls), industrial pollutants that are thought to cause health problems, possibly cancer, in humans. PCBs are pretty much everywhere in our environment, and they're showing up in farmed salmon (from their chow) and even wild salmon, though in much smaller amounts. Presently, eating salmon is still a good idea, but you can reduce your exposure to PCBs by following these guidelines:

- Buy wild salmon when possible.

- Use canned salmon—most of it is wild (check the label, though).

- If you buy farmed salmon, look for Chilean farmed salmon, which so far is lower in PCB's than that from the Atlantic.

- Before you cook salmon, remove the skin and the fat under it. Broil, bake, poach, or grill the fish rather than sautéing it. This will allow some fat to drain off but still keep some of those beneficial omega-3s.

Genetically Modified Organisms (GMOs)

Genetically modified organisms (GMOs) are life forms that have been altered by having genes from another organism inserted into their DNA. The promise behind this "genetic engineering" has been an even more abundant food supply, with less need for pesticides and other chemicals in its production, or foods with enhanced characteristics such as more of a certain vitamin. In some cases genes from a very different species are given to another species; for example, genes from a fish may be inserted into a plant. The corporations involved in the production of these foods, and many scientists, maintain that they are extremely safe. Other scientists and consumers, however, have expressed alarm at the rapid proliferation of GMOs in our food supply. Unintended health impacts from GMOs could be:

- Allergens—because introducing new genetic material changes proteins in the food.

- Antibiotic resistance—when an antibiotic-resistant gene is inserted into a plant, which could then transfer to disease-causing bacteria in our bodies.

- Increased toxins—when naturally occurring plant toxins are increased or a new toxin is formed.

- Harm to the environment—loss of insects that may die when eating modified plants, contamination of other plants with new transgenic material.

Whether any of these concerns will prove to be of great importance remains to be seen. But that could be the point. Despite involvement of three government agencies—the Department of Agriculture, the Environmental Protection Agency, and the Food and Drug Administration, oversight of this technology is weak and there are no mandated pre-market safety studies. Consumers have every right to feel outraged that a powerful technology, however helpful it may prove to be, has been allowed to penetrate our food supply to a great extent with so little testing beforehand. GMOs are not allowed in organic foods, and if you want to "vote" in favor of more caution, this is a good place to put your money.

Bovine Growth Hormone

A related issue is the use of recombinant bovine growth hormone (rBGH) or bovine somatotropin (rBST) to increase milk production in cows. Cows produce their own version of the hormone, and studies have not been able to detect any difference between the natural and genetically engineered forms in milk. Thus, milk that has been produced by cows receiving rBGH is not required to carry a disclaimer on its label stating that the hormone was used. Although there may be some other safety issues, drinking milk from cows receiving rBGH probably results in more harm to the cows than to humans. Cows producing increased quantities of milk are more susceptible to infections in their udders and must be treated with antibiotics (which again, is not good news for us). But more importantly, as a dairy farmer who had tried using the hormone was heard to say, "Those ladies work hard enough as it is."

While you won't find information that milk was produced using rBGH/rBST on the carton's label, milk producers who *don't* use the hormone are more than happy to advertise the fact. Look for something like "This milk comes from cows not treated with rBST." The cows will thank you for it.

Other Contaminants

Food (and water) may contain other contaminants as well. Fungal poisons, heavy metals like lead, industrial chemicals, antibiotic residues, chemicals that migrate into food from packaging, and food colorings, flavorings, and many other food additives have the potential to cause health problems. Some of this contamination occurs naturally; some is the outcome of poorly-handled industrial waste, agricultural practices, and consumer demand for foods that taste and look a certain way. Changes will be needed in industrial practices and governmental enforcement to solve some of these problems.

You don't have to feel like a victim, however; you can do a lot to make sure the foods you serve are as safe as possible. For one thing, realize that one of the greatest dangers we face is food poisoning from bacteria or viruses . . . often a product of our own mishandling of food. Serve a wide variety of foods and "spread out" the potential contaminants. Seek out foods that are organically grown or free of artificial colorings and flavorings. Remember, you "vote" with your shopping dollars! Know where your food comes from;

avoid, for example, buying fish caught in polluted waters. And you can keep yourself informed about these issues, perhaps even find ways to become involved, by visiting these websites:

Center for Science in the Public Interest Food Safety Program:
www.cspinet.org/foodsafety
National Resources Defense Council:
www.nrdc.org
Environmental Working Group:
www.ewg.org
Organic Consumers Association:
www.organic-center.org

Your Faithful Lunchbox Guide

Although most parents are thrilled to be spared the daily chore of packing lunches for their children, we realize that there are circumstances where it isn't possible for a childcare setting or school to provide meals on-site. For the parents who will be putting together lunches, here are some ideas for choices within the essential groups of foods, with suggested serving sizes for younger children. Mix it up!

Protein-Rich Foods

Roasted chicken or turkey breast (1–2 oz)
Tuna or leftover fish (1–2 oz)
Salmon patty/loaf (2 oz)
Hard-boiled egg (1) or egg salad
Nut butter—don't stop at peanut! (2 T)
Reduced-fat cheese (1–2 oz)
"String" cheese (2)
Baked marinated tofu cubes (½ c)

Tofu "eggless" salad
Tempeh "fingers" (2 oz)
Refried beans (mix with a little salsa) (½ c)
Hummus
Bean soups (½ c)
Veggie-burger

Starchy Foods

Bread (1 slice, small roll)
Bagel (½)
Flour or corn tortilla (1)
Pita points (6–8)
Rice or pasta salad (½ cup)
Crackers (3–4)
Bread sticks
Rice cakes (2, or 6–8 mini)
Unsweetened cereal (½ cup)
Muffin (1 small)
Tabouli (½ cup)

Calcium-rich foods

Skim or low-fat milk (6 oz)
Soy or grain beverage* (6 oz)
Yogurt (6 oz)
Reduced-fat cheeses (1 oz)
Tofu** (5 oz)
Cottage cheese (¾ cup)
Corn tortillas (2)

* Calcium-fortified
** Must contain calcium sulfate

Fruits and Vegetables (At least 2)

Carrot sticks
Celery "boats"
Zucchini sticks
Cucumber slices or boats
Turnip rounds
Jicama sticks
Broccoli "trees"
Tomatoes
Lettuce
Cabbage salad
Spinach leaves
Pepper rings or sticks
Apples, oranges, pears, berries
Bananas, pineapple, kiwi
Mango, papaya
Melon cubes

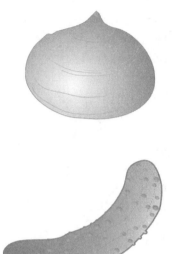

- Do use leftovers and combination foods: casseroles, pizza, dips made from cottage cheese or yogurt. See how your child likes cold leftover enchiladas at home first, though!

- Many children are happier with an assortment of finger foods than the classic sandwich and piece of fruit. Try a mix of vegetables and crackers or pita points with hummus, for example.

- Hot soups are much appreciated in cold weather. They should be packed in an insulated container, preferably metal.

- One reason that children throw out parts of their lunches or return them uneaten may be that the food is presented in a form that takes too long to eat. Consider this before packing hard-boiled eggs or fruit that needs to be peeled; peel and present in bite-size pieces for more success.

- It's best for lunches to be refrigerated until serving time, but frozen ice packs will work if no refrigerator is available.

In the interest of reducing lunchtime waste, we recommend that you avoid as much disposable food packaging as possible. **Laptop Lunches** makes the most thoughtful and fun lunchbox system we've ever seen—with colorful plastic inserts for different foods including dips or sauces and a carrying case that also functions as a tray. Insulated containers for beverages and soups or hot foods are also available. The company website not only has ordering information (and there's a discount for quantity orders) but an informative monthly newsletter as well: www.laptoplunches.com.

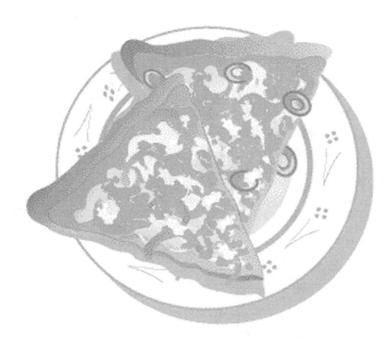

Snacks Are Important

Snacks can make important contributions to good nutrition. Children often can't eat enough to satisfy all of their needs at the standard three meals, and they may feel tired and miserable when opportunities to eat are spaced too far apart (so can adults, actually). The keys to making snacks work are *timing* and *food choices*.

- Establish regular snacktimes. Don't give handouts all day long, and don't let the children fill up on juice when they're thirsty.

- Schedule snacks a few hours before the next meal (so the children will be hungry enough at mealtime to eat, but not so hungry they are frantic), and a few hours after the last meal (so the children don't get the idea that they can refuse a meal and be rescued shortly thereafter).

- Snacks can be fairly substantial if it will be a long time before the children will eat again—lighter if you just need to hold off the hunger for a little while. When children are in child care for long afternoons, they may need a second, light snack around five o'clock. Parents facing the ride home and preparing late dinners are usually very appreciative when their children are fortified and reasonably cheerful!

- Be creative! Snacktime is a wonderful opportunity to use up leftovers, serve foods that are new and unusual, and have the kids participate in food preparation.

- Avoid serving foods that are highly sweetened or salted; make what you offer as nutritious as possible.

- Plan snacks to include a serving from at least 2 food groups. For ideas, see the sample menus beginning on page 177.

How Does Your Menu Measure Up?

A good menu does more than meet the basic requirements for servings from the 5 basic food groups of the food pyramid. With proper planning, you can make sure that the foods you serve are appealing, emphasize critical nutrients, and teach healthful eating habits. You also will be able to manage your costs and workflow better. Check your menu against the criteria below:

❑ Menu has some variety in:
  Color
  Texture
  Shape
  Temperature
  Flavors
  Preparation methods

❑ Whole-grain bread/cereal products are served often.

❑ Raw fruits and vegetables are served often.

❑ Good source of vitamin C is served daily.

❑ Good source of vitamin A is served at least three times/week.

❑ Good source of iron is served daily.

❑ Most of the foods are familiar to and enjoyed by most of the children.

❑ Some of the foods are new; some are familiar foods prepared in a different way.

❑ Higher-fat foods are balanced with lower-fat foods.

❑ Snacks fill in nutritional gaps in the main meals.

❑ Cultural, ethnic, and religious preferences are considered.

❑ Substitutions are planned for children with allergies.

❑ Holidays, birthdays, field trips, and special events have been planned for.

❑ Expensive foods are balanced with less expensive foods.

CHAPTER FOUR

The Recipes

About the Recipes . . .

In developing these recipes, we kept in mind that people who take care of children generally don't have a lot of time to cook. Even people who cook for children as a full-time job enjoy saving time! What we are promoting is the use of simple foods, made "from scratch." These foods are usually cheaper and taste fresher than processed foods. And very important, they give us more control over the amounts of fat, sugar, salt, and additives we serve.

Most of the recipes have been tested in very large quantities as well as very small ones. We aimed for testers in a variety of situations and in different parts of the country to make sure that we got a good picture of taste preferences and that ingredients would be readily available. Some recipes will obviously be unworkable due to time, transportation, or storage problems if you are running a centralized kitchen serving 500 children. They may, however, be useful as cooking projects in classrooms.

We have cut the fat, salt, and sugar in these recipes as much as possible, while still pleasing our obliging "taste testers," both children and adults. You may find at first that these recipes don't taste salty or sweet enough, but eventually your (and the children's) taste buds will get used to less salt and sugar. We also made the foods less spicy than we would ordinarily serve to adults. If you know that the children you're cooking for are very sensitive to spicy foods, you may want to cut the seasoning even further. On the other hand, some children have quite adventuresome palates, and you can be a little freer with the chili powder and such.

The serving sizes listed are the minimum amounts that must be served to count for reimbursement through the Child and Adult Care Food Program or the School Lunch Program.* You will want to make large enough quantities to allow for some second helpings, and you are probably aware, by now, of which items are likely to be especially popular with the children you're cooking for. In the interest of the children's health and of your budget, however, we don't suggest that you feel obliged to serve huge amounts of the meat or meat substitutes. Protein-rich foods (except dried beans) are usually the most expensive, and children don't need as much as you may think. If the children are still hungry, they can eat more vegetables, fruits, and grains instead. It's a habit that will serve them well when they grow up!

Bon Appetit!

---

* Unless otherwise specified, one serving of vegetables or fruit = ¼ cup. One serving of meat/meat alternate = 1 oz.

Recipe Table of Contents

Whole Grains

Introduction
In Praise of Oatmeal
Oatmeal Bar
Swiss Breakfast
Cereal Hash
Pancake Mixtures
    Basic
    Multigrain
    Wheatless
Chris's Pancakes
Gingerbread Pancakes
Banana Bread
Pumpkin Bread
Tropical Bread
"Bikini Bread"
Lemon Blueberry Muffins
Bulgur Pilaf
Pita Chips for Dips
Rice Cake Snacks
"Pizza Cake"
Savory Scrambled Cereals
Nori-Maki Rolls

Vegetables

Introduction

The Dark Green Vegetables
Chris's Lazy Method for Blanching Vegetables

Cream of Broccoli Soup
Senegalese Veggie Stew
Buttermilk Dressing

The Orange Vegetables
Sweet Potato Coins
Creamy Winter Squash Soup
Harvest Squash Bake
Pumpkin "Custard"

The Legumes (Dry Beans & Peas)
Lentil Soup
Garbo-Burgers
White Bean Soup
Vegetarian Chili
Hummus
Bean Dip

The Starchy Vegetables
Oven-Fried Potato Sticks
Mashed Potatoes and Carrots
A Different Potato Salad
Corn Soup
Homemade Potato Chips

The Other Vegetables
Roasting Vegetables
Far East Slaw
Shred-That-Salad!
Winter Salad
Fruit

Whole Grains

MyPyramid Daily Recommendation for Grains

Age group	Recommended Total Amount of Grains	Of Which at Least This Much Should Be Whole Grains
Childen 2-3 years	3 ounce equivalents	1½ ounce equivalents
Children 4-8 years	4 to 5 ounce equivalents	2 to 2½ ounce equivalents
Girls 9-13 years	5 ounce equivalents	3 ounce equivalents
Boys 9-13 years	6 ounce equivalents	3 ounce equivalents

An "Ounce Equivalent" of Grains Is Generally:*

1 slice of bread

1 cup of ready-to-eat cereal

½ cup cooked rice, pasta, or cooked cereal

½ mini bagel

5-7 crackers

½ English muffin

1 pancake (4½ inches)

1 corn tortilla

1 small flour tortilla

3 cups popped popcorn

*The Child and Adult Care Food Program has very specific requirements for grain foods based on weight. For adherence to regulations, it's essential to refer to the *Food Buying Guide for Child Nutrition Programs* (USDA, 2001).

Incorporating whole grains into your menu is easy. Breakfast is an especially good opportunity to serve whole grains, because several well-liked children's cereals are now made with 100% whole grains. Oatmeal, whole-grain toast (often better-accepted than whole-grain bread as a sandwich bread), and muffins, pancakes, and quick breads made with at least one-half whole grain flour are delicious ways to increase whole grain intake.

In Praise of Oatmeal

Oatmeal is simply one of the best breakfast cereals, nutritionally speaking and for the many ways it can be "dressed up" for eating fun.

Oats are a great source of slow-digesting complex carbohydrates, they are fairly high in protein as grains go, and they contain good amounts of thiamin, iron, and selenium. But it's the soluble fiber in oats that has gotten the most attention. This fiber seems to play a role in lowering blood cholesterol, especially the "bad" LDL cholesterol, and it may help control blood sugar as well.

Although all oatmeal is whole-grain, taste and texture are definitely sacrificed in the "instant" varieties. Those may be useful when traveling or for adult breakfasts eaten at the desk (there are even varieties specially fortified with women's needs in mind!). But to experience the true pleasure of a bowl of steaming oats, please use old-fashioned oats whenever possible. Cooking large quantities of oatmeal is a snap in a rice cooker. Use the usual proportions of oats to water (2 parts water to 1 part oats), add a little bit of salt, turn the rice cooker on, and walk away. You don't need to stand over the pot stirring when you undoubtedly have better things to do, and the oatmeal comes out perfectly fluffy.

"Oatmeal Bar"

The idea behind an "oatmeal bar" is similar to the salad bar. You set out the base, in this case the oats, along with an array of toppings from which the children can make their own special bowls of yummy oats. Children will enjoy making these choices even more if they are able to "do it themselves," so set out child-sized pitchers for milk and easy-to-use shakers for spices. Some suggestions for toppings are:

Sliced bananas

Berries (blueberries, raspberries)

Sliced strawberries

Chopped soft peaches or pears

Chopped apples*

Raisins*

Chopped dates*

Chopped prunes (dried plums)*

Toasted unsweetened coconut

Chopped nuts*

Cinnamon or pumpkin pie spice

Milk or soy, rice, or nut beverage

Yogurt

Be aware food safety regulations dictate that unused food that has been on the table in bowls will need to be thrown out after the meal. Plan your offerings with this in mind and you can avoid excessive waste. Spices in shakers and milk in covered pitchers should be fine to use later if the children haven't gotten their mouths or fingers all over the lids.

---

* Use with caution for children under age 4; these foods must be very finely chopped in order to avoid the risk of choking.

Swiss Breakfast

1¼ cups raw oats
1 cup water
2 T. wheat germ
2 T. honey or brown sugar

3–4 cups fresh fruit (bananas,
    blueberries, grated apples, etc.)
1 cup plain yogurt
1 T. orange juice

1. Stir oats and water together.
2. Let sit overnight in refrigerator.
3. In the morning, stir together the grains, yogurt, honey or brown
   sugar, and orange juice and serve with fruit . . . let the children add
   their own.

Note: Chopped toasted almonds and/or hazelnuts may be added.

Serves 8 preschool or 4 school-age children • 1 bread/grain + 1 fruit

Cereal Hash

Equal amounts of a variety of low-sugar cereals, which can include
naturally multicolored cereal rounds (available at health food stores).

Mix up a variety of cereals and store in an airtight container.
Aim for an interesting mix of shapes and sizes.

Preschool: ⅓ cup = 1 bread/grain

School-age: ¾ cup = 1 bread/grain

Pancake Mixtures

"Flying Saucers"

The following dry mixtures can be prepared in advance. When you wish to make pancakes, mix wet ingredients together, combine with dry mixture of your choice, and cook pancakes on a lightly greased skillet.

Basic:

4 cups unbleached flour	4 t. baking powder
4 cups whole-wheat flour	4 t. baking soda
2 cups buttermilk powder	2 t. salt
¼ cup sugar	

Combine 1¼ cups dry mixture with 1 cup water, 1 egg, and 2 T. oil.

Multigrain:

1 cup unbleached flour	2 T. sugar
1 cup whole-wheat flour	2 t. baking powder
1 cup cornmeal	2 t. baking soda
1 cup oat bran	1 t. salt
1 cup buttermilk powder	

Combine 1½ cups dry mixture with 1 cup water, 1 egg, and 2 T. oil.

Wheatless:

1 cup rice flour	1½ t. baking powder
1 cup oat bran	1 t. soda
1 T. sugar	¾ t. salt

Combine 1 cup dry mixture with 1 cup buttermilk, 1 egg, and 2 T. oil.

Eggless: Replace egg with egg substitute.

Each batch makes about 12 3-inch pancakes

Chris's Pancakes

1 cup whole-wheat flour
1 cup unbleached flour
1 T. sugar
1 t. baking soda
1 t. baking powder
½ t. salt
1 t. nutmeg

1½ cups buttermilk
½ cup orange juice
2 eggs
2 T. oil
1 t. vanilla
1 t. cinnamon

1. Mix dry ingredients together.
2. Mix wet ingredients together.
3. Mix wet and dry ingredients together.
4. Cook on lightly greased griddle.

Makes about 24 3-inch pancakes

Gingerbread Pancakes

"Gingerbread Frisbees"

1 cup whole-wheat flour
1 cup white flour
½ t. salt
1 t. baking soda
1½ to 2 cups buttermilk
2 eggs

3 T. molasses
1 t. ginger
½ t. cinnamon
½ t. ground cloves
1 T. oil

1. Mix dry ingredients together.
2. Mix wet ingredients together.
3. Mix wet and dry ingredients together.
4. Cook on lightly greased griddle.

Makes about 24 3-inch pancakes

Banana Bread

"Banana Gorilla Bread"

1 12.3-oz. package silken tofu
⅓ cup oil
1¼ cups sugar
2 eggs, slightly beaten
2 t. vanilla
2 cups very ripe mashed bananas
    (4 large or 5 small)

1 T. lemon juice
3½ cups whole-wheat pastry flour
2 t. baking soda
1 t. baking powder
1 t. salt
1 cup chopped walnuts or pecans
(optional)

1. Blend tofu and oil in food processor or blender until very smooth.
2. Add sugar, egg, and vanilla and blend very well.
3. Add bananas and lemon juice and process briefly.
4. Combine flour, soda, baking powder, and salt.
5. Gently combine liquid and dry ingredients. Fold in nuts (optional).
6. Put batter into 2 greased loaf pans.
7. Bake at 350° for 50–60 minutes or until done.

Each loaf serves 32 preschoolers or 16 school-age children • 1 bread/grain

Pumpkin Bread

1 12.3-oz. package silken tofu
¼ cup oil
1½ cups brown sugar
4 eggs
⅔ cup orange juice
1 15½-oz. can pumpkin (2 cups)
3½ cups whole-wheat pastry flour

1 t. baking powder
2 t. baking soda
1 t. salt
2 t. cinnamon
1 t. ground cloves
1 cup currants, raisins, or
   chopped nuts

1. Blend oil and tofu in blender or food processor until very smooth.
2. Add sugar, eggs, orange juice, and pumpkin, and blend again.
3. Stir together dry ingredients.
4. Add to pumpkin mixture.
5. Stir in currants or raisins (or chopped nuts).
6. Pour into 2 greased loaf pans.
7. Bake at 350° for about 1 hour or until toothpick comes out clean.

Each loaf serves 32 preschoolers or 16 school-age children • 1 bread/grain

Tropical Bread

1 cup whole-wheat flour
2½ cups unbleached flour
2 t. baking soda
½ t. salt
1 cup sugar

½ cup oil
2 eggs
2 very ripe bananas, mashed
1 cup crushed pineapple, drained
  (1 8-oz. can)
2 t. vanilla

1. Combine flours, salt, and soda.
2. Cream together sugar, oil, and egg.
3. Stir in bananas and pineapple.
4. Add flour mixture, stirring gently.
5. Stir in vanilla.
6. Bake in 2 greased loaf pans at 350° for 45 minutes.

Each loaf serves 24 preschoolers or 12 school-age children • 1 bread/grain

"Bikini Bread"

1 cup whole-wheat flour
1 cup unbleached flour
1½ t. baking powder
1 t. cinnamon
1 t. ground cloves
¼ t. baking soda
½ cup chopped walnuts

½ t. salt
⅓ cup oil
½ cup sugar
2 eggs
1 t. vanilla
2 cups grated zucchini

1. Sift or stir dry ingredients together.
2. Beat oil, sugar, eggs, and vanilla until fluffy.
3. Add dry ingredients to wet mixture.
4. Fold in zucchini and nuts.
5. Bake in greased loaf pan at 350° for 45 minutes.

Each loaf serves 32 preschoolers or 16 school-age children • 1 bread/grain

Lemon Blueberry Muffins

2 eggs
½ cup sugar
¼ cup oil
⅞ cup milk
rind and juice of 1 lemon
2 cups flour (whole-wheat pastry
   or ½ whole-wheat, ½ white)

1 T. baking powder
½ t. baking soda
½ t. salt
1½ cups blueberries
   (dredged in 1 T. flour)

1. Mix eggs, sugar, and oil, and beat until foamy.
2. Add milk and lemon.
3. Stir together flour, baking powder, soda, and salt.
4. Stir into liquid ingredients until just blended.
5. Gently fold in blueberries.
6. Spoon batter into muffin cups.
7. Bake at 425° for 20 minutes.

Makes 12 muffins • 1 bread/grain

Bulgur Pilaf

½ cup onion, chopped
1 T. oil
1 cup bulgur wheat
2 T. sesame seeds

2 cups water or stock
¾ t. salt
2 t. parsley flakes
1 clove garlic, whole

1. Sauté onion in oil for 5 minutes.
2. Add bulgur and sesame seeds. Sauté for 2 minutes.
3. Add remaining ingredients.
4. Bring to a boil, then simmer for about 15 minutes or until liquid is absorbed.
5. Remove garlic clove before serving.

Serves 12 preschool or 6 school-age children • 1 bread/grain

Pita Chips for Dips

"The Big Dippers"

1 lb. pita bread, preferably whole wheat

1. Cut pita breads in half and separate pieces where joined at the edges.
2. Stack and cut pieces into wedges.
3. Place in a single layer on a lightly oiled baking sheet.
4. Bake for 6–10 minutes at 400°, until brown and crisp.

Serves 32 preschool or 16 school-age children

Rice Cake Snacks

"Saucy Cheese Cake"

1 rice cake (brown rice is best)
2 T. grated cheddar or jack cheese
salsa

1. Spread cheese on rice cake.
2. Bake at 350° until cheese melts.
3. Top with salsa.

Serve 1 per preschool or 2 per school-age child for snack • 1 bread

"Pizza Cake"

1 rice cake (brown rice is best)
2 T. "Instant" Pizza Sauce (p. 174)
2 T. grated mozzarella cheese

1. Spread sauce, then cheese, on rice cake.
2. Bake at 350° until cheese melts.

Note: Can be microwaved, but they get soft.

Serve 1 per preschool or 2 per school-age child for snack • 1 bread

Savory Scrambled Cereals

5 cups unsweetened or low-sugar cereals,
    mixed (e.g., Cheerios, Wheat Chex,
    Rice Chex, Corn Chex, Crispix,
    Kix, Shredded Wheat)
1 cup small pretzel rings*
1 cup unsalted, roasted peanuts*

2 T. olive oil
1 T. Worcestershire sauce
1 t. seasoning blend such as
    Mrs. Dash
⅛ t. garlic powder

1. Stir Worcestershire and seasonings into the olive oil.
2. Toss in cereals, pretzels (optional), and peanuts (optional), stirring gently to coat.
3. Bake at 250° for 30–45 minutes, stirring about every 15 minutes, until toasty.

* Omit for children under 5 years old.

Serves (approximately) 15 preschool or 7 school-age children • 1 bread/grain

Nori-Maki Rolls

You may think kids won't like sushi, but you might be surprised!

2 cups medium-grain white rice
2½ cups water
3 T. rice vinegar (not the seasoned variety)

2 t. sugar
½ t. salt
5–6 sheets toasted seaweed
(sushi nori)

Fillings: About 2 cups altogether. (Use your imagination! This is a good way to use up little bits of leftovers):

Carrots, cut into thin strips and
steamed lightly
Cucumber, cut into thin strips
Spinach or chard, steamed and sprinkled
with toasted sesame seeds and a
little soy sauce

Green onions, cut into thin strips
Avocado
Cooked shrimp or crab
Canned or smoked salmon (lox)
Canned tuna (chunk light)

1. Rinse the rice and let it drain.
2. Place rice in saucepan with water. Bring to a boil, cover, turn heat way down, and cook for 20 minutes.
3. At the end of the cooking time, let the rice sit for 10–15 minutes. Resist the urge to remove the lid from the pot!
4. Turn rice out into a large bowl or roasting pan. Sprinkle the vinegar, salt, and sugar over it and mix well.
5. Allow rice to cool to room temperature.
6. Place a sheet of the seaweed (shiny side down) on a cutting board. The short side should be top-to-bottom.
7. Wet your hands and spread with ¾–1 cup rice, leaving about a ½-inch border at the bottom and 1 inch at the top.
8. Make an indentation in the rice horizontally along the middle. Arrange your choice of fillings over this. (It's okay if it's humped up.)
9. Start rolling from the bottom, squeezing with both hands as you go. Moisten the top border of the seaweed with some water, and keep rolling until the end.
10. Cover rolls tightly with plastic wrap and refrigerate until ready to serve (up to 48 hours, depending on the fillings).
11. At serving time, cut each roll with a sharp knife into 8 pieces and arrange on a platter. Mustard and pickled ginger are good accompaniments.

Serves 20 preschool or 10 school-age children • 1 bread/grain

Vegetables

MyPyramid Daily Recommendation for Vegetables

Age group	Recommended Amounts (Total, of a Variety of Vegetables)
Childen 2-3 years	1 cup
Children 4-8 years	1½ cups
Girls 9-13 years	2 cups
Boys 9-13 years	2½ cups

Weekly Recommended Amounts of Vegetable Subgroups

Age Group	Dark Green Vegetables	Orange Vegetables	Legumes	Starchy Vegetables	Other Vegetables
Children 2–3 years	1 cup	½ cup	½ cup	1½ cups	4 cups
Children 4–8 years	1½ cups	1 cup	1 cup	2½ cups	4½ cups
Girls 9-13 years	2 cups	1½ cups	2½ cups	2½ cups	5½ cups
Boys 9–13 years	3 cups	2 cups	3 cups	3 cups	6½ cups

A Cup of Vegetables Is:*

1 cup cooked vegetable

2 cups raw leafy vegetable

---

* More specific serving sizes can be found on the MyPyramid website: www.mypyramid.gov

The Dark Green Vegetables

Bok choy

Broccoli

Collard greens

Dark green leaf lettuce

Kale

Mesclun

Mustard greens

Romaine lettuce

Spinach

Turnip greens

Watercress

This group of vegetables, so rich in important nutrients like beta-carotene, vitamin C, iron, and often, calcium, can appear to be the most challenging to get children enthusiastic about. Yet, prepared well and offered frequently, these delicious gifts from the plant kingdom can become some children's favorites.

Sturdy greens like bok choy, kale, collards, mustard, and turnip greens are delicious when thinly shredded and sautéed with some olive oil and garlic, then covered so the steam finishes cooking the leaves. They are also fine added to stews and soups.

More delicate greens like romaine lettuce, mesclun, dark leaf lettuce, spinach, and watercress are wonderful bases for a salad bar. Remember that children, even very young ones, enjoy being able to assemble their meals to their own taste. The element of choice really helps with food acceptance.

Broccoli quickly becomes a favorite vegetable in groups of children—those who've been primed for vegetable acceptance, that is. Who can resist "little trees?" Some children do fine with raw broccoli, but we've found that blanched broccoli works even better. It's still bright green and has a little crunch to it, but the flavor isn't quite so pungent.

Chris's Lazy Method for Blanching Vegetables

Bring a big pot of water to a boil. Drop in vegetables that have been cut to a uniform size. Keep the heat on high; the water may or may not return to a boil by the time the vegetables are done. After 3 to 5 minutes, check a piece by piercing it with the tip of a knife. If it goes in easily, stop the cooking by draining the vegetables and spreading out on a baking sheet or plastic platter. Put in the freezer and set the timer for 5 minutes (so you don't get busy doing something else and end up with frozen vegetables!). Place the vegetables in the refrigerator to finish chilling.

Cream of Broccoli Soup

"Swamp Soup"

1½ lb. broccoli, chopped
   (include most of the stems)
½ medium onion, chopped
1 T. oil
2 cups water
2 cups milk

1 potato, scrubbed and cut into
   chunks
1 rib celery, sliced
1 carrot, chopped
½ t. nutmeg
¾ t. salt
½ t. pepper (preferably fresh ground)

1. Sauté onion in oil.
2. Add carrot and celery and sauté for 2–3 minutes.
3. Add broccoli, potato, and water, and simmer until vegetables are quite tender.
4. Stir in 1 cup of the milk, and purée the mixture in a blender or food processor.
5. Return to pan and add the other cup of milk and seasonings.
6. If too liquid, thicken with 1 T. cornstarch mixed into 2 T. cold milk and heat.

Note: Nice with Parmesan cheese on top!

16 vegetable servings at ¼ cup

Senegalese Veggie Stew

1 onion, chopped
1 T. oil
2 cups winter squash or sweet potato,
    peeled and cut into chunks
2 medium potatoes, cut into chunks
1 large carrot, cut into chunks
1 small bunch of greens (collards or
    turnip greens) *or* 1 10-oz. pkg.
    frozen greens

¼ t. cayenne
1 cup tomato sauce
1 to 1½ cups water
⅜ cup peanut butter (6 T.)
Salt to taste

1. Sauté onion in oil for a few minutes.
2. Add remaining vegetables one at a time, sautéeing each for a few moments
   before adding the next.
3. Add cayenne, tomato sauce, and water.
4. Simmer until vegetables are tender.
5. Mix some of the broth with the peanut butter.
6. Add to the vegetables and cook another 10 minutes.
7. Taste for seasoning and add salt if desired.
8. Serve over rice or millet.

16 vegetable servings at ¼ cup

Buttermilk Dressing

"Brontosaurus Milk Dressing"

1 cup buttermilk
¾ cup mayonnaise
½ t. pepper
2 t. dried minced onion

½ t. garlic powder
¼ t. salt
1 t. parsley flakes
¼ t. dill weed

1. Whisk ingredients together.
2. Let sit for at least 1 hour to blend flavors before using.

Makes 1¾ cup

The Orange Vegetables

Carrots

Pumpkin

Sweet potatoes

Winter squash

Sweet and nutritious, the orange vegetables have so much to offer—vitamin B6, iron, potassium, and impressive amounts of beta carotene. Carrots are the favorite of storybook bunnies, and especially in their raw "baby" form, of many children as well. Winter squash and sweet potatoes are often well-liked also—but please, let's move beyond the mountains of brown sugar and even marshmallows! These noble vegetables often benefit from clever seasoning, but they are sweet enough on their own.

A recipe for roasted sweet potatoes follows, but all of these hard orange vegetables develop an extra-rich flavor when roasted. See "Roasting Vegetables," page 149.

Sweet Potato Coins

2 lb. sweet potatoes   2–3 T. olive oil

1. Scrub and dry the sweet potatoes. Do not peel!
2. Slice into rounds ½ inch thick.
3. Spread the olive oil on a baking sheet big enough to fit your sweet potatoes in a single layer.
4. Spread the sweet potato rounds on the baking sheet, then flip over so that both sides are oiled.
5. Bake at 400°F for about 20 minutes, or until the sweet potatoes are soft to the touch and getting slightly golden.
6. Try serving these sprinkled with a little salt and lemon or lime juice.

Note: This recipe was tested with Garnet yams, a very moist and sweet variety of sweet potato common in California. It's worth experimenting with varieties available in your area to find those that aren't too dry and mealy.

16 vegetable servings at ¼ cup

Creamy Winter Squash Soup

2 lb. winter squash (butternut, acorn),   1 T. oil
   peeled and cubed   2–3 t. mild curry powder
1 onion, chopped   Salt to taste
1 red pepper, diced
10 oz. frozen corn *or* fresh corn cut from 2 ears

1. Lightly sauté onion and curry powder in oil.
2. Add squash and 3 cups water, and simmer until squash is very tender.
3. Purée mixture in batches in blender.
4. Return to pot and add enough water or milk for desired consistency.
5. Add red pepper and corn, and cook gently until they are tender.
6. Add salt to taste.

16 vegetable servings at ¼ cup

Harvest Squash Bake

"Harvest Moon Squash"

1½ lb. winter squash (butternut, acorn, banana), peeled, seeded, and cut into chunks
1 apple, cored and cut into chunks

2 T. raisins or currants
½ cup orange juice
1 T. butter, cut into pieces

1. Stir all ingredients together.
2. Put into greased shallow baking dish.
3. Bake covered at 375° for about 45 minutes, sitrring occasionally

10 vegetable servings at ¼ cup

Pumpkin "Custard"

"Jack O'Lantern Pudding"
(no milk, no eggs)

1 15-oz. can pumpkin purée (2 cups)
8 oz. tofu (regular or firm)
6 T. brown sugar
1 T. molasses

1 t. cinnamon
¼ t. ginger
¼ t. cloves

1. Blend all ingredients in food processor until very smooth.
2. Pour into oiled casserole.
3. Bake at 350° for 35–40 minutes.
4. Chill and serve.

Note: This can also be used as a dairyless pie filling.

7 vegetable servings at ¼ cup

The Legumes (Dry Beans & Peas)

Black beans

Black-eyed peas

Garbanzo beans (chickpeas)

Kidney beans

Lentils

Lima beans (mature)

Navy beans

Pinto beans

Soybeans

Split peas

Tofu

White beans

Legumes are low in fat and rich in protein and complex carbohydrates. They are unique in belonging to two groups within the MyPyramid system and also the Child and Adult Care Food Program meal patterns (they are also considered alternatives to meat). These marvelous and versatile foods contribute iron, vitamin B6, zinc, potassium, and often, folate to our diets—and children love them!

Dried beans are so inexpensive that cooking up a big pot may seem well worth the trouble of sorting, rinsing, and perhaps pre-soaking them. The new generation of pressure cookers makes cooking pre-soaked beans a ten-minute proposition—with consistently good results. Canned beans are a good and tasty option, however, and are still less expensive on a per-serving basis than many other protein-rich foods in the market.

Cooked dried beans make a wonderful addition to salad bars. It's best to set them out in their simplest form—no complex mixtures or dressing added—and let the children choose how to dress them up.

Lentil Soup

"Gentle Lentil Soup"

2½ cups lentils, rinsed and drained
7 cups water or stock
2 medium onions, chopped
3 cloves garlic, minced
Juice of one lemon
Salt and pepper to taste

2 stalks celery, chopped
2 T. olive oil
1 or 2 bunches spinach, chard, or collards, washed and chopped coarsely

1. Sauté onions, garlic, and celery in the olive oil, 5–10 minutes.
2. Add lentils and water or stock, and simmer until lentils are very soft. If necessary, add more water to get soup to desired consistency.
3. Add greens, salt, and pepper. Simmer for 10 more minutes or until greens are tender.
4. Stir in lemon juice right before serving.

24 1-oz. servings • meat alternative

Garbo-Burgers

"Beanie Burgers"

1 15½-oz. can garbanzo beans, drained
1⅓ cups rolled oats
1 cup water
1 t. Italian seasoning
a small onion, minced, *or* 1 t. onion powder

⅛ t. garlic powder
1½ T. soy sauce *or*
   2 t. Worcestershire sauce
1 T. olive oil

1. Run beans through food processor until they have a texture like ground meat.
2. Add remaining ingredients (except for oil) and allow to sit for 10–15 minutes so water is absorbed.
3. Heat olive oil in skillet.
4. Spoon large or small patties into the skillet; press down into burger shapes.
5. Cook on both sides until browned.

Note: Use as burgers or to fill in for the veal in a vegetarian version of "Veal Parmesan." Small patties can be eaten as finger food and/or dipped into sauces, too.

6 1-oz. servings • meat alternative

White Bean Soup*
"Speckled Soup"

1½ cups white beans
4 cups water or stock
2 cloves garlic, minced
2 stalks celery, chopped
2 carrots, chopped
1 onion, chopped
2 T. olive oil

2 t. dried basil
½ lb. green beans in 1" pieces *or*
   ½ lb. zucchini, sliced in half-moons
2 T. lemon juice
¾ t. salt
Pepper to taste

1. Soak beans in water to cover by 2" overnight. Drain in the morning.
2. Sauté garlic, onion, celery, and carrots in oil for about 10 minutes.
3. Add soaked beans and the 4 cups of water or stock.
4. Simmer until beans are tender, about 45 minutes.
5. Add basil and green beans or zucchini and simmer another 30 minutes or so, until tender.
6. Before serving, stir in lemon juice, salt, and pepper.

15 1-oz. servings • meat alternative

* Adapted from *Still Life with Menu* © 1988 by Mollie Katzen. Reprinted by permission of Ten Speed Press, Berkeley, California.

Vegetarian Chili
"Jack and Jilli Chili"

3 1-lb. cans pinto or black beans, drained
  (save liquid)
1 T. oil
1 large onion, chopped
1 bell pepper, chopped

3 garlic cloves, chopped
1 t. cumin
2 t. chili powder
1 1-lb. can tomatoes
½ t. salt

1. Sauté onion and green pepper in oil for about 5 minutes.
2. Add garlic and sauté another minute.
3. Add remaining ingredients and simmer about 20–30 minutes. Add bean liquid if necessary to retain moist consistency.

Variation: **Chili-Mac.** Toss with 6–8 oz. of macaroni, cooked.

18 1-oz. servings • 1 meat alternative (+1 bread/grain if macaroni is added)

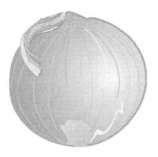

Hummus
"Quicksand"

1¾ cups chickpeas (15-oz. can)
1½ T. tahini
1½ T. lemon juice
½ t. garlic, crushed
½ t. cumin

¼ t. paprika
¼ t. salt
1 T. olive oil
¼ cup water

1. Blend all ingredients except water in food processor.
2. Add water 1 T. at a time, until you have the right consistency (a fairly thick purée).
3. Process until very smooth.
4. Use as spread with crackers, pita bread, or as a dip for vegetables.

6 1-oz. servings • meat alternative

Bean Dip
"Mud Dip"

1½ cups cooked (or canned) pinto or black beans
1 T. Mexican spice mix (below)
6 oz. grated jack or cheddar cheese

1. Mash beans with a fork or potato masher.
2. Stir in spice mix and grated cheese.
3. Heat until cheese melts, on the stove or in the microwave.

Mexican Spice Mix:
¼ t. garlic powder
1 T. onion powder

1 T. cumin
2 T. chili powder

12 1-oz. servings • meat alternative

The Starchy Vegetables

Corn

Green lima beans

Green peas

Potatoes

These vegetables are rich sources of complex carbohydrates and fiber, and they contain some protein and an array of vitamins and minerals as well. Unfortunately, children are getting too many servings of this vegetable group in the form of french fries and missing out on the nutrition these foods have to offer.

The majority of peas grown in this country are frozen or canned, and frozen peas are a very convenient food to have on hand. Simply defrosted, they are wonderful additions to salads and pasta dishes. Likewise, frozen corn retains a good texture and flavor and can be added to soups, stews, and our favorite—quesadillas!

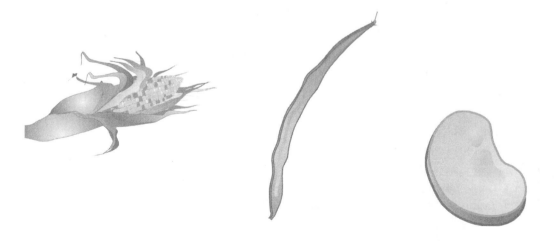

Oven-Fried Potato Sticks

"Fiddlesticks"

4 baking potatoes, scrubbed and dried (about 2 lbs.)
1 T. oil
¼ t. paprika

1. Cut each potato into 8–12 wedges.
2. Toss with oil and paprika.
3. Spread in shallow pan.
4. Bake until tender, 20–30 minutes at 450° *or* 35–40 minutes at 400°.

16 vegetable servings at ¼ cup

Mashed Potatoes and Carrots

"Monster Mash"

1 lb. raw potatoes (russet)
1 lb. raw carrots
2 t. butter or olive oil

Salt and pepper to taste
½ t. soy sauce (optional)

1. Wash potatoes and cut into eighths.
2. Scrub carrots and cut into 1" chunks.
3. Cook potatoes and carrots gently in about 1 cup of water. If they get too dry, add a little more water. If it looks too runny, let some of the water evaporate.
4. Mash, or put in food processor, with butter, salt, pepper, and the soy sauce (if desired).

Note: Thanks to Barbara Zeavin for this recipe.

16 vegetable servings at ¼ cup

A Different Potato Salad

4 medium potatoes, scrubbed
1 10-oz. pkg. peas and carrots
½ large dill pickle, chopped
¼ cup chopped onion
2 T. plain low-fat or nonfat yogurt

2 T. reduced-fat mayonnaise
2 T. lime juice
1 t. olive oil
Salt and pepper to taste

1. Steam the potatoes until tender. When cool enough to handle, cut them into cubes.
2. Steam the peas and carrots until cooked. Then cool.
3. Mix remaining ingredients in a large bowl.
4. Add the cooled potatoes, peas, and carrots.
5. Chill and serve.

12 vegetable servings at ¼ cup

Homemade Potato Chips
"Tato Pips"

1 lb. russet potatoes
Vegetable oil

1. Preheat oven to 400°.
2. Slice potatoes paper-thin. (A food processor will make this easier.)
3. Spread the slices out in a single layer on a foil-lined or lightly oiled cookie sheet.
4. Bake for 15 or 20 minutes.
5. Remove when cooked to a crisp, golden brown.

8 vegetable servings at ¼ cup

Corn Soup
"Uni-corn Soup"

1 medium onion, chopped
2 t. oil
2 10-oz. pkg. frozen corn *or*
    fresh corn cut from 6 ears
2¼ cups chicken or vegetable
    broth *or* water

2 cups milk
1 red pepper, chopped (optional)
¾ t. salt
1–3 cloves garlic, chopped
½ t. sugar

1. Sauté onion in oil until transparent.
2. Add corn, cover, and cook 15 minutes.
3. Add broth, 1 cup milk, salt, garlic, and sugar.
4. Simmer for 15 more minutes.
5. Take out about 1 cup of the corn; add 1 cup milk to the pot.
6. Purée in batches in blender until smooth.
7. Return to pot, add the reserved whole corn kernels and red pepper, and heat gently.
8. Season to taste with pepper.

12 vegetable servings at ¼ cup

The Other Vegetables

Artichokes

Asparagus

Bean sprouts

Beets

Brussels sprouts

Cabbage

Cauliflower

Celery

Cucumbers

Eggplant

Green beans

Green or red peppers

Iceberg lettuce

Mushrooms

Okra

Onions

Parsnips

Tomatoes

Tomato juice

Vegetable juice

Turnips

Wax beans

Zucchini

Don't let the term "other vegetables" give you the impression that the vegetables on this list are somehow inferior to the other vegetable groups—they just don't easily lend themselves to grouping with the others. Yet each has its unique and noteworthy nutritional qualities. Some are very high in vitamin C, others in iron, and the list of phytochemicals these vegetables contain is truly impressive. Serve and enjoy a variety of them often!

It's worth noting that many of the vegetables on this list are excellent for serving on "vegetable & dip" platters. Asparagus, brussels sprouts, cauliflower, and green and wax beans may be best appreciated when blanched. See "Chris's Lazy Method for Blanching Vegetables," p. 132.

Many of the vegetables on this list also develop a sweet, rich flavor when roasted, particularly the root vegetables (onions, parsnips, and turnips), asparagus, green beans, red and green peppers, mushrooms, and zucchini.

Roasting Vegetables

- Heat the oven to 425°.

- Wash the vegetables and dry well.

- Cut into uniform shapes (hard vegetables) or simply trim away the inedible parts and leave whole (asparagus, green beans, mushrooms).

* If you are roasting different types of vegetables, they may not have the same cooking time. Separate pans help.

- Toss in a bowl with a small amount of olive oil.

- Spread in a single layer in a baking pan and roast until the vegetables are soft and developing just a touch of caramelization (browning). That's what makes them sweet, but if it proceeds too far, the vegetables will taste bitter.

- Serve and enjoy!

Far East Slaw

6 cups finely shredded cabbage (1½ lb.)
1 red or green pepper, chopped fine
1 8-oz. can sliced water chestnuts

¼ cup chopped peanuts
Seasoned rice vinegar or
 Buttermilk Dressing to
 taste

1. Combine ingredients in a large bowl.
2. Dress with seasoned rice vinegar or Buttermilk Dressing (p. 135)

24 vegetable servings at ¼ cup

Shred-That-Salad!
"Confetti"

Salad Mix:
¾ lb. green cabbage
½ lb. red cabbage
2 carrots
2 green peppers

1. Shred in food processor and place
 in large bowl.
2. Toss with either Oil and Vinegar *or*
 Curry-Yogurt Dressing.

Oil and Vinegar Dressing:
3 T. olive oil
3 T. vinegar
Salt and pepper

Curry-Yogurt Dressing:
6 T. yogurt
6 T. reduced-calorie
 mayonnaise
2 t. curry powder
Salt

20 vegetable servings at ¼ cup

Winter Salad

½ head butter lettuce
1 large carrot, grated
2 medium-sized raw beets, grated
1 package radish sprouts *or* 1 piece of daikon (white) radish about the same size
    as the carrot, grated*
Seasoned rice vinegar to taste (the seasoned vinegar has some sugar and salt
    in it, which is important for the flavor of this salad)

1. Arrange lettuce leaves on a platter.
2. Arrange carrot, radish sprouts or radish, and beets in separate piles on top of
   the lettuce. It's fun to play around with decorative patterns.
3. Sprinkle some of the vinegar over each salad before eating.

* Young children should not eat sprouts.

12 vegetable servings at ¼ cup

Fruit

MyPyramid Daily Recommendation for Fruit

Age group	Recommended Amounts (Total, of a Variety of Fruit)
Childen 2-3 years	1 cup
Children 4-8 years	1 to 1½ cups
Girls 9-13 years	1½ cups
Boys 9-13 years	1½ cups

A Cup of Fruit Is:

1 cup sliced, diced, chopped, cooked, or canned fruit

½ cup dried fruit

1 cup of 100% fruit juice

It's a rare child who needs convincing to eat fruit. Fruits are naturally sweet, and they are so nutritious, too! They are low in fat, high in fiber and potassium, and depending on the fruit, they may be rich sources of vitamin A (beta carotene), vitamin C, iron, or folic acid. They offer a wide array of phytochemicals as well.

In general, fruit requires no special preparation beyond washing and perhaps slicing. Some recipes follow for times you'd like to add an extra twist to the fruits you serve. The important thing is to strive for variety in the fruits you offer.

Wiggly Fruit

2 t. (1 envelope) unflavored gelatin
2–3 cups sliced fruit

2 cups unsweetened fruit
    juice (not fresh pineapple)

1. Mix gelatin with ¼ cup juice in a bowl.
2. Measure another ½ cup juice and bring to a boil.
3. Add hot juice to gelatin mixture, stirring until all of the gelatin is dissolved.
4. Add remaining juice and chill until it begins to set.
5. Add fruit, stir, and chill until firm.

Note: Strong-flavored juices like grape, cherry, or raspberry work best. Apple-raspberry juice with peach slices is great!

8 fruit servings at ¼ cup

Micro-Fruit

1 lb. apples, halved and cored, *or* 1 lb. pears,
    halved and cored, *or* 1 lb. bananas,
    halved lengthwise

Cinnamon, ginger, *or*
    cinnamon sugar

1. Sprinkle fruit with cinnamon, ginger, or cinnamon sugar.
2. Place on microwave-safe dish.
3. Bake in microwave oven: pears, about 1½ minutes; apples, about 3 minutes; bananas, about 45 seconds to 1 minute.

Note: This is even yummier with a spoonful of plain yogurt on top!

6 fruit servings at ¼ cup

Soft-Serve Fruit

"Frosty Fruit"

2 lbs. bananas, peeled and cut into chunks
or 2 lbs. mangoes, peeled and cut into chunks

1. Freeze fruit (but not rock hard).
2. Run frozen fruit through food processor. (You may need to soften it up a bit first. Let it run long enough to whip a lot of air into the mixture, but not long enough to completely thaw the fruit.)
3. Serve right away.

Note: Cantaloupe, peaches, or strawberries may also be used, but you will need to use a little fruit juice to get the right consistency.

12 fruit servings at ¼ cup

Frosty Fruit Shakes

Peanut Butter Banana:
2 cups milk *or* 1½ cups plain yogurt
2–3 bananas, frozen (about 1 lb.)
3 T. peanut butter

Liquid Sunshine:
2 cups milk *or* 1½ cups plain yogurt
1 cup crushed pineapple
2–3 bananas, frozen (about 1 lb.)
½ t. vanilla

Bananaberry:
2 cups milk *or* 1½ cups plain yogurt
2–3 bananas, frozen (about 1 lb.)
1 cup strawberries or blueberries (may be frozen)
½ t. vanilla

Spicy Apple:
1½ cups plain yogurt
2 cups chunky applesauce
½ t. cinnamon
Ice cubes or crushed ice

Purée in blender and serve immediately.

8 fruit servings at ¼ cup

The Meat & Beans Group
(Includes Poultry, Eggs, Nuts, and Seeds)

MyPyramid Daily Recommendation for Meat and Beans Group

Age group	Recommended Amounts
Children 2-3 years	2-ounce equivalents
Children 4-8 years	3–4-ounce equivalents
Girls 9-13 years	5-ounce equivalents
Boys 9-13 years	5-ounce equivalents

An "Ounce Equivalent" of Meat Is:*

1 oz. cooked lean beef, pork, lamb, or skinless poultry

1 oz. cooked fish or shellfish

1 egg

½ oz. nuts or seeds

1 tablespoon nut butter

¼ cup cooked dry beans or lentils

¼ cup (2 oz.) tofu

2 tablespoons hummus

---

* The Child and Adult Care Food Program has somewhat different requirements in its meal pattern. If you depend on CACFP reimbursement, you must adhere to those quantities.

The foods in this group are protein-rich foods that supply the essential amino acids, vitamins, and minerals necessary for the growth and repair of body tissues. Our recipes emphasize fish, poultry, beans and lentils, and nuts because they are the choices that are lower in saturated fats, often rich in essential fatty acids, and gentler on the environment in their production.

Look for hearty recipes containing dried beans and lentils in the Vegetables section starting on page 130.

Yummy-for-the-Tummy Baked Fish

1 lb. fish filets (Pacific flounder,
    Pacific sole, tilapia)
2½ cups fresh whole-wheat bread crumbs
⅓ cup chopped onion
1½ T. lemon juice
½ t. Italian seasoning

1 t. parsley flakes
¼ t. salt
⅛ t. pepper
1 T. olive oil
3 T. Parmesan cheese
⅛ t. garlic powder

1. Spread out fish filets in oiled baking pan.
2. Combine remaining ingredients and spread over fish.
3. Bake at 400° for about 15 minutes or at 375° for 20 minutes.

11 1-oz. servings • meat

Homemade Fish Sticks

"Sea Sticks"

1 lb. pollock or Pacific cod, cut into sticks
1 egg white, beaten
1½ T. oil
¾ cup cornflake crumbs

½ t. onion powder
1⁄16 t. garlic powder
Salt and pepper to taste

1. Mix together beaten egg white and oil.
2. Combine cereal crumbs, onion powder, garlic powder, salt, and pepper.
3. Dip fish sticks into egg white mixture, then roll in seasoned flakes.
4. Bake at 400°, 10–15 minutes, turning once.

11 1-oz. servings • meat

Salmon Cakes or Muffins

1 1-lb. can of salmon, flaked
½ cup chopped onions
2 T. lemon juice
1½ t. dill weed
¼ t. tabasco *or* dash of cayenne pepper

¾ cup cracker meal
2 egg whites
½ cup milk
¼ t. salt
¼ t. pepper

1. Mix all ingredients well.
2. Shape into patties and place on a greased baking sheet or portion into greased muffin cups.
3. Bake at 400° for about 20 minutes.

11 1-oz. servings • meat

Tuna Salad

"Looney Tooney Salad"

2 6½-oz. cans water-packed chunk light
    tuna, drained and flaked
½ cup plain yogurt or a mixture of
    ½ yogurt and ½ mayonnaise
2 minced scallions

2 minced celery ribs
½ t. curry powder
¼ t. salt
4 T. water chestnuts,
    chopped (optional)

1. Mix all ingredients together.
2. Eat as salad or sandwich spread.

10 1-oz. servings • meat

Nuts About Peanuts

Peanuts aren't true nuts; they are actually the shell-enclosed seeds of a legume that's related to peas and beans, and the pods grow underground!

Delicious, inexpensive, and a favorite food of many children, peanut butter provides protein, niacin, folic acid, magnesium, vitamin E, and even fiber. The fats in peanut butter are primarily the kinds that are good for your heart, but peanut butter is high in fat and therefore calories, so it's a good idea to serve lower-fat foods along with it for balance.

For reasons that aren't well-understood, an increasing number of children are being diagnosed with peanut allergies, and their reactions can be so severe that it may be necessary to ban all peanut products from your premises. If this does occur, it's essential to have a plan in place and good communication among all parents and staff members involved, in order to avoid any unnecessary incidents where a child accidentally encounters peanut products and suffers a life-threatening reaction.

For those who can eat it, however, peanut butter is a versatile and healthful addition to your menu. Try it:

- On top of toast, pancakes, and waffles, to add some extra protein in the morning

- As a dip not just for celery, but also for carrots, cucumbers, apples, and bananas

- As an addition to smoothies

Peanut Butter Ping Pong Balls

Version 1:
½ cup peanut butter
¼ cup honey

½ t. vanilla
2–3 cups Rice Krispies or
    crispy brown rice cereal

1. Stir together peanut butter, honey, and vanilla.
2. Stir in cereal.
3. Wet hands and form the mixture into balls.
4. Place on waxed paper and chill. Store in covered container in refrigerator.

Version 2:
½ cup peanut butter
¼ cup molasses

½ t. cinnamon
2–3 cups Rice Krispies or
    crispy brown rice cereal

Repeat directions as above.

Serves 6 preschool or 4 school-age children for breakfast or snack
• 1 meat alternative + 1 bread/grain

Magical Peanutty Simmer Sauce

½ cup peanut butter

1¾ cups chicken or vegetable broth, water, or half broth/half water

2 oz. (½ small can) chopped mild green chiles

2 cloves garlic, chopped, or ½ tsp crushed garlic in a jar

1 tsp. grated ginger (again, you can use the bottled variety)

1 tsp. salt (less if your broth is very salty)

¾ tsp. chili powder

½ tsp. pepper

1. Put all ingredients in the blender and blend away!
2. Let the mixture sit to meld flavors as you prepare other ingredients (this sauce can be made in advance and kept refrigerated, up to 2 days, until you are ready to cook with it).

How to Use the Simmer Sauce:

Chicken in Simmer Sauce: Sauté 1 cup chopped onion in a small amount of oil for 5–10 minutes, until soft. Add 1¼ pounds boneless, skinless chicken breast or thigh meat, in bite-size pieces, and stir for a minute or two. Add the simmer sauce. Cook over low heat until the chicken is done and the sauce has thickened somewhat, about 15–25 minutes. The sauce will thicken more as it stands.

Tofu in Simmer Sauce*: Sauté 1 cup chopped onion and 20 ounces firm tofu in ¾ inch cubes, in a small amount of oil until the tofu has begun to brown on all sides. Add the simmer sauce and cook over low heat until the tofu is heated through and the sauce has thickened somewhat, about 15 minutes.

- Serve on plain brown rice. Allow the sauce to spill over onto these great go-withs: steamed carrots, spinach, or greens, or chunks of baked sweet potato.

- For a yummy Thai-inspired sauce, substitute 1 cup of light coconut milk for 1 cup of the broth or water and 2 Tbsp. low-sodium soy sauce for the salt in the original recipe.

With chicken: 18 1-oz. servings meat
* Since tofu is not yet reimbursable for CACFP, the peanut butter itself would account for 4 1-oz. servings of meat "alternate"

Chow Mein Salad

½ lb. Napa (Chinese) cabbage, shredded
⅓ lb. mung bean sprouts
¼ lb. snow peas
1 or 2 scallions, tops only, thinly sliced
1 rib celery, thinly sliced
1 8-oz. can water chestnuts, sliced
9 oz. cooked chicken meat, shredded
1 5-oz. can chow mein noodles
(crispy type)

Dressing:
2 T. plain rice vinegar
2 T. toasted sesame oil
1 T. vegetable oil
2 T. soy sauce
1 garlic clove, pressed, *or*
⅛ t. garlic powder
½ t. powdered ginger
½ t. sugar

1. Blanch bean sprouts and snow peas separately, about 2 minutes, in boiling water. Let cool in refrigerator.
2. Combine all salad ingredients in large bowl.
3. Combine dressing ingredients and toss with salad.

Variations:
Romaine lettuce can be used instead of Napa cabbage.
You can substitute 9 oz. cooked shrimp for the chicken.

8 1-oz. meat servings + 8 vegetable servings

Marek's Chicken

4 lbs. chicken pieces
2 cloves garlic, pressed
Juice of one lemon
1-inch piece ginger root, peeled and
    chopped fine

2 bunches scallions, cut into
    1-inch pieces
1 T. curry powder
2 T. oil
Salt to taste

1. Remove skin from chicken pieces.
2. Brown chicken and ginger in oil, about 5 minutes.
3. Add scallions, garlic, and curry powder, and sauté about another 5 minutes.
4. Add lemon juice, about ¼ cup water, and salt. Cover the pan and simmer until chicken is thoroughly cooked, adding more water if necessary to keep the mixture very moist. Serve with rice.

Note: Chris's friend, Marek, learned to cook this dish in Nepal.

24 1-oz. meat servings

Chicken Fingers
"Slim Pickin' Chicken Fingers"

The meat:
1 lb. boneless, skinless chicken breasts sliced across the "grain" in ¾-inch strips, or 1 lb. chicken "tenders"

The coating mix:
1 cup fine dry breadcrumbs or cornflake crumbs (ready-made crumbs are cheaper than the cereal)
½ t. salt
½ t. garlic powder
½ t. onion powder
½ t. poultry seasoning
¼ t. pepper
¼ t. paprika

The "glue"
2 egg whites *or* ½ cup buttermilk

1. Combine the cereal crumbs and seasonings.
2. Mix the chicken pieces with the buttermilk *or* beat the oil with the egg whites and combine with the chicken pieces.
3. Roll the chicken in the crumbs, pressing lightly if necessary, and spread out on a baking sheet that has been oiled or sprayed with pan spray.
4. Bake at 400°, turning over once, for 15 minutes, or until a sample piece shows no pink when you cut it.

10 1-oz. servings • meat

Three Marinades for Chicken

Each is enough for about 2 lbs. chicken pieces or strips of chicken breast

Mustard-Honey Marinade
¼ cup honey
2 T. Dijon-type mustard
1 clove garlic, pressed *or* ⅛ t. garlic powder
2 T. rice vinegar
1½ t. dark sesame oil
1½ T. soy sauce

Teriyaki Marinade
¼ cup soy sauce
¼ cup orange juice
1 T. brown sugar
2 cloves fresh garlic, pressed, *or* ¼ t. garlic powder
1 t. fresh grated ginger *or* ½ t. powdered ginger

Mint-Garlic Marinade
1 cup plain yogurt
2 T. chopped onion
1 t. dried mint
2 cloves garlic, pressed, or ¼ t. garlic powder
½ t. salt

For each marinade, mix all ingredients together.
Bake or grill chicken until no pink remains.

Sloppy Josephines

1¼ lbs. ground turkey
¾ cup onion, chopped
1 cup tomato sauce
2 T. prepared mustard
1 T. Worcestershire sauce

1 t. brown sugar
⅛ t. garlic powder
Salt and pepper to taste
Whole-grain hot dog or
   hamburger buns

1. Sauté onion and turkey gently until turkey is cooked through, breaking up large clumps. Add small amount of oil if necessary to prevent sticking.
2. Add remaining ingredients and simmer 15 minutes.
3. Serve on hot dog or hamburger buns.

14 1-oz. servings • meat

Turkey Loaf
"Loafin' Turkey"

1¼ lbs. ground turkey
1 10-oz package frozen broccoli
1 cup sharp cheddar cheese, grated
1 cup soft whole-wheat bread crumbs
1 egg

⅓ cup milk
½ cup chopped onion
1 t. fines herbes
2 t. prepared mustard
½ t. salt
⅛ t. pepper

1. Steam broccoli until just barely cooked.
2. Mix with all other ingredients in a large bowl.
3. Pack into a loaf pan and bake about 1 hour at 350°.

18 1-oz. servings • meat

Turkey "Lollipops"

1¼ lbs. ground turkey
1 T. oil
2 T. chopped cilantro (optional)
½ t. salt

1 cup chopped onions
1 T. curry powder
1 cup soft whole-wheat breadcrumbs
¼ t. pepper

Sauce: Plain yogurt and apple butter
You'll need popsicle sticks, available from restaurant supply or craft stores.

1. Sauté onion in the oil until translucent.
2. Add curry powder to the onions and sauté for about 5 minutes, being careful not to burn the curry powder.
3. Mix all the ingredients together with your hands.
4. Form the mixture into 14 balls for toddlers and school-age children and into 9 balls for preschoolers. Flatten slightly to form patties about ¾ inch thick.
5. If you are making a small batch, fry in a skillet, using pan spray, for 15–20 minutes over medium heat. Cook until the temperature in the middle of a patty reaches 165°F.
6. For larger batches, baking on baking sheets is more practical, though the patties won't brown as nicely. Spray a baking sheet with pan spray and bake at 375°F for 15–20 minutes, or until the temperature in the middle of a patty reaches 165° F.
7. Insert popsicle sticks into the patties to make "lollipops."
8. Serve with ketchup or a dipping sauce made of equal parts plain lowfat yogurt and apple butter.

Ground turkey varies in its cooking qualities. If you find that the patties come out dry, the next time add one beaten egg to the recipe above.

Servings:
14 1-oz. meat servings for toddlers (1 each)
9 1½-oz. meat servings for preschoolers (1 each)
7 2-oz meat servings for school-age childen (2 each)

Green Eggs and Ham

8 eggs
½ cup minced fresh parsley (chives are
    also nice, but optional)
½ cup milk

Oil
4 oz. cooked turkey ham
    or Canadian bacon
Salt and pepper to taste

1. Beat eggs, parsley, and milk together.
2. Scramble egg mixture in a heavy or nonstick pan in a small amount of oil.
3. Serve with small amounts of turkey ham or Canadian bacon on the side.

20 1-oz. servings

The Milk, Yogurt, and Cheese Group

MyPyramid Daily Recommendation for the Milk Group

Age group	Recommended Amounts
Childen 2-3 years	2-cup equivalents
Children 4-8 years	2-cup equivalents
Girls 9-13 years	3-cup equivalents
Boys 9-13 years	3-cup equivalents

A "Cup Equivalent" of Milk Is:*

1 cup skim, low-fat, reduced-fat, or whole milk

8 oz. (1 cup) yogurt

1½ oz. hard cheese

⅓ cup shredded cheese

½ cup ricotta cheese

2 cups cottage cheese

---

* The Child and Adult Care Food Program has different requirements in its meal pattern. Only fluid milk "counts" as milk. The other dairy foods are considered meat alternatives, and CACFP uses different quantities to determine acceptability. If you depend on CACFP reimbursement, you must adhere to those quantities.

Milk and milk products provide not only calcium for building and maintaining bone mass, but potassium, which may help to maintain healthy blood pressure, and vitamin D, which helps to maintain the correct levels of calcium and phosphorus in the body. Calcium-fortified beverages such as soy milk or fruit juices may supply calcium in amounts at or close to dairy milk, but they don't necessarily have the other nutrients that dairy foods offer.

Much of the artery-clogging saturated fat in the American diet can come from dairy foods. Be sure to make choices lower in fat such as skim or low-fat milk and yogurt (for children 2 years and older) and reduced-fat cheeses. Use the stronger-flavored hard cheeses sparingly, when their flavor and texture really counts, and balance them with lower-fat foods.

Chilaquiles*

1 dozen corn tortillas, several days old
1 cup onions, chopped
2 cloves garlic, pressed *or* ¼ t.
  garlic powder
2 t. chili powder

1½ cups low-fat cottage cheese
1½ cups canned crushed tomatoes
6 oz. grated jack or cheddar
  cheese
Salt to taste

1 t. cumin powder   1 T. oil

1. Cut tortillas into wedges or tear into strips.
2. Sauté onions in oil for 5 minutes. (A nonstick or cast-iron skillet that's ovenproof is ideal for this.)
3. Add tortilla pieces, chili powder, garlic, cumin, and salt.
4. Toss until the tortilla pieces are wilted.
5. Purée cottage cheese and tomatoes in blender until smooth.
6. Stir gently into tortilla pieces.
7. Sprinkle with grated cheese.
8. Bake at 350° for about 20 minutes.

12 1-oz. meat servings • 12 grain/bread servings

* Adapted from *Laurel's Kitchen* by Laurel Robertson, Carol Flinders, and Bronwen Godfrey. Petaluma, Calif.: Nilgiri Press, 1976.

One-Pot Macaroni and Cheese

8 oz. dry macaroni or other pasta
2 cups low-fat milk
1½ T. cornstarch
¾ t. salt
¼ t. fresh ground pepper
½ t. dry mustard

¼ t. paprika
12 oz. sharp cheddar cheese,
   grated
2 scallions, green part only,
   thinly sliced *or* chives (optional)

1. Cook macaroni.
2. While macaroni is cooking, combine milk and dry ingredients in a jar and shake very well.
3. When macaroni is tender, drain it and return to pan.
4. Add milk mixture and stir gently over medium heat until sauce thickens.
5. Add cheese and optional scallions or chives, stir until melted, and serve.

12 1-oz. meat servings • 12 grain/bread servings at ¼ cup

Easier-Than-Lasagna

8 oz. macaroni or spiral pasta
1 onion, chopped
4 cloves garlic, chopped
2 T. olive oil
2 t. oregano
1 t. basil
1 bay leaf

1 28-oz can (3¾ cups) crushed
   tomatoes
1 t. salt
½ cup water
2 cups cottage cheese or
   ricotta cheese
½ cup Parmesan cheese
9 oz. brick or jack cheese, grated

1. Sauté onion and garlic in the oil.
2. Add tomatoes, herbs, salt, and water and simmer 30 minutes.
3. Cook pasta until just tender.
4. Stir all ingredients together except the brick or jack cheese to sprinkle on top. Bake for 20 minutes at 375°.

18 1-oz. meat servings • 18 grain/bread servings at ¼ cup

Taco Salad

8 cups shredded lettuce
1 lb. fresh tomatoes, diced
6 oz. cooked chicken or turkey, shredded or diced
    or 6 oz. cooked ground beef
    or 1½ cups cooked dried beans (kidney, pinto, or black beans)
6 oz. grated cheddar or jack cheese
1 cup crumbled tortilla chips

Dressing:
3 T. oil
1½ T. red wine vinegar
2 T. water
⅛ t. garlic powder
½ t. oregano
½ t. chili powder
¼ t. cumin powder
¼ t. salt

1. Combine dressing ingredients.
2. Toss lettuce and tomatoes with dressing.
3. Spread meat or beans and cheese over top.
4. Sprinkle crumbled tortilla chips over all.

Optional additions: Fresh raw corn cut from the cob, scallions, cilantro, avocado

12 1-oz. meat servings + 12 vegetable servings at ¼ cup

Build-a-Sundae

1½ cups yogurt *or* cottage cheese
1 lb. chopped fruits

Optional toppings:
  Nuts
  Unsweetened cereals
  Honey or maple syrup

1   Put yogurt or cottage cheese in individual bowls.
2. Add fruits (applesauce, raisins, chopped dates, berries, bananas, etc.).
3. Top with nuts, cereals, and/or honey or maple syrup (optional).

6 1-oz. meat servings • 6 fruit servings at ¼ cup

Hot Chocolate

4 cups milk
1½ T. sugar

1½ T. cocoa powder

1. Combine cocoa powder and sugar with about ¼ cup milk.
2.   Whisk in the remaining milk.
3. Cook over medium heat, stirring constantly, until milk is hot but not boiling. *Or,* heat in microwave 2–3 minutes, or until milk is hot.

4 cups milk (servings vary)

Mock Sour Cream
"Make Believe Sour Cream"

2 cups cottage cheese   2 T. lemon juice
2 T. low-fat milk

1. Run the ingredients through the food processor or blender until the mixture is absolutely silky smooth. Makes about 2 cups.

8 1-oz. servings • meat

Creamy Dill Dip
"Dippity Doo Dah Dip"

2 t. parsley flakes
1 t. dill weed
2 small garlic cloves, pressed

1. Add to 2 cups Mock Sour Cream.

Toasted Onion Dip

2 T. dry minced onions, toasted lightly 3–5 minutes at 350°
2 t. soy sauce
Dash of garlic powder

1. Add to 2 cups Mock Sour Cream.

Sunshine Dip

2 cups plain nonfat or low-fat yogurt   2 T. orange juice concentrate

1. Mix together.
2. You can experiment with concentrates of other juices, too! Try grapefruit, tangerine, lemonade, or limeade.
3. Use as a dip for pieces of raw fruit—peaches, strawberries, kiwi, bananas, and so on.

8 1-oz. meat servings

"Instant" Pizza Sauce

2 cups canned crushed tomatoes   1½ t. oregano
¾ t. garlic powder   ½ t. salt
1 t. basil   ¼ t. pepper

1. Stir all ingredients together.
2. Let sit at least 1 hour.
3. Use as sauce for pizzas.

Makes 2 cups

Quick Pizzas
"Road Runner Pizza"

For each child:

Base:
English muffin half, or flour tortilla, or pita bread, split, or slice of French bread

2 T. "Instant" Pizza Sauce (recipe on previous page)
2–4 T. (½–1 oz.) cheese—mozzarella, cheddar, jack, provolone, or a mixture, grated or sliced

1. Spread "Instant" Pizza Sauce over base.
2. Cover with cheese and any other toppings you fancy.
3. Bake at 425° until bubbly.

Toppings:
Sliced mushrooms, green peppers, onions, olives, artichoke hearts, and so on.

1 meat alternative + 1 bread per serving for snack

CHAPTER FIVE

• •

Sample Menus Using Our Recipes

In spite of many, many years of experience planning menus for children and adults (for our own families, too), inevitably an afternoon comes when we face a menu-planning form littered with blank spaces. Sometimes we need to get out of a rut, for example, serving the same vegetable with the same meat and grain combination for years. Sometimes we're trying a new recipe and aren't sure what flavors, colors, and textures will go well with it, and sometimes a menu-planning session comes at the end of a day that has already been way too long. Whatever the reason, all of us need inspiration now and then, and sample menus offer just that.

The following menus feature recipes from this book and aim for nutritional balance, fun for the children, and ease for the cook!

Ten Breezy Breakfasts

It's easy to help children get a good start on the day when you have healthful make-ahead foods on hand. Quick breads and muffins can be made in large batches and frozen until needed. The dry ingredients for pancakes can be measured out the night before or made up in large quantities as a "mix." You can cook hot cereals and stew fruit very successfully in a microwave oven. And you needn't restrict your thinking to traditional "breakfast foods." Sandwiches and even pasta can taste great in the morning!

Banana Gorilla Bread Peanut butter Sliced apples Hot chocolate	Scrambled eggs **Pumpkin Bread** Orange slices Milk	**Multigrain Pancakes** Applesauce Milk
English muffins **Micro-Fruit** Yogurt topping Milk	**Swiss Breakfast** Milk	Cottage cheese **Bikini Bread** Sliced pears Milk
Lemon Blueberry Muffins Banana chunk Milk	Oatmeal Assorted fruits and nuts Milk	**Cereal Hash** Strawberries Milk

Bagels Sliced turkey & low-fat cheese Tomatoes Milk

Fine Finger Feasts

Most children love eating with their hands. Although we certainly think that they should get lots of practice with flatware, we know that meals that can be eaten entirely with the fingers are a fun change of pace. They're also easy on the cook.

Cold sliced omelets
Nori-Maki Rolls
Sliced cucumbers
Tangerines
Milk

Cold **Turkey Loaf** cubes
Oven-Fried Potato Sticks
Broccoli and carrot sticks
Crackers
Milk

Chicken Fingers
Bread sticks
Assorted raw vegetables
Apple wedges
Milk

Quick Pizzas
Assorted raw vegetables
Apples
Milk

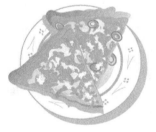

Bean Dip
Tortillas (corn or flour), heated
and cut into strips or wedges
Jicama sticks
Fresh pineapple spears
Milk

Homemade Fish Sticks
Sweet Potato Coins
Zucchini and green pepper strips
Bread
Milk

Teddy Bear Tea Parties

Tea parties, complete with teddy bears or other favorite stuffed animals, are a delightful and relaxing ritual for snacktime. The "tea" can actually be warmed apple cider, hot cocoa, or basic herbal tea, such as peppermint (chamomile, although mild, can cause problems for children with ragweed allergies). If you have some sturdy teacups, by all means use them. Lots of foods are appropriate for teatime—as long as they are dainty.

Assortment of crackers
Slices of cheese
(preferably reduced-fat varieties)
Assorted fruits
"Tea"

Peanut butter and honey
sandwiches, cut into triangles
Sliced peaches
"Tea"

Peanut Butter Ping Pong Balls
Banana
"Tea"

Open-faced **Tuna Salad**
sandwiches on toast points
Apples and raisins
"Tea"

Bikini Bread
Strawberries with **Sunshine Dip**
"Tea"

Lunch Around the World

Few of the ethnic recipes in this book are authentic. That's because we found that traditional preparation methods were too lengthy, ingredients were difficult to find, or the authentic versions contained too much fat or salt. Similarly, the menus listed below are not truly representative of meals eaten in certain cultures. However, these menus do illustrate typical flavor principles of a variety of cuisines and include foods that might be eaten together in a meal. If you're interested in presenting truly ethnic meals to the children, ask friends or the children's parents for family recipes and menu outlines.

Baked chicken or fish
Rice or millet
Senegalese Veggie Stew
Bananas
Milk

Chicken baked in **Mint-Garlic Marinade**
Bulgur Pilaf or pita bread
Cucumber slices
Dried figs
Milk

Chicken baked in **Teriyaki Marinade**
Rice
Steamed broccoli
Plums
Milk

Marek's Chicken
Rice
Steamed greens
Apricots
Milk

Chilaquiles
Shred-That-Salad!
Papaya
Milk

Easier-Than-Lasagna
Green salad
Grapes
Milk

Chow Mein Salad
Bread
Oranges
Milk

Vegetarian Menus

One-Pot Macaroni and Cheese
Steamed broccoli
Apple wedges
Milk

Easier-Than-Lasagna
Carrot and zucchini sticks
Milk

White Bean Soup
Whole-wheat bread
Assorted raw vegetables
Pears
Milk

**Taco Salad with
Beans and Cheese**
Crackers
Milk

Vegetarian baked beans
Cornbread or crackers
Shred-That-Salad!
Oranges
Milk

Red beans
Rice
Sweet Potato Coins
Far East Slaw
Milk

Chilaquiles
Cabbage salad
Pineapple chunks
Milk

Scrambled eggs
English muffins
Oven-Fried Potato Sticks
Fresh fruit salad
Milk

Lentil Soup
Bread sticks
Green salad
Apples
Milk

Quick Pizzas
Spinach salad
Pears
Milk

Peanut butter or cheese toast points
Creamy Winter Squash Soup
Apples
Milk

Garbo-Burgers in pita bread
with lettuce and tomato
Melon wedges
Milk

Snacks by the Dozen!

Hummus **Pita Points**	Peanut butter Apples to dip	Baked sweet potato Milk
Turkey Loaf cubes Cucumber slices	Whole wheat toast Cottage cheese	**Build-a-Sundae**
Oven-Fried Potato Sticks **Mock Sour Cream** dip	**Spicy Apple Fruit Shake** Whole-wheat crackers	**Banana Bread** Milk
Tuna Salad Pita bread Lettuce and tomato	Assorted nut and seed butters Bread triangles	Cottage cheese Sliced bananas
Soft-Serve Fruit Whole-wheat crackers	**Hummus** Cucumbers and baby carrots	**Quick Pizzas** Celery sticks
Sliced fruits **Sunshine Dip**	**Bean Dip** Tortilla wedges	Grilled cheese sandwich Apple slices
Nori-Maki Rolls Tangerines	**Lentil Soup** Whole-wheat breadsticks	**Peanut Butter** **Ping-Pong Balls** Bananas
Sliced cheeses and turkey breast Tomatoes	**Gingerbread Pancakes** Applesauce	**Green Eggs and Ham** Toast
Vegetable platter with **Buttermilk Dressing** Crackers	String cheese Breadsticks **Instant Pizza Sauce** to dip	Yogurt Strawberries Sliced almonds

More Snacks by the Dozen!

Corn tortillas Shredded cheese Avocado slices	**Cereal Hash** Blueberries Milk	**White Bean Soup** Crackers
Peanut butter Carrots, celery, and cucumbers to dip	**Liquid Sunshine (fruit shake)** Toast	**Lemon Blueberry Muffins** Milk
Micro-Fruit (Apples or pears) Cheese slices	Hard-boiled egg Vegetable platter with dip	French toast Applesauce
Vegetarian Chili Crackers	Oatmeal Sliced bananas Milk	Mixed nuts Sliced apples
Pumpkin Bread Pears		

Are You Still Stuck in a Meal-Planning Rut? Have a Little Fun with These Ideas!

- Serve "breakfast" foods for lunch.

- For a fun change, serve any kind of sandwich filling in an ice-cream cone (sorry, not reimbursable on the Child and Adult Care Food Program) or a whole-wheat hot dog bun.

- Make a "dip-it" lunch with a serving of protein-rich dip (examples: hummus, cottage cheese, nut butter, or Bean Dip), an assortment of vegetables and/or fruit, and crackers, soft tortillas, or bread strips.

- Plan a "shapes" week: Monday all square-shaped food, Tuesday all rounds, Wednesday all sticks, Thursday all triangles, Friday all stars (use small cookie cutters, usually available at cake-decorating shops).

- Plan a "colors" week: Monday all yellow food, Tuesday all red, Wednesday all green, Thursday all orange, Friday all white (if you're feeling really adventurous, try blue!).

- Plan a meal with foods that begin with the same letter (examples: chicken, crackers, corn, cantaloupe).

- Fill a flour tortilla with unconventional fillings and take advantage of children's enthusiasm for burritos: scrambled eggs, cheese, and potatoes or broccoli; peanut butter and bananas; Yummy-for-the-Tummy Baked Fish, lettuce, and tomato or tartar sauce; Tuna Salad, sprouts, and tomatoes; teriyaki chicken and Far East Slaw; shredded chicken in barbeque sauce and coleslaw . . . you get the idea!

- Set up stuffed baked potato bars and let the children put together their own "personal potatoes." Here are some possibilities: broccoli, cheese, and ham or turkey ham; spinach, ricotta and mozzarella cheeses, and marinara sauce; chili with beans, cheese, lettuce, tomato, and olives; chicken in barbeque sauce and corn. Some light sour cream (thinned with milk if desired) or Buttermilk Dressing may be appreciated to moisten the mixture.

Meal Planner

Week of: _____

Meals	Monday	Tuesday	Wednesday	Thursday	Friday
Breakfast Bread or Grain Fruit or Veggie Milk					
Snack Choose from 2 groups					
Lunch Bread or Grain "Meat" Vegetable Fruit or Veggie Milk					
Snack Choose from 2 groups					
Supper Bread or Grain "Meat" Vegetable Fruit or Veggie Milk					

Shopping List

Week of: _____

❑ Fresh Fruits

    ❑ _____   ❑ _____
    ❑ _____   ❑ _____
    ❑ _____   ❑ _____
    ❑ _____   ❑ _____
    ❑ _____   ❑ _____

❑ Canned Goods

    ❑ _____   ❑ _____
    ❑ _____   ❑ _____
    ❑ _____   ❑ _____
    ❑ _____   ❑ _____
    ❑ _____   ❑ _____

❑ Fresh Vegetables

    ❑ _____   ❑ _____
    ❑ _____   ❑ _____
    ❑ _____   ❑ _____
    ❑ _____   ❑ _____
    ❑ _____   ❑ _____

❑ Baking Supplies

    ❑ _____   ❑ _____
    ❑ _____   ❑ _____
    ❑ _____   ❑ _____
    ❑ _____   ❑ _____
    ❑ _____   ❑ _____

❑ Frozen Foods

    ❑ _____   ❑ _____
    ❑ _____   ❑ _____
    ❑ _____   ❑ _____
    ❑ _____   ❑ _____
    ❑ _____   ❑ _____

❑ Beverages

    ❑ _____   ❑ _____
    ❑ _____   ❑ _____
    ❑ _____   ❑ _____
    ❑ _____   ❑ _____
    ❑ _____   ❑ _____

❑ Poultry/Fish/Meat

    ❑ _____   ❑ _____
    ❑ _____   ❑ _____
    ❑ _____   ❑ _____
    ❑ _____   ❑ _____
    ❑ _____   ❑ _____

❑ Spices/Condiments

    ❑ _____   ❑ _____
    ❑ _____   ❑ _____
    ❑ _____   ❑ _____
    ❑ _____   ❑ _____
    ❑ _____   ❑ _____

(continues on next page)

Shopping List (continued)   Week of: _____

❑ Dairy Products
- ❑ _____
- ❑ _____
- ❑ _____
- ❑ _____
- ❑ _____
- ❑ _____

- ❑ _____
- ❑ _____
- ❑ _____
- ❑ _____
- ❑ _____
- ❑ _____

❑ Other Items
- ❑ _____
- ❑ _____
- ❑ _____
- ❑ _____
- ❑ _____
- ❑ _____

- ❑ _____
- ❑ _____
- ❑ _____
- ❑ _____
- ❑ _____
- ❑ _____

❑ Staples
- ❑ _____
- ❑ _____
- ❑ _____
- ❑ _____
- ❑ _____
- ❑ _____

- ❑ _____
- ❑ _____
- ❑ _____
- ❑ _____
- ❑ _____
- ❑ _____

❑ Paper Products
- ❑ _____
- ❑ _____
- ❑ _____
- ❑ _____
- ❑ _____
- ❑ _____

- ❑ _____
- ❑ _____
- ❑ _____
- ❑ _____
- ❑ _____
- ❑ _____

❑ Breads/Cereals/Grains
- ❑ _____
- ❑ _____
- ❑ _____
- ❑ _____
- ❑ _____
- ❑ _____

- ❑ _____
- ❑ _____
- ❑ _____
- ❑ _____
- ❑ _____
- ❑ _____

❑ Household Items
- ❑ _____
- ❑ _____
- ❑ _____
- ❑ _____
- ❑ _____
- ❑ _____

- ❑ _____
- ❑ _____
- ❑ _____
- ❑ _____
- ❑ _____
- ❑ _____

❑ Cleaning Supplies
- ❑ _____
- ❑ _____
- ❑ _____
- ❑ _____

- ❑ _____
- ❑ _____
- ❑ _____
- ❑ _____

- ❑ _____
- ❑ _____
- ❑ _____
- ❑ _____

- ❑ _____
- ❑ _____
- ❑ _____
- ❑ _____

CHAPTER SIX

Running a Ship-Shape Kitchen

Many of us find ourselves in the position of cooking for 6 children, or 60, without the benefit of professional cooking training or even a high-school home economics course! Managing a kitchen, even at home, requires shopping with budget *and* nutrition in mind, impeccable hygiene and safety practices, efficient setup and techniques, a well-organized food storage system, and a good working knowledge of ingredients and food preparation techniques. It's not as hard as it sounds, though. Tracking down information like cooking temperatures for meat or substitutes for buttermilk in a recipe used to take hours, but not any longer. We put it all in one place for you, and you might even be able to teach your mom a thing or two.

How to Save Money on Food

You don't have to spend a lot of money to provide good nutrition. Some of the most nutritious foods are very inexpensive, and some expensive foods aren't very healthful. So go ahead, save some money—you aren't being cheap, you're being smart!

- Decide how much money you can spend on food.

- Plan menus ahead of time. Make a shopping list and stick to it!

- Shop no more than once a week. The more often you walk into a store, the more you'll be tempted by impulse items.

- Serve less meat and more beans, grains, fruits, and vegetables.

- Have children drink water instead of juice or milk when they're thirsty between meals.

- Be very careful to transport and store foods properly so they don't spoil before you can use them.

- One day a week, make a soup with odds and ends of vegetables, or a fruit salad or smoothies with leftover fruits.

- Use leftovers, but handle them carefully!

- Have a garden and grow your own (or let the children do it).

- Shop smart . . .

  - Eat before you go shopping.

  - Leave children at home, unless you can say "no" and mean it!

  - *Read labels*—know what you're buying.

  - Compare unit ("per pound") prices to decide which size and brand of an item is the better buy. See *Anatomy of a Shelf Pricing Label* (page 191).

  - Compare the price of convenience foods with their "from scratch" counterparts.

  - Be aware of the high cost of packaging. Buy in bulk when you can.

  - Take advantage of seasonal specials on produce, meats, and groceries.

  - Buy house brands rather than name brands when their quality suits you as well.

– Don't run all over town to save ten cents; you'll spend more on gas!

– Use coupons *when they're for items you would use anyway.*

– Look into opportunities for cooperative food buying with other families, child care providers, or feeding programs.

– *Buy only what you can use.*

Anatomy of a Shelf Pricing Label

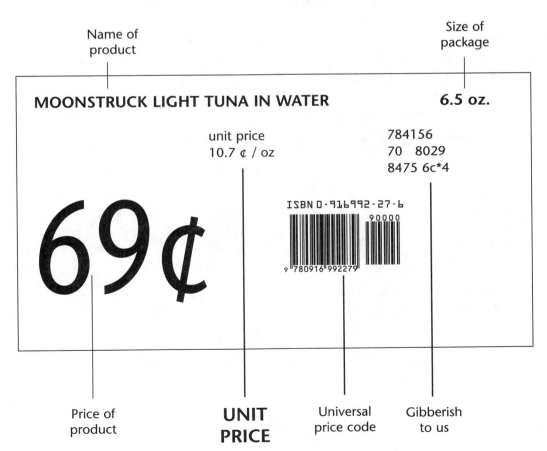

How Much Am I Spending on Protein?

Meats and meat substitutes can be the most expensive items on your menu. If you are interested in saving money on food, you have several options. You can serve the less expensive protein foods more often. You can combine inexpensive and more costly protein foods at the same meal (for example, bean chili with cheese on top). You can avoid overloading children with high-protein foods (you should offer at least the minimum serving size, of course, but you don't need to offer a child 9 ounces of meat at one meal). And if you would like your children to experience the taste of shrimp or other expensive food, serve it as a snack, in small portions.

Price isn't everything, and you should consider whether a food has much to offer nutritionally, as well. For example, turkey franks are relatively cheap, but they are also high in fat and sodium.

How to Calculate the Price Per Serving of any Food

Divide the price for the purchase unit (pound, piece, package) by the number of servings you will get from the unit. You can refer to "How Much to Buy?" on page 203 for information on servings per unit for some foods. Your local Child and Adult Care Food Program office can give you information about purchasing their buying guides.

For example, chicken drumsticks were $1.39/lb. According to our buying guide for the Child and Adult Care Food Program, a pound of drumsticks yields 4.3 servings (1½ oz):

$$\$1.39 \div 4.3 = \$0.32 \text{ per serving}$$

Don't Let Those Nutrients Get Away!

Nutrients can be destroyed when foods aren't handled properly. Long storage times, exposure to air and light, and prolonged cooking are notorious nutrient-robbers. Make the foods you serve as nutritious as possible by following these basic guidelines:

Buy it Right

- Avoid food that looks wilted, bruised, or spoiled.

- Check expiration dates on packages.

- Fresh produce is generally preferable. However, fruits and vegetables that have been sitting in storage or in produce bins for a long time will gradually lose their advantage. In that case, frozen foods will be better. Some foods that don't freeze well, like tomatoes and pineapple, are okay canned.

Store it Right

- When you're taking food home from the store, or if you've received a delivery of perishable foods, don't delay putting them away.

- Keep foods at the proper temperature:

  - 65° or below for canned foods

  - 40° or below in the refrigerator

  - 0° or below in the freezer

- Use foods within their recommended storage times (see *How Long Will It Keep?*, pages 194-196).

Cook it Right

- Don't overcook foods.

- Serve raw fruits and vegetables often.

- Wash produce before cooking or serving, but don't soak it.

- Cut fruits and vegetables as close to serving time as possible. If you must prepare them ahead of time, seal in air-tight bags and refrigerate.

- Cook vegetables in a minimum of water and only until tender-crisp. Steaming, microwaving, and pressure-cooking are better than boiling.

How Long Will It Keep?

	Canned/Dry Storage (months)	Refrigerator (days)	Freezer (months)
Produce			
Asparagus	6	4–6	8–10
Broccoli	—	3–5	10–12
Carrots	12	7–14	10–12
Corn	12	1	10–12
Green peppers	—	4–5	10–12
Greens	12	1–2	10–12
Lettuce	—	7–10	—
Onions	1–3 weeks	—	—
Potatoes	1–2 weeks	—	—
Sweet potatoes	5–7 days	—	—
Tomatoes	6	1–2	2
Apples	12	2–4 weeks	10–12
Bananas	—	7	3
Grapefruit	6	10–14	10–12
Oranges	6	10–14	10–12

	Canned/Pantry (months)	Refrigerator (days)	Freezer (months)
Peaches	12	3–5	10–12
Strawberries	—	3–5	10–12
Watermelon	—	7	10–12
Dairy Products			
Butter	—	1–3 months	6–9
Cheese, cheddar	—	1–2 months	6
Cheese, cottage	—	7	—
Cheese, mozzarella	—	2–4 weeks	6
Cheese, Parmesan	—	12 months	—
Fluid milk (opened)	—	7	3
Infant formula	12–18	2 (opened)	—
Nonfat milk powder	12	2–3 months	—
Puddings, etc., with milk	—	2–3	1
Yogurt	—	7–14	1
Meats/Meat Substitutes			
Beans, dried	12	—	—
Beef, roast	—	3–5	6–12
Beef, ground	—	1–2	3–4
Beef, cooked in casserole	—	3	2–3
Beef, cooked in gravy	—	1–2	2–3
Chicken parts	—	1–2	9
Chicken, cooked, plain	—	3–4	4
Chicken, cooked, in sauce	—	1–2	6
Eggs, fresh	—	4 weeks	—
Eggs, hard-boiled, in shell	—	7	—
Eggs, hard-boiled, peeled	—	7	—
Fish, fatty	—	1-2	3
Fish, lean	—	1-2	6
Frankfurters	—	4–7	1–2
Frozen prepared entrees	—	—	3–4
Lunch meats, opened	—	7	1-2
Peanut butter	12	3–4 months	—
Turkey parts	—	1–2	3–6

	Canned/Pantry (months)	Refrigerator (days)	Freezer (months)
Grain Products			
Breads, tortillas	2–4 days	4–7	4
Cereal, cooked	—	2–3	—
Cereal, ready-to-eat			
Opened	3	—	—
Unopened	12	—	—
Pancakes, waffles	—	1	2–3
Oats, rolled	12	—	—
Wheat flour, unbleached	6–12	12 months	12
Whole-wheat flour	1	12 months	12

Sources:
Bailey, Janice, *Keeping Food Fresh*. New York: Harper & Row, 1989.
Duyff, Roberta, *The American Dietetic Association's Complete Food & Nutrition Guide*, 2nd ed.
 John Wiley & Sons, Inc. 2002.
USDA, Food Safety and Inspection Service

Know Your Ingredients

- **Bulgur** is cracked parboiled wheat. It cooks very quickly and is terrific in pilafs and salads.

- Look for whole-grain or enriched **cornmeal,** not the degerminated variety, for baking. **Polenta,** or coarsely ground cornmeal, is cooked like a hot cereal.

- **Couscous** is a tiny round pasta made from semolina wheat; it comes in whole-grain and refined varieties and is great as a breakfast cereal and in pilafs.

- The flavors of **fresh garlic, fresh ginger,** and **fresh onion** are far superior to their dehydrated, powdered, frozen, and paste versions. However, when saving time is a consideration, you can get good results with the processed forms of these seasonings.

- **Honey, brown sugar,** and **turbinado ("raw") sugar** are not much more nutritious than white table sugar. In the case of honey and "raw" sugar, you pay a lot more for trace amounts of vitamins and minerals. Honey and brown sugar can lend a unique taste to a recipe, however. We urge you to exercise moderation in the use of *all* sweeteners.

- Our preferred vegetable oils for cooking are **olive oil** and **canola oil,** both of which are low in saturated fat and high in monounsaturated fat. Both are high in fat and calories, though (about 2,000 calories per cup!), so use as little as you can to get the job done.

- **Peanut butter** often has shortening and sugar added, which contribute nothing worthwhile nutritionally. Buy "natural" peanut butter made only from peanuts. It tends to separate, so stir it up after you open the jar and refrigerate it.

- We suggest that you use **reduced-sodium soy sauce** in place of regular soy sauce—same rich flavor, less sodium.

- Foods labeled **"sugar free"** may contain artificial sweeteners. Check the ingredients, and if the food is artificially sweetened, avoid serving it to children. Artificial sweeteners can cause diarrhea in susceptible children. They can also train children to expect a very sweet taste in foods.

- **Toasted sesame oil,** which you may also see as "oriental sesame oil," is a very dark and richly flavored oil that is added sparingly to some Asian dishes. Light-colored sesame oil won't do the trick.

- **Tofu** is sometimes called "soy cheese" or "soy bean curd." It is made from soy milk and, though rather bland by itself, is much appreciated by vegetarian (and nonvegetarian) cooks for its ability to accept a wide variety of seasonings. It is a good source of protein, is low in saturated fat, and can be a good source of calcium if it is made with calcium sulfate. As this book goes to press, tofu is not yet acceptable for reimbursement under child-feeding program guidelines. However, we believe that because it is a healthful food that many children like, it may be worth your while to serve a little of it along with other reimbursable items. If you are not concerned with meal program reimbursement, go ahead and use this wonderful food frequently! We have found that "silken" tofu in aseptic packages makes a nice replacement for some of the fat in quick breads and muffins, so you will see it as an ingredient in some of our recipes. Check the Resources (Appendix D) in the back of the book for information about tofu and other soy foods.

- Ground **turkey** can be used in place of ground beef in most recipes, or even substituted for half the beef, and is lower in fat. You have to be careful when you cook it, as it can get dry and tough when cooked too long; cook just until no pink remains.

- **Whole-wheat pastry flour** is best for making muffins and quick breads; regular **whole-wheat flour** is used in making yeasted breads.

How to Get the Most Information from a Product Label

The nutrition label on a food product can help you decide whether it would be a good choice for a healthful diet. Today's food labels contain ingredient listings; *Nutrition Facts,* which give specific information on calories and nutrients; and occasionally a *nutrition description,* for example, "reduced fat" or a health claim describing the relationship between a particular food and health.

- Nutrition labeling is *required* on most packaged foods. Some fresh fruits and vegetables, meat, poultry, and seafood are labeled as well.

- A nutrition label *must* list the total calories, calories from fat, total fat, saturated fat, trans-fat, cholesterol, sodium, total carbohydrate, dietary fiber, sugars, protein, iron, vitamins A and C, and calcium content of the product. Labels on foods specifically for children ages 4 and under are somewhat different because their dietary needs don't fit neatly into the recommendations of the Dietary Guidelines for Americans. A label may list the calories from saturated fat, stearic acid, polyunsaturated fat, monounsaturated fat, potassium, soluble fiber, insoluble fiber, sugar alcohol, other carbohydrate, percent of vitamin A as beta carotene, and other vitamins and minerals. If a food is enriched with one of these voluntary components or if a health claim is made regarding one of them, its content must be listed on the label.

- Check the serving size carefully. Although serving sizes on the present labels are more realistic than in years past, they still might not reflect what you actually eat or serve.

- The ingredients in a food product are listed in order by weight, from the most to the least. For example, if butter is the first ingredient on the list, there is more butter in the product than any other ingredient.

- You will need to know alternative names for certain food components in order to get a clear picture of how much of them a product contains.

Sugar:

brown sugar	dextrose	high fructose corn syrup
honey	fructose	glucose
corn syrup	sucrose	malt syrup
corn syrup solids	maltose	fruit juice concentrates
invert sugar	molasses	
maple syrup		

Sodium:

salt	monosodium glutamate
baking soda	sodium benzoate
sodium caseinate	sodium nitrate
sodium nitrite	sodium phosphate
sodium propionate	

- Know what the various terms on labels *really* mean:

  Sodium free = less than 5 mg sodium/serving

  Very low sodium = 35 mg or less sodium/serving

  Low sodium = 140 mg or less sodium/serving

  Reduced sodium = at least 25% less sodium compared with the usual product

  Unsalted, no salt added = no salt added during processing of a food usually made with salt

  Sugar free = less than 0.5 g per serving

  No added sugar, without added sugar, no sugar added = no sugars added during processing

  Reduced sugar = at least 25% less sugar per serving than the usual product

Calorie free = fewer than 5 calories per serving

Low calorie = 40 calories or less per serving

Reduced or **fewer calories** = at least 25% fewer calories than the usual food product

Cholesterol free = 2 mg or less cholesterol and 2 g or less saturated fat per serving

Low cholesterol = 20 mg or less cholesterol and 2 g or less saturated fat per serving

Reduced or **less cholesterol** = 25% or more reduction in cholesterol from the usual product and at least 2 g less saturated fat

Fat free = less than 0.5 g fat per serving

Saturated fat free = less than 0.5 g and less than 0.5 g *trans* fatty acids per serving

Low fat = 3 g or less fat per serving

Low saturated fat = 1 g or less per serving and not more than 15% of calories in the food

Reduced or **less fat** = 25% or less than the usual food product

Reduced or **less saturated fat** = 25% or less than the usual food product

Extra lean = meat or poultry contains no more than 5 g total fat, 2 g saturated fat, and 95 mg cholesterol per 3-oz. serving

Lean = meat or poultry contains no more than 10 g fat, 4.5 g or less saturated fat, and 95 mg cholesterol per 3-oz. serving

Light, lite = contains one-third fewer calories or one-half the fat of the reference food

High fiber = 5 g or more per serving

Good source of fiber = 2.5 to 4.9 g per serving

More or **added fiber** = at least 2.5 g more than the reference food.

Cook's Tour of a Nutrition Facts Label

The heading, Nutrition Facts, indicates that you're about to learn specifics about the nutrient content of the food!

Note carefully the serving size and number of servings in the package (located right underneath Nutrition Facts)!

The Amount Per Serving, Calories, and Calories from Fat tell you how the calories from fat compare to the total calories in a serving. It does not tell you the percent calories from fat.

The % Daily Value tells you how a serving contributes overall to a 2,000-calorie diet. Use these figures to get an idea of whether the food contains a little or a lot of a certain nutrient. A food is "high" in a nutrient if it contains 20% or more of the Daily Value.

The nutrients listed (from Total Fat through the Vitamins and Minerals) are the biggest concerns for most consumers today. In general, we need to be alert to getting too much of certain items like fat rather than too little of most vitamins and minerals.

The footnote on the right with the headings of "Calories, 2,000, 2,500" helps consumers learn basic recommendations for a healthful diet—upper limits for fat, saturated fat, cholesterol, and sodium, and minimum targets for carbohydrate and fiber.

At the bottom, a conversion guide helps you learn the caloric value of the energy-producing nutrients.

Nutrition Facts

Serving Size 2 waffles (78 g)
Servings Per Container 6

Amount Per Serving

Calories 280   Calories from Fat 45

	% Daily Value*
Total Fat 5 g	7%
Saturated Fat 2 g	10%
Trans Fat 0 g	
Polyunsaturated Fat 1 g	
Monounsaturated Fat 1.5 g	
Cholesterol 20 mg	7%
Sodium 540 mg	22%
Potassium 330 mg	10%
Total Carbohydrate 49 g	16%
Dietary Fiber 3	12%
Sugars 7 g	
Protein 10 g	

Vitamin A 4%	Vitamin C 4%
Calcium 15%	Iron 4%

* Percent Daily Values are based on a 2,000 calorie diet. Your daily values may be higher or lower depending on your calorie needs:

	Calories	2,000	2,500
Total Fat	Less than	65g	80g
Sat Fat	Less than	20g	25g
Cholesterol	Less than	300mg	300mg
Sodium	Less than	2,400mg	2,400mg
Potassium	Less than	3,500mg	3,500mg
Total Carbohydrate		300g	375g
Dietary Fiber		25g	30g

Calories per gram:
    Fat 9 • Carbohydrates 4 • Protein 4

How Much to Buy?

Food	Purchase Weight or Measure	Approximate Yield
Fruits		
Apples	1 lb.	3 cups sliced
Apricots, dried	1 lb.	3 cups
Bananas	1 lb.	3–4 medium, or 1½ cups mashed
Oranges	1 lb.	3–4 medium, or 2 cups pieces
Raisins	1 lb.	3 cups
Vegetables		
Broccoli, fresh	1 lb.	2⅓ cups cooked
Cabbage	1 lb.	4 cups shredded raw, 2 cups cooked
Carrots, fresh	1 lb.	3¾ cups shredded raw
Lettuce, romaine	1 lb.	7¾ cups chopped
Onion	1 medium	1¼ cups chopped
Pepper, green	1 large	1 cup chopped
Potatoes, fresh	1 lb.	2½ cups cooked, 2 cups mashed
Tomatoes, fresh	1 lb.	3–4 medium, 2½ cups chopped
Grains		
Cornmeal, coarse	1 lb.	3 cups dry, 12 cups cooked
Oatmeal	1 lb.	6 cups dry, 12 cups cooked
Rice, brown	1 lb.	2½ cups dry, 4⅜ cups cooked
Rice, white	1 lb.	2½ cups dry, 7½ cups cooked
Macaroni	1 lb.	9¾ cups cooked
Spaghetti	1 lb.	5¼ cups cooked
Wheat flour	1 lb.	4 cups
Whole-wheat flour	1 lb.	3¾–4 cups
Dairy Foods		
Butter	1 lb.	2 cups, 4 sticks
Cheese, hard	1 lb.	4 cups shredded

Food	Purchase Weight or Measure	Approximate Yield
Meat, Poultry		
Beef, 10% fat, ground	1 lb.	12 oz. cooked meat
Canadian bacon	1 lb.	11 oz. cooked meat
Chicken breast halves	1 lb.	8⅞ oz. cooked chicken meat
Chicken drumsticks	1 lb.	6½ oz. cooked chicken meat
Tuna, water packed	12½-oz. can	10½ oz. drained, 1⅜ cups
Turkey, ground	1 lb.	11 oz. cooked meat
Other		
Beans, dried	1 lb.	2¼ cups dried, 6 cups cooked
Peanut butter	1 lb.	1¾ cups

Source: *Food Buying Guide for Child Nutrition Programs*, USDA, 2001.

Equivalents and Substitutions

Food	Amount	Equivalent
Baking powder	1 t.	¼ t. baking soda + ½ t. cream of tartar *or* ¼ t. baking soda + ½ cup buttermilk or yogurt and reduce liquid by ½ cup
Bread crumbs	1 cup	4 slices dried bread, crushed and run through a food processor *or* ¾ cup cracker or cereal crumbs
Buttermilk	1 cup	1 cup plain yogurt *or* 1 T. lemon juice *or* vinegar + enough milk to make 1 cup; let stand 5 minutes
Catsup	1 cup	1 cup tomato sauce + ¼ cup sugar + 2 T. vinegar + ¼ t. ground cloves
Eggs, in baking	1 egg	1 t. cornstarch + 3 T. more liquid in recipe *or* 2 T. liquid + 2 T. flour + ½ T. oil + ½ t. baking powder
Flour, for thickening	1 T.	1 T. quick-cooking tapioca *or* 1½ t. cornstarch *or* 2 T. granule cereal (e.g., farina or cornmeal)
Garlic, fresh	1 clove	⅛ t. garlic powder *or* ½ t. garlic salt and omit ½ t. salt from recipe
Herbs, fresh	1 T.	1 t. dried herb *or* ¼ t. ground herb
Lemon juice	1 t.	1 t. vinegar
Milk	1 cup	1 cup soy, rice, or nut milk *or* 1 cup fruit juice for baking (add ½ t. baking soda if the juice is acidic)*

* Remember, these are not nutritional equivalents.

Food	Amount	Equivalent
Sour cream	1 cup	1 cup plain yogurt *or* 1 cup low-fat cottage cheese + 1 T. lemon juice + 1 T. nonfat milk, pureed in blender or food processor to desired consistency
Sugar, brown	1 cup	1 cup white sugar + ¼ cup molasses
Sugar, white	1 cup	1 cup brown sugar, packed *or* ¾ cup honey or maple syrup and reduce 2 T. of other liquid in recipe *or* 1 cup date sugar *or* 1½ cup fruit juice concentrate and reduce liquid in recipe by 2 T.
Tomatoes, fresh	1 lb.	1 cup tomato sauce
Tomato juice	1 cup	1 cup tomato sauce + 1 cup water
Tomato sauce	2 cups	¾ cup tomato paste + 1 cup water
Tomato soup	10¾-oz. can	1 cup tomato sauce + ¼ cup water

Basic Guide to Measurements

Reminder: Help with measuring is a great way to enable children to participate in the cooking process. In fact, checking the accuracy of your measuring equipment can make an interesting math and science activity.

Standard U.S. Liquid Measurements

3 teaspoons	= 1 tablespoon
4 tablespoons	= ¼ cup or 2 ounces
5⅓ tablespoons	= ⅓ cup or 2⅔ ounces
12 tablespoons	= ¾ cup or 6 ounces
16 tablespoons	= 1 cup or 8 ounces
2 cups	= 1 pint
2 pints	= 1 liquid quart
4 quarts	= 1 liquid gallon

Canned Goods Weights and Measures

8 ounces	= 1 cup
10½–12 ounces	= 1¼ cups
14–16 ounces	= 1½ cups
16–17 ounces	= 2 cups
1 lb. 4 ounces	= 2½ cups
1 lb. 13 ounces	= 3½ cups
No. 10 can	= 12–13⅔ cups

Keeping Food Safe to Eat Is Up to You

We live in a time when many people are suspicious, almost afraid, of their food. Some fears about the safety of our food supply are reasonable, and some are not. It's important to realize that most of the dangers associated with food are due to the way *we* handle it in our own kitchens. In the United States, about 76 million people get sick, and 5,000 people die from food poisoning every year. Millions and millions of others have an uncomfortable few days with what they think is "stomach flu." Most of these illnesses could have been prevented through careful handling of food by the cook.

Food-borne illnesses are usually caused by bacteria. Some are caused by viruses or poisonous chemicals. We'll refer to bacteria and viruses together as **germs.**

Germs are found everywhere—in soil, in air, on animals' bodies (including ours), on fruits and vegetables, in milk—but before you swear you'll never eat or breathe again, realize that most aren't harmful to us (some are even helpful, like the bacteria that make yogurt). Other germs are a problem only if there are a *lot* of them around, or if they've had the chance to manufacture toxins that will hurt us even when the germs are dead. To survive, germs need:

- Food and water

- *Time* to reproduce or make toxins

- The right *temperature*

- A way to get around (they can't wiggle into our custard by themselves, but they *can* hitchhike on our fingers)

When we talk about preventing food poisoning, most of what we're dealing with involves giving the germs as little time as possible at the temperatures they like, so they can't do their dirty work. We also want to introduce as few bacteria as we can into our stew, or salad, in the first place. Food becomes unsafe to eat through six main mistakes:

- Poor personal hygiene on the part of people working with food

- Preparing food that may already have been spoiled or contaminated by poisons

- Storing food without proper care

- Handling food carelessly

- Using unclean equipment or working in a dirty kitchen

- Allowing insects or rodents to infest food supplies

Food safety is *very* serious business. What follows might seem like an impossibly long list of guidelines for keeping food safe to eat. But every point in the list is crucial, so it's worth reviewing over and over until all of these practices are second nature to you. Items that specifically apply to group settings are marked with a ✪.

Start with Personal Hygiene

- Always wash your hands before you handle food.

- Wash your hands again after you:
  - Use the toilet.
  - Change a child's diaper or assist a child in the bathroom.
  - Touch your face, hair, or any infected part of your body.
  - Blow your nose, sneeze, or cough.
  - Touch dirty rags, clothing, or work surfaces.
  - Clear away dirty dishes and utensils.
  - Touch raw food, especially meat, fish, or poultry.
  - Handle money or smoke a cigarette.

- Keep your fingernails clean and short.

- Avoid wearing rings (except a simple band), bracelets, and anything that would dangle into the food.

- Keep your hair clean and long hair tied back.

- Wear clean clothing.

- Don't work with food when you're sick.

- Don't smoke in the kitchen.

Use the STOP DISEASE Method of Handwashing*

Use liquid soap from a dispenser and running water.

Rub your hands vigorously as you wash them.

Wash all surfaces, including:
    Backs of hands
    Wrists
    Between fingers
    Under fingernails

Rinse your hands well with running water.

Dry your hands wth a paper towel.

Turn off the water using a paper towel instead of bare hands.

Discard towel in covered trash can controlled by a foot pedal.

* Source: *Childhood Emergencies—What to Do, A Quick Reference Guide* by Marin Child Care Council (formerly Project Care for Children), Bull Publishing Company, 1987.

Be Picky About the Foods You Serve

- Buy only from reputable stores or dealers.

- Don't buy or accept for delivery foods that look spoiled or infested with insects.

- Use only pasteurized milk.

- ✪ Don't serve home-canned foods to children you take care of.

- Don't serve raw eggs in any form (like eggnog), and don't allow children to taste items like raw cookie dough containing eggs. Liquid pasteurized egg products are fine.

- Don't serve spoiled or moldy foods, food from a bulging or leaky can, or anything else that looks or smells suspicious. If you have doubts, toss it, and don't take a little taste to test it! Some very dangerous foods taste okay.

- Pay attention to "use by" or "sell by" dates on food packages.

Store Foods Carefully

- Store foods at the right temperatures:

Refrigerator:	32–40°F
Freezer:	0°F or below
Pantry:	65°F or below is best

- Immediately put perishable foods into the refrigerator or freezer after shopping or receiving a delivery.

- Stored foods should be dated, labeled if necessary, and kept off the floor.

- Place newer foods behind older ones in the storage area— "first in, first out."

- Don't store opened food in cans in the refrigerator. Transfer the food to glass or plastic containers.

- Cover all stored foods.

- Leave space for air circulation in the refrigerator. Don't line the shelves with foil. Keep it clean and check every day for food that should be tossed out. Check the thermometers in the refrigerator and freezer.

- Cool leftovers quickly in shallow containers in the refrigerator.

- Store cooked foods *above* raw foods in the refrigerator.

- Store packages of thawing meat or poultry in bowls or shallow pans so their juices can't drip on foods below.

☻ Leftovers should be kept in the refrigerator for no more than 24 hours.

- Store foods separately from chemicals, cleaners, and so on.

☻ Lunches and other perishable foods that children bring from home should be refrigerated until serving time.

If the Power Goes Out . . .

A fully stocked freezer will keep foods at safe temperatures for up to 2 days, a half-full freezer for 1 day. Keep the door closed!

A refrigerator will keep foods safe for only 4–6 hours. Perishable foods should be discarded, but generally fresh fruits and vegetables, hard and processed cheese, butter, margarine, and most condiments will be okay for longer periods. Discard anything that looks suspicious.

Handle Food with Respect

- Keep perishable foods at safe temperatures. If they're to be eaten cold, keep them at 40°F or below. If they're supposed to be hot, they must be 140°F or above. If you aren't going to serve hot foods soon, refrigerate them in uncovered shallow pans. The center of the food must reach 450°F or less within 4 hours. Don't leave perishable foods out on the counter while you're working on a recipe with many steps.

- Wash fruits and vegetables thoroughly before using them.

- Wipe the tops of cans before you open them.

- Thaw frozen foods in the refrigerator or in the microwave. Bacteria can be happily setting up colonies on the outside of the food even when the center is frozen.

- Use oven temperatures of at least 325°F, and when using a crockpot, bring the food to a boil before setting the heat on "low."

- Cook fish, poultry, eggs, and meat thoroughly.

- Taste those delicacies you're concocting with two spoons, the professional way. Spoon One goes into the food and then transfers it to Spoon Two (the spoons can't touch). Spoon Two goes into your mouth.

- ✪ Avoid touching foods with your hands. Use scoops, tongs, other utensils, or disposable gloves when handling food that will be served uncooked to another person (for example, it's all right to cut carrots for soup with your bare hands, but not carrots that will be served raw).

- *Never* serve food that's left on anyone's plate to another person.

- ✪ Discard any food that remains in serving bowls after family-style meal service in a child care setting.

- Don't mix leftover food and fresh-cooked food unless it's in good condition and the mixture will be used up immediately.

Final Cooking Temperatures

Egg-based dishes	160°F	Fish	145°F
Ground poultry	165°F	Ground beef, pork, lamb	160°F
Poultry pieces: breasts	165°F	Other cuts of meat	145°F
Poultry pieces: thighs, wings,		Leftovers, casseroles	165°F
legs	180°F		
Whole poultry	165°F		

Scrambled eggs are done when no visible liquid remains, poached and fried eggs when the whites are completely set and the yolk is starting to thicken.

How to take a chicken's temperature: A quick-read or digital thermometer is recommended. Insert the thermometer into the inner thigh area near the breast of the bird but not touching the bone. If stuffed, the stuffing must reach 165°F.

To test other foods for doneness, insert the thermometer into the thickest part of the food, away from fat, bone, and the pan itself. For thin items like meat patties, the thermometer can be inserted sideways, though a special thermometer called a thermocouple is even better. If your food wasn't done on first testing, clean your thermometer with hot soapy water and an alcohol prep pad before inserting it into the food again, to avoid introducing contamination into the food.

Source: IsItDoneYet.gov

Keep the Kitchen and Your Equipment Clean

- Don't allow animals or cat litter boxes in the kitchen.

- Regularly clean your equipment, kitchen, and eating area (see *The Squeaky-Clean Kitchen Scrubbing Schedule,* p. 218).

- Don't let anyone sit on counters or work surfaces.

- Keep rugs out of food preparation areas.

- Wash the can opener in between uses. It's one of the most overlooked sources of germs in the kitchen!

- Air-dry rather than towel-dry dishes and utensils.

- Make sure plates, bowls, and glasses are dry before stacking them on shelves.

- Hold plates by the rims, drinking glasses by the bottoms, cups and silverware by the handles.

- Clean any cutting board or utensil that has touched raw meat, poultry, or eggs before any other cooked or raw food comes in contact with it. It's a very good idea to have separate cutting boards for raw meat, fish, poultry, and for other foods.

- The debate over cutting board material continues, but plastic cutting boards are probably preferable to wooden boards because they can be cleaned more easily. Discard any board that has deep grooves in it.

- Don't use cracked tableware or containers; bacteria can find food and a nice place to live in the cracks.

- Don't serve or store foods in antique or imported pottery (especially from Mexico, China, Hong Kong, or India) unless it has been verified to be lead-free. Lead from the glazes can leach into food and has caused many cases of lead poisoning in the United States.

- Use freshly laundered towels and rags.

- Sanitize sponges occasionally with a bleach solution or run them through the dishwasher.

✪ Tableware and serving pieces used in group settings must be sanitized. A dishwasher works; so does a bleach dip.

To Sanitize with a Bleach Solution . . .

Wash the table- or serviceware with hot water and detergent, rinse, then dip for 1 minute in a solution of ⅓ cup chlorine bleach to 5 gallons of water. Air-dry.

✪ Disposable tableware is meant to be disposed of after a single use. *Do not* try to save money or the environment by washing and reusing it. The risk of spreading germs among children is too great.

Don't Put Out the Welcome Mat for Insects and Rodents

- Keep your kitchen immaculate.

- Store opened packages of food within tightly sealed containers.

- Remove garbage promptly and keep the outdoor garbage area clean.

- Don't store food under the sink.

- Keep doors and windows tightly screened. When screens get holes, fix them.

- Caulk openings and cracks around sinks, drain pipes, and water pipes. Repair cracks in walls.

- Inspect containers and cardboard boxes that you bring into your building. Cockroaches, especially, like to hitchhike in them.

- If you notice some pests around, take care of the problem before it gets bigger. Should you find that you'll have to use an insecticide, follow the directions carefully.

CAUTION!!
These foods are among the most common sources of food poisoning:

- Undercooked or improperly handled meat, poultry, eggs, fish, and dairy products

- Raw milk

- Cooked plant foods (fruits, vegetables, beans, or grains) or tofu left at room temperature for more than 2 hours

- Homemade ice cream (with unpasteurized eggs)

- Improperly canned low-acid foods, such as green beans, corn, spinach, mushrooms, olives, beets, asparagus, pork, beef, and seafood

---

The Squeaky-Clean Kitchen Scrubbing Schedule

We know that cleanup isn't usually the most attractive aspect of any job. A well-used kitchen can rapidly turn into a public health hazard, though, without conscientious cleaning. Then it's *really* no fun. The grime in a kitchen will never get out of hand if you set up a cleaning schedule and follow it. So here it is—preventive medicine for your kitchen:

Constantly

❑ Wipe up spills and splashes from:

Work surfaces   Range
Floors   Microwave
Walls   Refrigerator

❑ Wash equipment after each use:

Can opener   Blender
Mixer   Food processor

Daily

❑ Make sure all dishes, utensils, and so on, are washed.

❑ Wipe down work tables and counters and sanitize with a solution of 1 tablespoon chlorine bleach in 1 quart water.

❑ Wipe down range, microwave, refrigerator, and dishwasher.

❑ Sweep and damp mop kitchen floor.

❑ Take out the trash.

❑ Check refrigerator and freezer temperatures.

Weekly

❑ Scrub kitchen floor.

❑ Remove burners from range and clean underneath them.

❑ Clean the inside of the refrigerator. Throw out old food. A mixture of baking soda and water may be used to wipe the shelves and walls.

❑ Clean out the food trap in the dishwasher.

❑ Clean the filter from the smoke hood.

Saving Time in the Kitchen

If you're taking care of children by yourself, you know it's important to be supervising *them*, not a gourmet dish that's bubbling out of control on the stove. And even if you are in the position of cooking primarily for children, it's still nice to save time here and there so you can do other important things—like cleaning, maintaining equipment, doing bookwork, developing new recipes, and training staff. Here are some time-saving tips, learned the hard way during years of collective experience:

❑ Plan menus ahead of time, check for ingredients on hand, make a detailed shopping list, and shop only once a week.

❑ Remember that the children probably won't appreciate three elaborate menu items in a meal. *Keep it simple.* Skip the fancy sauces.

❑ For your "meat" dishes, use foods that require little or no cooking, like eggs, tofu, cheese, canned fish, canned dried beans, and nut or seed butters.

❑ Generally, fresh foods taste the best and give you the most control over amounts of sodium and other ingredients. But there are some convenience foods that can save you time and still taste good. You'll need to decide if they're worth the extra cost:

- Bottled crushed garlic and ginger puree

- Vegetable and chicken broth in aseptic boxes

- Grated cheese

- Prewashed salad greens in bags

- "Baby" carrots and broccoli or cauliflower florets in bags

- Frozen corn, chopped spinach, and peas

- Bottled pasta sauce

- Canned dried beans, tomatoes, and applesauce

❑ It's okay to serve some cold foods, or even a full meal of them.

❑ Plan for leftovers that can show up later in another form. (Example: turkey loaf, served later as a cold sandwich filling or as cubes on a snack tray).

❑ Do as much in one pot or pan as possible. Avoid recipes that lead to a tower of dirty dishes in the sink. See if you can revise your old favorites to save steps.

❑ Make larger portions than you need and freeze some for later. Casseroles, soups, sauces, and quick breads lend themselves readily to this.

❑ Do as much of the food preparation as possible when the children aren't around or are napping, unless you want them to pitch in. You may find it works to set up an activity for them in the kitchen while you're doing certain phases of the food preparation.

❑ Use time-saving appliances like food processors, when they really will save time. Consider setup and cleanup time.

Safety for Adults in the Kitchen

Burns, cuts, and falls can put a damper on your fun in the kitchen. Don't let them happen to you! Follow these guidelines:

- Allow yourself enough time for the job. Most accidents happen when you're in a hurry or aren't paying attention to what you're doing.

- Wipe up grease or wet spots and pick up loose items from the floor immediately.

- Don't run or allow running in the kitchen.

- Use a ladder if you're reaching for items stored on high shelves.

- If you can, store heavier items on lower shelves.

- Keep your knives sharp; you are more likely to be cut by a dull knife, since you need to use more pressure.

- Store knives separately, not loose in a drawer with other utensils.

- Don't soak knives in a dishbasin; you could cut yourself reaching into the water.

- Make sure that your hands (and feet) are dry before plugging in or unplugging electrical appliances.

- Don't reach into a toaster with a metal utensil unless the toaster is unplugged.

- To unplug an appliance safely, turn it off, then hold the plug close to the electrical outlet and pull gently.

- Keep equipment in good repair. Be on the lookout for frayed cords and straining motors.

- Keep items that burn easily (pot holders, towels, curtains, billowy sleeves, and the like) away from burners and other sources of heat.

- Keep the oven and broiler clean. Grease buildup could lead to a fire.

- When cooking with a covered pan, take the lid off facing away from you to avoid being scalded.

Making a Kitchen Safe for Young Children

- Keep all poisonous products in locked cupboards.

- Keep all poisonous products in their original containers; don't transfer them into soda bottles or coffee cans.

- Use safety latches on cabinets.

- Keep potentially dangerous items like knives, matches, boxes with serrated edges, toothpicks, and plastic bags in one place, out of reach.

- Make sure that your drawers have safety catches so they don't crash to the floor when they're pulled out too far.

- When you're using the stovetop, keep pot handles turned toward the center of the stove.

- Watch out for appliance cords dangling over the counter. If you leave toasters, coffeemakers, and other appliances on the counter, unplug them when not in use, place them against the wall, and tuck the cords behind them.

- If you can, get a garbage disposal that operates only with a lid in place.

- Don't store alcoholic beverages, vitamins, and medicines in the refrigerator or any place accessible to a young child.

- Keep vanilla, almond, and other alcohol-containing extracts out of children's reach, too.

- Many children are burned by hot water from the tap. Supervise them closely at the sink.

- Teach children the proper way to use a knife (some don't realize which side of the blade is the cutting edge) and supervise always.

- Keep a first aid kit handy.

- Set aside child-safe kitchen equipment in a lower cabinet so the children can "play cooking" while you're working in the kitchen.

Using Your Microwave Safely

Because there is a wide array of models on the market, and because, with the speed of technology, new and different versions will be out each year, we recommend that you read the instructions that come with the microwave oven you are using and keep them handy for reference and service information.

Microwave ovens, when used and maintained properly, are considered to be extremely safe. There are some basic safety rules, however, that everyone who uses a microwave oven should know.

Important Safety Rules

- Follow the manufacturer's instructions for use.

- Keep the oven clean, especially around the door seal.

- Never tamper with any part of the oven.

- If you suspect any damage to the oven, be sure to call a qualified service person to check it out.

- Heat-proof glassware and glass-ceramic (Corning Ware type) cookware seem to be the best choices for use in the microwave, with round containers resulting in more even heating than square or rectangular ones. Here's how to test glass for microwave-cooking safety: Fill a glass measuring cup with 1 cup of water and put it in the microwave oven next to the container you are testing. (The cup of water is included because the oven should never be operated without food or liquid in it to absorb the energy.) Run the microwave oven on HIGH for one minute. *If the container stayed cool, it's okay to cook in it. If it was only luke-warm, it's okay to reheat in it. Don't use it in the microwave if it got warm.*

- Always choose containers that are colorless and plain; color and decoration can interfere with the transmission of microwaves.

- Other types of containers such as plastic yogurt or margarine tubs, and *even plastic containers that are marked "microwave-safe,"* may have chemical components that can "migrate" into the food at high temperatures.

- For the same reason, if you cover food with plastic wrap while cooking or heating, do not let the covering come in contact with the heating food. Also, be sure to use only the kind of plastic wrap that is recommended for use in the microwave, since other types can melt into the food.

- Avoid heat-susceptor packaging. At this time, its safety has not been thoroughly established.

- Recycled paper products should not be used in the microwave. They may contain small metal fragments that can set the paper on fire during cooking.

Preventing Microwave Burns

- Beware of microwave burns. The container or some portions of the food may be cool enough to touch, while other portions may be hot enough to cause external or internal (mouth and esophagus) burns. Fats and sugars can get especially hot in the microwave and must be handled with extreme caution.

- Puncture foods that have unbroken skins, such as potatoes, tomatoes, and sausage, to allow steam to escape and prevent bursting. Do not cook eggs in the shell for the same reason.

- To prevent being burned by escaping steam, puncture plastic wrap if you are using it to cover the cooking food.

- Stay with the oven if you're popping popcorn. Heat buildup can cause a fire.

Children's Use of Microwave Ovens

It is a fact of modern life that children are frequent users of microwave ovens. Thus, the potential is great for serious accidents. Here are some things to consider when assessing a child's ability to use a microwave oven safely.

- Does the child have the ability to understand cause and effect, for example, "If I do this, then that will happen"?

- Can the child competently read, understand, and follow directions?

- Is the child tall enough to remove food easily from the oven with both hands? Many of the serious burns reported have resulted from hot food spilling on the child who attempts to remove it from the oven.

- Is the child capable of understanding and upholding all of the safety rules on pages 223–224, "Using Your Microwave Safely"?

There is no age at which using any stove or oven is completely risk-free. However, the risk to children, because of their smaller size and limited experience, is likely to be greater than to adults. We strongly urge adults who permit children to use microwave ovens (or any stove or oven) to do so with extreme caution, thorough explanation of safety rules, and considerable practice in the presence of an adult. Here are a few additional safety tips if children will be using the microwave oven:

- Be sure that the oven is on a sturdy surface and can't be tipped.

- Have a table or counter nearby so that the cookware can be set down nearby immediately after removing it from the oven.

- Be sure that the child always uses oven mitts to minimize the risk of burns. Portions of the dish may be hot or hot food may spill over the edge.

- Make sure the child always lifts a lid or plastic wrap slowly, starting at the side away from the face.

Checklist: Is Your Kitchen Ready to Feed Groups of Kids?

Feeding Necessities

❑ Child-appropriate tableware, serving utensils (serving spoons, tongs, pitchers, etc.)

❑ Infant or adaptive feeding equipment, if applicable

❑ High chairs and child-size tables and chairs

❑ Menu guidelines and recipes for kid-pleasing foods

❑ Forms for recording individual children's feeding needs and, if applicable, reports to parents

❑ Emergency food supplies

❑ Recycling setup, preferably one that the children can use

Food Safety

❑   Thermometers for refrigerator and freezer (be sure to check these appliances to make sure they are at the appropriate temperatures)

❑   Refrigerator, freezer, and pantry storage containers with tight-fitting lids or good seals

❑   Separate cutting boards—one for raw meats, poultry, and fish and another for raw produce and foods that have already been cooked

❑   Setup for air-drying dishes and food preparation equipment after washing

❑   Sanitizers (such as bleach) and appropriate storage/application containers (be sure you know the correct mixing proportions and safety precautions)

❑   Meat or "quick-read" thermometer to test food temperatures and alcohol prep pads to disinfect the thermometer

❑   Disposable gloves approved for food service

❑   Hair restraints

Child Safety

❑   Safety devices for appliances and cupboards

❑   First aid kit

❑   Easily accessible instructions for performing the Heimlich manuever.

Food Safety and Sanitation Mini-Inspection

If you are serving children in a group setting, it's a good idea to do periodic checkups on the cleanliness and food handling practices in the kitchen. Although the following list is not a complete food safety inspection, it will direct you to problem areas that are commonly responsible for outbreaks of food-borne illness.

Personal Hygiene

❑   Food preparers must wash hands before handling food, between tasks, and before putting on gloves.

❑   Food preparers must wear clean clothes, restrain hair, have short, clean fingernails, and wear only simple jewelry.

❑   No one smokes in the kitchen.

Food Purchasing and Storage

❑   Purchase foods from reliable stores or vendors.

❑   Use only pasteurized milk and apple juice.

❑   Purchase food before the "sell by" date and use it within maximum storage times.

❑   Store food off the floor.

❑   Store newer foods behind or under older foods.

❑   Store food in a way that protects it from contamination (for example, covered containers).

❑ Stored foods must be free of mold, insect infestation, or other forms of spoilage.

❑ Check thermometers in the refrigerator and freezer daily to be sure they are at the appropriate temperature.

❑ Store chemicals and cleaners separately from food.

Food Handling

❑ Thaw food in the refrigerator, in the microwave, or under cold running water.

❑ Do not allow food to be in the "danger zone" for more than 4 hours *total*. That includes transport and during preparation, cooking, and serving.

❑ Taste food using two spoons—one for the food and one for the mouth.

❑ Food handlers must use gloves or utensils when touching food that will be served without further cooking.

Kitchen Cleanliness

❑ Work surfaces, equipment, utensils, and food storage areas must be clean to sight and touch.

❑ Air-dry washed items.

❑ Use separate cutting boards—one for raw meat, poultry, or fish, and another for other foods.

❑ Dishes and containers must be free of cracks.

❑ Use freshly laundered towels and rags; sanitize sponges regularly.

❑ Sanitize tableware after each use.

❑ Store garbage in appropriate containers; keep kitchen garbage cans clean.

❑ Keep window and door screens in good repair.

❑ Be sure there are no signs of insect or rodent infestations.

. . . .

Environmental Concerns

At first glance, running a child care center or day care home, with the many regulations for sanitation, severe time constraints, and a tight budget, may seem incompatible with caring for the environment. Please don't give up yet! Among the many decisions you make about which cleaning products to use, how to dispose of garbage, and even such details as whether to run a half-full dishwasher, it's likely that you can find a few hassle-free ways to lessen the environmental impact of your business. You'll teach the children by your good example at the same time, and you may find them to be enthusiastic allies in your efforts.

Hints for an Earth-Friendly Kitchen

Each of us makes many choices every day that have an impact on the environment and affect the kind of world we're building for our children. With just a little thought and effort we can develop and maintain habits that contribute to a healthier planet. Try posting a reminder list in the kitchen of three or four earth-friendly improvements you are pretty sure you can make. When those become second nature, post a new list. What you do *does* make a difference.

To Save Water

- Wash dishes in a dishpan instead of under running water.

- Rinse the dishes with the faucet on halfway and only on while in use (50% of wasted water in homes is due to letting the tap run unnecessarily).

- If you use a dishwasher, run it only when it is full.

- When peeling fruits or vegetables that will need to be washed, set them aside in a colander until they're all peeled, then wash them all at once.

- Fix leaky faucets right away. Even tiny leaks waste lots of water. Meanwhile, catch the drips in a container for watering plants.

- Use a low-flow aerator (available at most hardware stores) on your faucet.

- If you have a water meter, check it to find hidden leaks. (If there is a leak, it will register use even when all the water in the house is turned off.)

To Save Energy

- Use cold water instead of hot whenever possible.

- Keep a container of cold drinking water in the refrigerator to avoid having to let the faucet run until the water gets cold.

- Keep the refrigerator and freezer only as cold as you need to—refrigerator 32–40°, freezer 0°.

- Make sure the refrigerator door seal is tight.

- Periodically use a brush or vacuum to clean the condenser coils on the back of the refrigerator. (Unplug it while doing this.) Dirt and dust make it more difficult for the coils to stay cool.

- If you have a manual-defrost freezer, defrost it regularly. Frost buildup causes the motor to run longer.

- Defrost frozen foods in the refrigerator—it will help keep the refrigerator cold, using less energy.

- Don't leave the refrigerator door open unnecessarily.

- For cooking small portions, pressure cookers, toaster ovens, and microwave ovens are more energy-efficient than conventional ovens. For large items such as turkeys, microwaving is the least efficient.

- Preheat the oven only when it is really necessary, and then, for the shortest possible time. (Ten minutes is usually adequate.)

- Don't open the oven door while baking; you'll let a lot of heat escape. Use a timer and look through the oven window.

- Match the pot size to the burner, using the smallest of both for the job, and use lids on pots to speed up cooking.

- Use glass or ceramic baking dishes for baking—they retain heat well and you can lower the oven temperature 25°.

- Use compact fluorescent lights, which are three to four times more energy-efficient than incandescent bulbs.

- Insulate your hot water heater and accessible hot water pipes.

Planning a Kitchen for Energy Efficiency

If you are designing a new kitchen, or remodeling an existing one, you have a great opportunity to build energy efficiency right into your plans.

- Purchase energy-efficient appliances—check their federally mandated Energy Guide Labels to compare and rate them.

- Choose a refrigerator with a top freezer compartment rather than a side-by-side model, which uses up to 35% more energy.

- Choose a chest-type freezer over an upright if you have the space. They are 10–15% more energy-efficient. Also, an automatic-defrost model consumes 40% more electricity than an equivalent-size-and-style manual-defrost model.

- Select a dishwasher with a built-in water heater. With an insulating water heating jacket for your hot water heater, you will be able to keep your household water temperature lower (110–120°). The dishwasher will only heat the amount of water necessary to wash the dishes at the required 140°F.

- Plan to install the dishwasher away from the refrigerator or freezer. If that's not possible, put insulation between them. Heat and moisture from the dishwasher make the refrigerator or freezer use more energy.

- Purchase a gas range with electric ignition instead of a pilot light. You will be cutting gas consumption by about 40% a year.

- Choose a convection oven over a conventional one. You will be able to lower temperatures and shorten cooking times.

- Install a solar hot water system.

- Include a built-in recycling system that is designed to coordinate with local recycling requirements.

- Refer to David Goldbeck's book, *The Smart Kitchen: How to Design a Comfortable, Safe, Energy-Efficient and Environmentally Friendly Workspace* (Woodstock, N.Y.: Ceres Press, 1989), and also to the other resources listed in Appendix D to help you with your planning.

Think of Mother Earth When You're Shopping

Most of us grew up during the "disposables" or "throw-away" generations. Now that we are faced with the dire consequences, we find ourselves struggling to change some very ingrained environmentally harmful habits. With less than 5% of the world's population, our nation generates 25% of its pollutants and more than 30% of its garbage. Every day, each American throws out an average of 4 pounds of garbage. That totals a *daily* garbage heap of 438,000 tons—enough to fill 63,000 garbage trucks! By becoming "green" consumers, we can directly reduce the amount of waste.

Here's how to shop with ecology in mind:

- First and foremost—if you don't really need it, don't buy it!

- Choose reusable items over disposable items whenever possible.

- Emphasize plant foods rather than animal foods in your menus.

- Be picky about packaging:

  - Look for products that have minimal packaging.

  - Choose products packaged in recycled (look for the ♲ symbol) or recyclable materials, or in reusable containers.

  - Choose products packaged in materials that are most easily recyclable in your community.

  - Buy eggs in cardboard cartons rather than foam plastic.

  - Avoid purchasing anything in foam plastic.

— Let the store manager know why you are making these choices.

— Write or call the manufacturers and let them know why you've chosen to buy or not to buy their products. (You can usually find their address and phone number on the container. Many companies list an 800 phone number for consumers.)

- Bring your own canvas or string bags with you when you shop.

- Paper or plastic? It's debatable which is better. Whichever bag you choose, reuse it as much as possible, then recycle.

- Read labels—try not to purchase products with harmful ingredients.

- Buy the large size or buy in bulk.

- When you do make purchases in recyclable containers, be sure to actually recycle them.

- Talk to your children about why you are making these choices; this will help them develop their own "ecology awareness."

- Complete the loop by buying consumer goods made from recycled materials. This is critical to keeping the demand for recycled materials high and our recycling systems viable.

Making Everyone a Part of Your Recycling Plan

Whether it's in the home or in the child care setting, establishing a recycling program works best if everyone is involved. Adults can take responsibility for gathering or purchasing necessary supplies and transporting wastes to the recycling center; older children can help with research, planning, setup, and maintenance of the program; and younger children can help by decorating boxes to use as storage containers and helping to decide where to keep them and by sorting recyclables.

Here are some ideas to help you establish a successful recycling program:

- Find out what local recycling programs are available in your community and what items can be recycled.

- If you do not have a curbside pick-up program in your community, decide on a practical schedule for going to the recycling center.

- Decide on the most convenient place(s) to store the recyclables — kitchen, garage, back porch, closet, and so on. If you don't have lots of space in a nearby, convenient spot (e.g., the kitchen), use small containers there and, when full, empty them into larger bins in another storage area (e.g., the basement). The more convenient your system, the quicker you will adapt to using it.

- Select containers, preferably with handles or on wheels, that won't be too heavy or bulky to carry when they fill up. Some possible choices: sturdy cardboard cartons, paper grocery bags, empty milk crates, plastic laundry baskets, rattan baskets, or recycling storage units specially designed for the purpose. (See "Appendix D—Resources" for places to order these.)

- As they accumulate, sort your recyclable items into the containers to be set out for curbside pick-up or delivered to the recycling center.

- If you have a yard, establish a compost for recycling food waste (other than meat products) and other organic materials (see page 244).

- Be creative about recycling items that can't be taken to the recycling center. Clothes and household goods that are in usable condition can be donated to nonprofit organizations. Many items are usable for arts, crafts, and science projects with children. A current fashion trend is jewelry, art pieces, and clothing made of recycled material—a sign of the times!

- If there is no recycling program in your community, join with other concerned residents and get one started. *The Recycler's Handbook: Simple Things You Can Do*, by The Earthworks Group, will tell you how to begin.

Nationwide Recycling Information:
1-877-EARTH911
www.earth911.org

Homemade and Nontoxic Cleaning Products

What's a safe and economical way to keep your home and center squeaky clean? You can make your own nontoxic cleaning products.

Many of the commercial household cleaning products that we have become accustomed to using contain harsh, toxic chemicals that add to environmental pollution and may also be harmful to our skin and lungs. (The average American home uses approximately 25 gallons of hazardous chemicals per year!) When you purchase cleaning products, read labels and avoid buying products that include harmful ingredients (these are required by law to have some type of warning label or hazard symbol).

Examples of some of the more common and familiar hazardous substances included in cleaning products are **ammonia**, which is harmful to the skin, eyes, and lungs; **chlorine bleach**, which can be highly irritating to the eyes, nose, throat, and lungs, and *can result in deadly fumes if mixed* *with ammonia;* and **cresol**, an ingredient in many disinfectants, which can cause poisoning by ingestion and inhalation.

More and more companies are responding to consumer demands for environmentally safe products. With a bit of kitchen chemistry, you can make your own safe and effective alternative cleaners, too.

Here are some cleaning products for you to try. The ingredients can be found in your grocery or hardware store or pharmacy.

General All-Purpose Cleaners

- Mix equal parts of white vinegar and water for general cleaning.

- Mix 3 tablespoons washing soda with 4 cups warm water. Rinse with clean water.

- Dissolve 4 tablespoons baking soda in 1 quart warm water or use baking soda on a damp sponge to clean and deodorize surfaces. Baking soda can also be made into a paste and used with an old toothbrush to clean tile grout.

- Dr. Bronner's Sal Suds is a very effective and safe pine-scented cleaner.

Sanitizers

(*Note:* It is possible that these alternatives will not pass muster with child care licensing authorities.)

- Mix ½ cup borax with 1 gallon hot water. Use on a sponge or cloth to sanitize kitchen and/or bathroom surfaces.

- Hydrogen peroxide will sanitize surfaces.

- Isopropyl alcohol wiped on surfaces and allowed to dry is another effective sanitizer.

Dishwashing Soaps

- Use any phosphate-free dishwashing liquid.

- Use pure bar soap rubbed on a cloth or sponge.

Scouring Powders

- Sprinkle baking soda, borax, table salt, or washing soda on any surface where you would normally use a scouring powder. Scrub with a damp cloth or plastic mesh scrubber and rinse.

Oven Cleaners

- Sprinkle water and then lots of baking soda in the oven. Scrub with steel-wool pads and more water as needed.

- To maintain an already reasonably clean oven, mix 2 tablespoons non-phosphate dishwashing liquid soap with 1 tablespoon borax in a spray bottle and fill with warm water. Spray the solution in the oven and leave for 20 minutes or more before wiping clean. Spread newspapers on the floor to catch drips.

Silver Polish

- Apply a paste of baking soda mixed with water. Then rub, rinse, and dry the silver.

- Line the bottom of the kitchen sink with a sheet of aluminum foil. Fill with hot water and add ¼ cup of baking soda, rock salt, or table salt. Put the silver into the water for 2–3 minutes, then wash in soapy water and dry.

- Use toothpaste on an old toothbrush to remove tarnish from crevices. Rinse with warm water and polish with a soft cloth or chamois.

Brass and Copper Polish

- Use lemon juice or a slice of lemon sprinkled with baking soda. Rub with a soft cloth, rinse, and dry.

Glass Cleaner

- Put club soda in a spray bottle. Spray on window or mirror and dry with crumpled newspaper or paper towels.

Drain Cleaners

- Prevent clogging by keeping a drain strainer over the sink drain and never pour grease down the drain. Pour a pot of boiling water down the drain once or twice a week.

- For clogged drains, first try a plunger or a mechanical snake. If it's still clogged, pour ½ cup salt and ½ cup baking soda down the drain, followed by 6 cups of boiling water. Let it sit for several hours before flushing with more water.

- Another formula for clearing clogged drains is to pour ½ cup of white vinegar and a handful of baking soda down the drain and cover it tightly for 1 minute. Then rinse with hot water.

Air Freshener

- Simmer vinegar or herb mixtures or spices (e.g., cinnamon sticks or cloves) in water.

Furniture Polishes

- Use plain mayonnaise, straight from the jar. Rub on the wood with a soft cloth.

- Mix 2 parts olive oil with 1 part lemon juice.

- Mix 3 parts olive oil with 1 part white vinegar.

Source: Debra Lynn Dadd, *Nontoxic & Natural: How to Avoid Dangerous Everyday Products and Buy or Make Safe Ones*, Jeremy P. Tarcher, Inc., Los Angeles, 1984; and Debra Lynn Dadd, *The Nontoxic Home*, Jeremy P. Tarcher, Inc., Los Angeles, 1986.

Building a Compost Heap

Composting is a great way to teach children the importance of feeding the soil in order for the soil to grow healthy vegetables to feed them! The type and size of your compost system will depend very much on your location and your access to growing spaces. If you live in an apartment and do not have yard wastes your best bet is to recycle your organic kitchen vegetable scraps in a worm bin. If you have a yard and you want to grow vegetables just follow the steps below to make your own compost.

• Place your compost bin on a level, well-drained spot that is easy to access and as close to your garden as possible. If there is extra space adjacent to your bin to store bags of leaves, grass clippings, a bale of straw, manure, or other organic materials, so much the better, as you will need these "dry" materials to balance your "wet" kitchen scraps when loading-up your compost bin.

• The minimum size for a compost bin to ensure that it is capable of reaching temperatures high enough to kill most weed seeds (130°) is 3' X 3' X 3.' Your pile can be larger, but if heaps are taller than 5 feet they tend not to get enough oxygen in the center, thus slowing down the millions of microorganisms turning your organic wastes into gardener's delight.

• A compost bin can be made from a range of materials. A simple low-cost bin is made of chicken wire held up with metal stakes. People have had good success using four wooden pallets wired together at the corners. Whatever type bin, it needs a top to keep out unwanted rain—maintaining the right moisture is a key to making good compost.

• Given enough time all organic material decomposes. For a gardener, the challenge of composting is to accelerate the process by having adequate air flow, moist but not wet conditions, and a good mixture of nitrogenous materials to increase bacterial activity, which hastens decomposition.

- Once the bin is ready, line the bottom with materials that do not compact and will encourage a constant air flow in the heap; e.g. corn stalks, branches, etc. The second layer should be high in nitrogen, with materials such as manure and/or grass clippings. The third layer is garden soil or old compost so as to introduce the required microorganisms. From then on build up your compost heap with a mixture of wet (kitchen scraps) and dry (leaves and/or hay), occasionally covering the mixture with soil. During dry seasons add water. Ideally, working compost feels as moist as a squeezed sponge.

- There are organic materials that should be avoided including: diseased plant material; really difficult weeds like Bermuda grass; meat; grease; cat or dog feces; and materials that are greater than ¼ inch thick. Also do not use plant material contaminated with pesticides.

- If you have the time and space you can turn the compost, forking it from one bin to another. However, if you do not have the time or energy, simply cap the heap and leave it for several months. It will eventually be ready to apply to your garden. Whatever method you have used, to now create top-quality potting mixture, sift your compost through a ¼-inch screen.

---

* Thank you, David Haskell, for writing this piece!

CHAPTER EIGHT

....

A Basic Scheme for Nutrition Education

A child starts to learn about food the day she is born. As she receives her first feeding by breast or bottle, she learns that it is pleasurable to eat; her hunger is satisfied and she enjoys the contact with her caregiver. When she takes her first spoonful of mashed bananas, she learns that her hunger can be quieted by something new—something sweet and slightly lumpy that slides from a spoon into her mouth. Each new food is a profound experience! As she grows and sits at the family table, reads books, watches television, and helps prepare foods, she learns more about the place food has in her social structure and what adults consider to be appropriate foods for nourishment. Learning about food happens constantly and automatically.

But are the messages this child gets regarding food likely to teach her what she needs to know about eating healthfully, enjoying eating, and becoming a savvy and socially responsible consumer? If this child is typical, she will have picked up a mish-mash of ideas about food, some of which are fine and some of which aren't helpful at all. This should be no great surprise, because the typical adult is in the same situation!

Recognizing that children need a good knowledge base about food and nutrition, many child care centers, homes, and schools have implemented nutrition education programs. The best is comprehensive in its approach, meaning that the site's menus, the example set by teachers and other adults, books, videos, and toys used, formal nutrition education activities and field trips, and participation by parents reinforce consistent messages about eating well and happily. For example, children are unlikely to learn about the pleasures of trying new foods if the center's menus rotate among hamburgers, hot dogs, and spaghetti with meat sauce. They will continue to think that sweet foods always accompany celebrations if every holiday or birthday is celebrated with cupcakes or candies. They will not learn to recycle waste if containers are not provided for recyclable material in the lunchroom.

Teaching children what they need to know about food starts with adults learning about good nutrition and applying its principles in their own lives every day. The children who eat brown rice and broccoli enthusiastically are generally those who have seen their parents and teachers or caregivers doing it; they think that's how people are *supposed* to eat. Too often nutrition education for child care staff and parents focuses on children's nutrition issues. It's important for people who work with children to know about these things, but at least as much effort should go into helping them improve their own nutrition.

There are many fine nutrition education resources available, especially for older children. The purpose of this section of the book is to outline a rather simple organic approach to teaching children about food, not to deliver a pre-packaged curriculum. It works best if you have a system, but with your own special flavor to it.

Teaching Kids About Food, Step by Step

Build the Foundation

- **Learn and practice the basics of good nutrition yourself.** A class at your local college or adult education center may be available; if not, some suggested books are listed in Appendix D. Keep abreast of nutrition news by reading reliable magazines or journals.

- **Serve meals that are consistent with current nutritional guidelines.** If children are bringing their own food to the site, how do their bag lunches or snacks look? Some child care centers and schools encourage parents to refrain from sending foods high in sugar or salt to school and have guidelines regarding appropriate foods for celebrations.

- **Fill the children's environment with nutrition-positive decorations, toys, books, and videos.** Take a look at your classroom, child care site, or home. Are there posters of healthful foods or families from around the world sharing meals? When you decorate the children's paperwork with stickers, do you use "lollipops" or "apples"? Does the math textbook teach that 4 candy bars + 5 candy bars = 9 candy bars?

Construct a Framework of "Natural" Learning Experiences

- **Equip your classroom for food preparation activities.** This need not be costly; many inexpensive kitchen tools are available that are easy for children to manage. Projects should be fairly simple and geared to the children's level of development. Even assembling a salad can be exciting for a young child. There are many good children's cookbooks; stick with those having recipes for more than cookies and candy. And remember that constant adult supervision is a must.

- **Set up some food-growing experiences for the children.** A children's garden is wonderful, but if space or time isn't available, many foods can be grown in pots outside or in a windowsill.

- **Take children shopping for food.** Regular grocery stores offer plenty of opportunities for "food education," but be sure to check out other shopping resources; for example, farmer's markets and ethnic groceries.

- **Arrange field trips to places where food is grown or manufactured.** Your local cooperative extension agent can usually provide you with listings of farms that conduct tours or allow you to "pick your own." And there is probably a bakery, restaurant, or food-processing plant in your area that arranges tours.

- **Establish a system of environmentally conscious waste disposal.** Have the children sort their own trash for recycling and use a minimum of nonrecyclable materials in food service. Maintaining a compost heap with certain food wastes is a wonderful adjunct to your garden as well.

- **Use mealtimes as occasions to talk about food origins, cultural food habits, and various nutrition concepts.** For example, preschoolers might be asked which of the foods served come from animals, whereas older children might be asked to identify those high in fat or vitamin C. Children can be encouraged to share information about how (or whether) their own families use certain foods.

- **Plan for reinforcement at home in order to ensure consistent messages.** Parents and caregivers or teachers need to be in communication with each other about the values and concepts they are working to impart to their children.

Supplement with Other Nutrition Education Activities

- **Games, riddles, puzzles, art projects, flannelboard stories, songs, puppets, dramatic play, and science experiments can all be used to enrich the program of "food education" you've established.** Numerous curricula and idea books are available. You may want to organize your nutrition education around certain concepts, say, on a monthly basis. Cooking projects, stories, games, and menus can help teach a particular theme. Assess what the children already know about food and nutrition before you choose the themes you will develop; knowledge and skills will vary widely within the same age group. Be sure the children are well grounded in the simpler concepts before moving on to more sophisticated ones.

Making the Most of Your Position as a Role Model

Children are constantly learning from what adults do and say. By "labeling" our actions, and explaining the "why's" when we make choices, we are making the most of our opportunity to help childen learn. Remember to talk with children (without "lecturing") about what you are doing and why you are doing it. Also consider how your conversations with other adults may influence children who might be listening.

Here are some examples:

- "Let's clear our food garbage into this empty carton and add it to the compost. Instead of filling up the garbage dumps, we'll be making new soil."

- "I'll rinse this jar and add it to the recycling bin. Glass can be reused over and over again."

- "Let's bring our canvas bag to the grocery store. That way we don't need to use either paper or plastic bags."

- "While we're brushing our teeth, let's turn off the faucet so we won't be wasting water."

- "I was going to buy this cereal, but I just read the label and saw how much salt and sugar it had. I'll buy this other kind instead."

- "Let's buy the eggs in the cardboard carton instead of in the plastic foam one. That way we can recycle and we won't be adding to pollution."

Acknowledge efforts that the children make to follow your examples. Let them know that you notice when they learn something new.

Developing Nutrition Learning Objectives

Review "What Every Child Should Learn About Food and Eating" on page 14. There are numerous themes you can develop in order to support these basic concepts. Some are simple enough for a toddler to grasp; others are more complicated and are best used with older children. For example, a preschooler can learn that we need food in order to live and grow; a sixth grader can learn the role of protein or calcium in maintaining our bodies' functions.

Here are enough themes to last you for years! Remember, the simpler concepts serve as a foundation for learning the more complicated ones.

Simpler

- I need to wash my hands before handling food or eating.

- I must behave in an acceptable fashion at the meal table.

- There are lots of different foods I can eat.

- I can name foods of different sizes, shapes, colors, and preparation methods.

- I can enjoy and identify foods using all of my senses.

- I need to eat a variety of good foods in order to grow and stay healthy.

- I can identify foods that come from animals.

- I can identify foods that come from plants.

- I know how the plants that we eat grow.

- Many people work to give me the food I eat . . . farmers, food processors, truck drivers, grocers, bakers, parents, caregivers . . .

- People in different cultures eat different foods, and families within those cultures eat different foods and use certain foods to celebrate special occasions.

- Television advertising will try to get me to buy foods that aren't always good for me.

- Food has to be stored and handled carefully or it can make me sick when I eat it.

- I should avoid wasting food.

- When I eat, I make waste that I should dispose of in a way that is best for the earth.

- I can describe the relationship between what I eat and the health of my teeth.

- I can make myself healthful snacks and help grownups prepare meals.

- I can identify practices that ensure my safety while cooking.

- I need to balance my food intake with work and play activities.

More Difficult

- I can classify foods by food group.

- I can name one major nutrient provided by each of the food groups.

- I can plan a nutritionally adequate meal.

- I can name at least one function for each of the six major nutrient groups.

- I can describe the basic process of digestion.

- I can name foods that are significant sources of protein, starches, sugar, fat, sodium, and fiber.

- I can name several health professionals that give advice regarding the relationship between food and health.

- I can recognize the main ingredients in certain products by reading their food labels.

- I can use unit pricing to decide what's the best buy when purchasing foods.

A Food Education Planner

Now, it isn't our intention to lay out an entire nutrition curriculum for you. But we would like to encourage you to look at your nutrition education program systematically, and give you some of our ideas for activities, along with some resources for others.

We have found it helps to be able to organize your thoughts on paper. The Food Education Planner on page 257 is an example using the theme "There are lots of different foods I can eat." We discuss this below. We have included a blank form on page 258 for you to photocopy and use when planning your program.

First, let's walk through the different ways one of the themes discussed earlier could be taught. Suppose, for example, we want four-year-olds to get the idea that "there are lots of different foods that I can eat."

Theme:	There Are Lots of Different Foods I Can Eat
The Menu:	A variety of tasty and attractive foods are served, some familiar to the children and some new to them.
Modeling:	The children see adults enjoying a variety of foods and being willing to taste new ones.
Concepts in Environment	Books and posters portray a vast assortment of foods, some familiar and some more unusual. Some books that talk about eating a variety of foods are: *Bread and Jam for Frances* (R. Hoban, Harper & Row, New York, 1964); *Gregory the Terrible Eater* (M. Sharmat, Scholastic Book Service, New York, 1980); and *Green Eggs and Ham* (Dr. Seuss, Random House, New York, 1960).
Activities and Trips:	Take a field trip to an ethnic grocery store, a farmers' market, or the produce department of a local supermarket. Help the children pick out some food items they've never tasted, then go back home or to the classroom and have a tasting party.
	Make a flannelboard story out of *Green Eggs and Ham*. (For added fun, the next day let the children tell you the story.)
	Sing a song together about trying new foods (see page 296).
Cooking:	Make "Green Eggs and Ham" together (recipe on next page).
	Prepare some of the foods from the above field trip with the children.

Green Eggs and Ham

8 eggs

½ cup minced fresh parsley (chives are
also nice, but optional)

½ cup milk

Oil

4 oz. cooked turkey ham
or Canadian bacon

Salt and pepper to taste

1. Beat eggs, parsley, and milk together.
2. Scramble egg mixture in a heavy or nonstick pan in a small amount of oil.
3. Serve with small amounts of turkey ham or Canadian bacon on the side.

20 1-oz. servings

At Home: Send recipes home to parents, using new foods introduced in school or child care.

SAMPLE: Food Education Planner

Central Idea: There are lots of different foods to eat

Menu

Try new vegetables (with dip): jicama, asparagus, snow peas.

Try Vietnamese soup recipe from Tran's mom.

Role Modeling

Talk about how much fun it is to explore new foods, while we're eating lunch.

Environment

Put "Green Eggs and Ham" in book area (also read during circle time).

Put up poster of exotic produce.

Activities

Field trip to Asian Food Mart for materials for Nori-Maki rolls.

Cooking Projects

Green Eggs and Ham

Nori-Maki rolls

Parents / "Homework"

Send recipes home for Nori-Maki rolls and Tran's mom's soup, along with write-up of tips for introducing new foods.

Food Education Planner

Central Idea: _____

Menu	**Role Modeling**
Environment	**Activities**
Cooking Projects	**Parents / "Homework"**

Food-Based Activities for Kids

What Children Learn Through Cooking Activities

Cooking is an ideal vehicle for nutrition education for young children. It allows them to become familiar with foods they might not otherwise see, and often children will eagerly eat foods which they have prepared, even when they refused them previously. Cooking activities also allow children to share the process of working toward a goal and sharing the fruits of their labors with friends and family.

Cooking develops many concepts and skills, including:

Motor Skills:	Scrubbing, tearing, dipping
	Pouring, mixing, shaking, spreading
	Rolling, kneading, juicing, peeling
	Cutting, grating, slicing
Language Arts:	Naming—foods, actions, equipment, processes, categories
	Comparisons
	Time designations
	Following directions
	Letter/word recognition
Mathematics	Measuring
	Counting
	Sequencing
	Classification
	Numbers on tags and labels

Socialization   Sharing

Teamwork

Self-care

Cultural food habits

Food-related professions in the community

Science: Heat and coolness

Floating

Dissolving

Evaporation

Browning

Leavening

Melting

Gelatinization

Sense awareness

Be sure to include parents in cooking activities, or send the recipes you've made with the children home. This will help ensure consistent messages about healthy eating.

Survival Guide for Cooking With Children

The 5 Laws of Successful Cooking Projects

1. Plan projects at the childrens' level of development (see below).

2. Keep your participation in the project to a minimum, but supervise constantly.

3. Plan cooking activities to fit within the day's menu of nutritious foods.

4. Insist upon good safety practices and have a first aid kit handy.

5. Insist that the children help with cleanup.

Remember that food-handling skills develop over time. Here is a guide to help you understand what kids of different ages are capable of.

2-year-olds: ***Big Arm Muscles***

Scrub

Tear, Break, Snap

Dip

3-year-olds: ***Medium Muscles / Hands***

Wrap

Pour

Mix

Shake

Spread

4-year-olds:	***Snall Muscles / Fingers***
	Peel
	Roll
	Juice
	Crack eggs
	Mash
5 and up:	***Fine Coordination / Working Against Resistance***
	Measure
	Cut
	Grind
	Beat with egg beater

Kitchen Safety While Cooking With Children

Young children can get so many things out of cooking projects; let's make sure injuries aren't among them! The major dangers to children while cooking are burns and cuts. Thus, they need to start learning about two major concepts, very hot and sharp.

Very Hot!

Talk about what's hot. Is a book hot? Milk in the refrigerator? A pan on the stove? Let the children know that very hot things can burn and hurt us, and for now, only grownups will touch them (for example, taking food out of the oven).

• Never leave children alone in the kitchen when heat-producing appliances or items that are cooking are within reach.

- Keep a fire extinguisher in the kitchen and make sure you know how to use it. To prepare in case someone's clothes should catch fire, children should be drilled on *Stop, drop, and roll!*

- Tie long hair back and roll back billowy sleeves, or have children wear short-sleeved shirts, to avoid contact with flames.

- Turn pot and pan handles toward back of work area.

Sharp!

Young children can generally cut soft food with plastic knives or serrated dinner knives. They need to learn how to hold a knife, which is the sharp edge of the blade, and that sharp can hurt. Demonstrate by cutting an orange. If you cut with the dull side, nothing happens unless you press down on the sharp edge, which hurts. When you apply the sharp edge to the orange, you get slices.

- Many teachers wrap colored tape around the handles of knives to remind children which end to hold.

- Children also need to learn to keep the fingers of the other hand out of harm's way. You can teach them about the "other hand" by making it a game. ("One of your hands is holding a car. What is the 'other hand' doing?").

- Small cutting boards help focus the child's attention; just make sure they're stable. A damp cloth underneath can prevent sliding.

- It often helps to practice cutting on playdough before moving on to real food.

- If you're cutting something round, like a peach, cut it in half first so there's a flat side to rest on the cutting board.

- Allow the children to cut objects only while sitting down.

- Never leave children alone in the kitchen when they're working with knives!

Other Precautions

- Don't allow running in the kitchen.

- Wipe up spills immediately so no one slips and falls.

- Teach the children not to use electrical appliances unless you're there to supervise. It's best to leave blenders, electric skillets, etc., unplugged and tucked away when not in use.

- Make sure everyone's hands are dry when using electrical appliances.

- Have everything the children will be working with at their level, or else provide a secure stool or chair for children to stand on.

- Make sure that you allow plenty of time for your cooking project; accidents are more likely to happen when you're feeling rushed. Maintain a calm and focused atmosphere in your kitchen.

Single-Portion Cooking

Two main approaches to children's cooking projects are commonly used in group settings. One is giving each child a task that contributes to making a finished product that everyone will eat. The other is single-portion cooking, sometimes called "cup cooking."

The advantage of the former is that it allows a child the cooperative experience of cooking and generally requires less setup time. However, it's sometimes difficult for the adult in charge to ensure that everyone keeps interested, and it isn't always clear to the child how his or her task related to the outcome.

Single-portion cooking lets the child participate in the cooking process each step of the way. It also conveys the idea that (at least sometimes) "if you don't work, you don't eat," a handy notion for children to keep in mind as they grow up. And for the squeamish, it requires the child to touch only her own food. It does take considerably more advance preparation to cook this way, and some recipes or equipment don't lend themselves easily to this method. But we highly recommend giving the technique a try.

The general idea here is to set up a number of work stations that correspond to specific steps within a recipe. Generally a picture illustrating the directions for the step would be placed behind the tools and ingredients a child would need to complete the step. The child should move systematically through the "stations" with little (or no) adult help. The pictures should illustrate every task, starting with handwashing and ending with eating (and cleanup if a picture helps!).

On the next page is an example of how our recipe for Peanut Butter Ping-Pong Balls would look in single-portion format. Don't let what you feel is a lack of drawing talent deter you from trying this with other recipes!

If you would like to convert a favorite recipe into a single-portion cooking project, we have some advice for you:

- Think through the logistics of the project. Will all of the steps work in individual bowls or containers? Do you have the equipment for each step?

- Rather than have the children measuring out miniscule amounts of herbs, spices, or other ingredients, you may want to make up a "spice mixture" or "flour mixture."

- Convert your recipe to single portions by division. For example, if your recipe calls for 2 cups of flour, and you want 8 portions, it's probably easiest to first convert the cups to tablespoons: 2 cups = 32 tablespoons. Then divide by the number of servings: 32 tablespoons ÷ 8 = 4 tablespoons per portion. You may find a table of measurements on page 207. If you end up with some intimidating fraction, you can often combine ingredients, as in the "spice mixture" example above, or change the portion size (like making the recipe serve 8 instead of 10).

PEANUT BUTTER PING PONG BALLS

① Wash Hands

② Add to Bowl — 2 T. Peanut Butter

③ Add — 1 T. Honey

④ Add — ⅛ t. Vanilla

⑤ Add — ¾ cup crispy rice cereal

⑥ Roll into balls

⑦ Refrigerate 1 hr.

⑧ Eat!

- *Do a trial run before you attempt the recipe with children.* You want them to feel successful

The book *Cook and Learn, Pictorial Single Portion Recipes* (Beverly Veitch and Thelma Harms, Addison-Wesley Publishing Company, Menlo Park, Calif., 1981) is an excellent guide (with recipes) to the single-portion cooking method.

Taste Testing Is A Fun Way to Get to Know Foods

Exposing children to as many healthful foods as possible, even those you won't be able to incorporate into your menus, is easy and fun doing "taste testing." This is also an ideal way to introduce new foods that will be appearing at the meal table by allowing the children to experience tiny amounts and talk about the foods' characteristics. You can taste test one food at a time, different varieties of the same food (for example, yellow, plum, beefsteak, and cherry tomatoes), or different foods within a food group.

Taste tests can be done with small groups of children or in a larger group, as at "circle time." Small groups allow younger children to have plenty of time to explore the sensory characteristics of the food beyond taste: smells, textures, colors. Larger groups lend themselves to activities like taking votes and graphing favorite varieties of foods. Whichever method you choose, prepare sufficient samples for testing (and you may need several plates so that children don't have to wait too long for a turn).

Make sure that the children don't put their hands all over other children's food. Also, prepare a list of questions that you'll ask the children about the foods they're tasting. Here are some examples of questions you can ask:

Before cutting up samples:

- What does the food feel like? Smooth? Bumpy? Soft? Hard? Sticky? Gooey?

- Is this food wet? Dry?

- Which of these varieties is the largest? The smallest?

- What color is this food?

- What color do you think the inside is?

While tasting:

- What does the food smell like? Sharp? Spicy? Sweet? Toasty?

- Is this food easy to chew?

- How does the food feel on your tongue?

- What does the food taste like? Salty? Bitter? Sweet? Sour? Spicy? Hot?

- Does this taste like anything else you've eaten?

- Do you eat this food at home?

- How does your family eat this food?

- Which of these foods is your favorite? Why?

Remember the division of responsibility! Allow each child to decide whether to eat a food or not.

Smelly Boxes and Feelie Socks

This activity is a fun way for young children to learn about the sensory characteristics of foods. It requires them to play detective, identifying foods using only one clue (sense) at a time.

Feelie Socks
(Touch)

Place sturdy foods inside clean socks. Ask the children to put their hands into the socks and identify the foods only by touch. Talk with them about how the foods feel. Are they smooth, bumpy, fuzzy? Are they round, irregular, long, large, or small?

Mystery Solutions
(Taste)

Stir flavoring agents (below) into plain water. Give each child four spoons to dip into the solutions for tiny tastes.

Sweet: sugar
Salty: salt
Sour: white vinegar
Bitter: unsweetened grapefruit juice

Smelly Boxes
(Smell)

Make slits in the lids of boxes (like the slit in a piggy bank). Ask the children to identify the foods by smell alone. Ideas: lemons, onions, garlic, tuna, cotton balls saturated with vanilla.

Can You Believe Your Ears?
(Hearing)

Ask the children to close their eyes and identify foods using only the sense of hearing. Examples: popcorn popping, soda water fizzing, apples or carrots crunching.

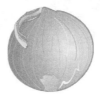

Gardening With Children

One of the most exciting and enjoyable ways to teach children about where food comes from is through gardening activities. Even toddlers love to participate—they can fill pots with dirt, smash up dirt clods, and water plants with a sprinkling can. If you don't have a garden area, you can start with an egg carton, some soil, and a windowsill.

When children plant vegetable or fruit seeds and watch them grow, they are learning many things, such as:

- Food does not start out at the grocery store.

- Some of our food comes from the earth.

- Plants need soil, water, and sunlight.

- Plants have seeds, roots, and leaves.

- There are seasons and life cycles.

- Plants are living things and need to be cared for.

- I can grow some of my own food.

- Seeds that I find in my fruits and vegetables can be planted to grow more fruits and vegetables.

Children who successfully plant and grow their own food will feel pride in their accomplishment and can develop respect for nature and for their surroundings. They may even be more willing to taste a new vegetable if they've grown it themselves.

Here are some planting activities that are fun to do with children. The more they can do independently, the more they are likely to learn.

- **Grow a baby citrus tree:**

    1. Have the children save seeds from an orange, tangerine, lemon, or grapefruit and soak them overnight.

    2. Provide the children with individual containers for planting (egg cartons, milk cartons, peat pots—just be sure to make drainage holes to prevent the seeds from rotting) and let them fill their containers with good potting soil.

    3. Have each child plant 2 or 3 seeds about 1 inch deep in their container. (Have some rulers on hand to talk about how deep 1 inch is.)

    4. Have the children keep them in a warm, sunny spot, water them as the soil begins to feel dry, and watch for the seeds to sprout.

- **Grow a vegetable:**

    1. Follow the steps for planting citrus seeds, but use vegetable seeds. Follow instructions on the seed packet for planting depth. Beans or peas are good choices because they sprout quickly and grow fast.

    2. When the seedlings are big enough, if you have an outdoor garden, the children can transplant them.

- **Provide the children with some large seeds** such as beans or peas and let them sprout the seeds in wet paper towels or cotton in a transparent container. This will enable the children to watch the whole process and have a better idea of what's going on under the soil.

- **When you are involved in planting activities with children, their learning can be enhanced by asking questions and encouraging experiments, such as these:**

  1. What's inside a seed?

  2. Does it have a top and a bottom?

  3. If we plant seeds in different directions, will the roots and leaves still know which way to grow?

  4. What does a seed need in order to grow?

  5. Let the children study plants and seeds under a magnifying glass.

  6. Let the children experiment by planting in different soils, under varying lighting conditions and temperatures, with more or less water, etc.

  7. Compare and discuss the results.

  8. Measure daily or weekly growth of plants and keep a chart or graph.

  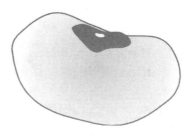

  9. Do all seeds grow at the same speed? Compare the growth of beans or peas to the growth of an avocado seed.

As much as possible, let the children discover their own answers to these questions:

- Learn the names of the parts of plants. (You can cut out flannelboard pieces to show the parts that grow above and below the ground—seeds or bulbs, roots, leaves, stems, buds, and flowers.) Then talk about the different parts of plants that we eat—e.g., carrots and potatoes are roots, broccoli and cauliflower are flowers, lettuce and spinach are leaves, celery and asparagus are stems.

- Have the children save the seeds from fruits and vegetables they eat. They can cut out pictures of the foods from magazines and make charts showing which food grows from which seed.

- According to the ages of the children, your own interest in gardening, and the space that is available, gardening activities can be more extensive. Older children can research, plan, and develop an entire vegetable garden. Work with them to decide what needs to be done, how to divide up the work, etc.

Here are some good books about gardening with children:

Linnea's Windowsill Garden by Christina Bjork and Lena Anderson, Translated by Joan Sandin, R&S Books, Stockholm, 1988.

Gardens for Growing People: A Guide to Gardening With Children by Ruth Kantor Lopez, Gardens for Growing People, California, 1990.

Kids Gardening: A Kids' Guide to Messing Around in the Dirt by Kevin Raftery and Kim Gilbert Raftery, Klutz Press, Palo Alto, California, 1989.

Roots, Shoots, Buckets, & Boots: Gardening Together With Children by Sharon Lovejoy, Workman Publishing Company, 1999.

The Growing Seeds: A Guided Fantasy

Here is a guided fantasy for children who are participating in planting activities. Playing a tape of soft music or sounds of nature will enhance the experience. Adapt it to a longer or shorter version depending on the age and attention span of the children. Pause between sentences to give the children time to visualize.

First curl up into a comfortable little ball. Now, close your eyes and pretend that you are a tiny seed being planted in the ground and covered gently by rich fertile soil. Keep your eyes closed and curl up as small as you can.

Now, imagine that it's early morning and you are beginning to feel the warmth of the sun on the soil. You feel warm and cozy as the sun comes up. Soon someone comes along with a sprinkling can and gently waters all of the little seeds. (The adult can walk around the room gently patting heads to feel like water drops.) *Take a deep breath and enjoy the smell of the moist earth.*

Notice how the water keeps you cool and damp through the hot afternoon sun. Before long it is evening, and then, night.

Now imagine the next day . . . and the next night . . . and another day . . . and another night . . . and slowly, very slowly, you feel your seed covering begin to open as your tiny roots reach down into the soil. Then your stem and leaves begin to reach up and out toward the sun. You are happy because you have had just enough sunshine and water to help you grow. (Suggest they begin to unfold and reach up, gradually stretching up to standing position.) *When you have stretched your stem and leaves up as tall as you can, take a deep breath of clean, fresh air, and stop and think about what kind of plant you have grown into. When you are ready, open your eyes and stand or sit quietly until all of the other seeds have finished sprouting.*

You might then encourage the childen to talk about their experiences and what kind of plants they became. They may also wish to draw pictures based on their seed-growing fantasy.

Science Experiments for Older Children

Kids can learn a lot about science by experimenting with food, and a lot about food by learning the science of it. Older children love to make bubbling concoctions and peer into microscopes. Some of the scientific concepts that can be experienced while doing food experiments are:

- Solutions and crystals (sugar, salt)

- The properties of acids and bases (baking soda, vinegar)

- Emulsification (mayonnaise)

- The properties of starches and sugars (caramelized sugar, tapioca)

- Denaturing of proteins (sour milk, scrambled eggs)

- Oxidation (apples treated with lemon juice)

- The life cycles of organisms like yeasts, molds, and bacteria (yogurt, bread)

- The action of enzymes (meat tenderizer)

Interested in learning more? (We must confess to a fascination with science experiments ourselves. Some things you never outgrow!) There are some very good books available that can show you how to set kids up in their own "laboratories."

Science Experiments You Can Eat by Vicki Cobb, Harper Trophy, 1984.

Foodworks: Over 100 Science Activities and Fascinating Facts That Explore the Magic of Food by Ontario Science Centre, Massachusetts, Addison-Wesley Publishing Company, Inc., 1987.

Science Fun with Peanuts and Popcorn by Rose Wyler, New York, Julian Mesner, 1986.

The Social Aspects of Food

Planting Seeds for Healthy Children and a Healthy Planet

Food preparation and mealtimes offer opportunities to model and teach healthy and responsible behavior toward self, others, and our world. The experiences we provide help to plant the seeds of curiosity, interest, understanding, and caring in children. Some of the concepts we can begin to teach in relation to mealtime include:

- How food is grown, produced, transported, marketed, cooked, etc.

- How to be smart, thoughtful shoppers—economically, environmentally, and healthwise.

- How to responsibly dispose of leftover food and food packaging.

- What responsibilities we have toward others—from appropriate behavior when eating together to awareness of global issues such as world hunger, environmental protection, etc.

- Respect and appreciation for the diversity of lifestyles among people.

Knowing how much our day-to-day actions influence the development of children in our care can be a strong motivating factor in helping us to keep striving toward more healthy and environmentally sound habits. By functioning in a way that reflects concern and caring for our own well-being and that of others, we are taking the first step toward helping the children we care for begin to grow into healthy and responsible adults.

Food and the Development of Social Awareness

The need for food is, of course, one of the primary things that all human beings have in common. Because of this, mealtime can serve as the first setting for developing a child's social awareness.

This development takes place in many stages and in many "arenas." In a preschool setting, this awareness is very direct and personal. For example, children begin to gain a sense of manners and consideration for others (such as passing food at the table, not taking "seconds" until everyone has had "firsts," the concept of sharing) which they can, hopefully, start to apply to other non-mealtime areas of interaction. They are also learning about the ways in which they are the same as, as well as different from, each other, through seeing and hearing about each other's families.

More appropriate at a later age, 5 years and up, when a child begins to see the world as involving more than just his direct experience, is the fostering of an awareness of a larger scope of social concerns and cultural traits. Children are learning that there is a whole world of people, and that there is an immense diversity of customs, beliefs, ways of life—and an equally immense, and shocking, diversity of economic conditions and abilities to meet nutritional needs.

Teaching Children About Hunger

How and when do children become aware that for many people hunger means far more than just having to wait half an hour until snack time? What role can adults take in helping children (who have not experienced it first-hand) understand and deal with this awareness?

Again, it is most appropriate to introduce these concepts to children of 5 years and up because:

• They may be hearing or seeing things that make them curious. What is Ethiopia? Why was that man back there sleeping on the street?

- They are getting old enough to learn about some harsh realities without becoming overly frightened or seeing themselves as being in danger.

- They are capable of taking some actions (participation in food drives, etc.) that have results they can see and/or understand; this helps to instill a sense of empowerment—"I can help solve the problem!"

The purpose of teaching children about hunger is not to get them to eat their broccoli. Telling them to "finish your vegetables, there are children starving in India" to an adult means "you should appreciate the fact that *you* have food." But a child might easily miss the connection and feel confused: What does *my* broccoli have to do with someone I don't even know?

Ideally, as we teach children about hunger and other social problems and injustices, we are helping them grow into adults who will care about society and the world, and who will feel capable and motivated to keep improving it. We need to teach them in a way that neither minimizes nor exaggerates the problem of hunger. How can we accomplish this?

The book, *Discover the World: Empowering Children to Value Themselves, Others and the Earth*, edited by Susan Hopkins and Jeffry Winters, offers many suggestions and "activity charts" designed to help adults teach children about social concerns. We have included their activity chart related to the issue of hunger on pages 280–281. The activities are appropriate for use with preschool and early elementary school-age children.

Older elementary school children and junior high and high school age children are capable of learning, understanding, and doing much more in relation to hunger.

Teaching Children About Cultural Diversity

Another area in which mealtime can be used to further children's global awareness is in regard to cultural diversity. It is one of the opportunities to nurture the development of enthusiasm, appreciation, and respect for the differences as well as the similarities of all people.

Often, multicultural education is included in ways that, though unintended, might actually promote stereotypes and present incorrect information. For example, serving "ethnic" foods and presenting "ethnic" dances and music only on "ethnic" holidays may emphasize and misportray differences; showing pictures of cultural groups dressed in "traditional" clothing does not convey the reality of daily life, etc. This approach might also give the impression that all people of a particular cultural group do things in the same way.

The following guidelines, adapted from the book *Anti-Bias Curriculum: Tools for Empowering Your Children* by Louise Derman-Sparks and the Anti-Bias Curriculum Task Force, will help ensure that efforts to teach multi-cultural education at mealtime won't backfire.

- Prepare foods that children regularly eat at home. Include foods eaten by every child's family. Integrate culturally diverse cooking regularly at snack and lunch. Ask parents for recipes that you can include. Also, include foods from cultures not represented within the group.

- Don't stereotype. Be sure to avoid generalizations. Though certain foods may be traditionally identified with a particular cultural group, remember to point out that families within the same culture may eat differently from each other.

- Explain the difference between daily foods and holiday foods.

- Don't mix cultures up. Families from El Salvador do not eat the same foods as families from Mexico. Families recently from Mexico may not eat the same foods as third-generation Chicanos.

Learning About Hunger: Activity Chart

Concept	Good nutrition involves eating a balanced diet of various foods.	We can grow food.	
Art Experience	Make a collage with food pictures representing the food groups.	Paint pictures of gardens or farms.	
Science Experience	Make a food group mural to hang up in the eating area.	Have a drought in one part of the garden. What happens?	
Music/Movement		Sing "The Garden Song" ("Inch by Inch") by Dave Mallet.	
Fine Muscle	Cut out pictures of foods for mural.	Plant seeds.	
Large Muscle		Cultivate the soil.	
Language	Discuss food groups and "balanced diet."	Discuss seeds to be sown. Contrast mature fruits and vegetables.	
Special Activities	Conduct a food drive this week. Ask families to bring in dried and canned foods to donate to a local food bank.	Start a garden.	

From *Discover the World: Empowering Young Children to Value Themselves, Others and the Earth.* Edited by Susan Hopkins and Jeffry Winters, Concerned Educators for a Safe Environment. New Society Publishers: Philadelphia, Penn., Santa Cruz, Calif., and Gabriola Island, BC; 800-333-9093. Reprinted with permission.

Learning About Hunger: Activity Chart

Not everyone has as much food as they would like.	Sharing means giving of ourselves to help.	We can share our food with our neighbors.
	Make a picture book about sharing.	
Discuss with the group that sometimes people don't have enough food. Then have a snack with only one serving per child. Afterward, discuss: Did you want more? How did it feel not to be able to have more?	Share garden work.	Make breads together. Send home copies of recipes with all the children.
	Make a salad from garden produce to share with others.	Each child kneads a small amount of bread dough and adds it to class loaf.
	Discuss taking your portion of food and leaving enough for others.	Vocabulary—label food and put cans into categories. Make a grocery store.
Problem-solve: We have one piece of watermelon and 4 children want it. What shall we do?		Pack up food with children to send to the food bank.

- Children may not like the new food they are supposed to be learning to appreciate. Teach children ways to decline food politely. Serve small portions and invite, but don't force them to try it. Help them understand that sometimes we like new things and sometimes we don't. If children make fun of the food or call a food "yucky," intervene immediately, explaining that it is not okay to respond in those ways, and offering other ways: "I've never tasted that before; what does it taste like?" or "It tastes different to me"; or, if a child really doesn't want to try, say, "No, thank you; I don't want any today."

The World Foods: Activity Chart on pages 283–284 will give you some good ideas regarding your activities for children.

Handling Holidays and Special Occasions

Holidays almost always involve special foods, meals, cooking, and baking. Often they also involve lots of excitement, high expectations from adults and children, and a fair share of hard work and stress. For child care providers, they also include many questions such as: What do I expect of myself? What do I expect of the children? How can I involve the children and their families?

Some careful planning and evaluating can help you create celebrations that will leave you exuberant . . . instead of exhausted. Here is a checklist to help you evaluate your plans.

Expections and Assumptions

- What is your purpose in choosing to celebrate this holiday?

- Are you planning activities automatically, just because you've always done them that way?

- Are your plans based on what you really enjoy doing rather than on what you think the children or other adults expect you to do?

- Are you making any automatic assumptions about what children will enjoy and understand?

- Have you talked to the children about what would make the celebration special for them? Their hopes and ideas may be simpler than you think.

- If you think the children have specific expectations, are they reasonable and agreeable with you?

"Age-Appropriateness"

- Are your plans appropriate for the level of development of the children who will be participating?

- If there are children of mixed age range, are there activities that can be adapted to various ages so that everyone can participate?

- How will the experience be meaningful for the children who will be participating?

- What do you hope or think that the children will learn from the experience?

- If cooking activities are a part of your plans, are they appropriate for the ages of the children who will be participating?

Cultural Awareness

- Are your plans appropriate for the ethnic background of the children who will participate?

World Foods: Activity Chart

Concept	Everyone eats.	There are many foods around the world that are similar.
Art Experience	Collage with food pictures cut out from magazines.	
Science Experience	Eat something from each basic food group. Discuss taste, smell, and texture.	Make or buy and taste pancakes, won tons, tortillas, crepes. Compare. Discuss origins.
Music/Movement	Play games from Malvina Reynolds' album, *Artichoke, Griddle Cake and Other Good Things.*	
Fine Muscle	Cut out pictures of people marketing, preparing, and eating a variety of foods.	Prepare and eat foods of various cultures with appropriate utensils such as rice with chopsticks.
Large Muscle	Walk to store and buy an item from each food group.	
Language	Food Lotto. Make a set of cards representing many cultures.	Learn food names and associate with countries of origin.
Special Activities	Set up a grocery store.	

From *Discover the World: Empowering Young Children to Value Themselves, Others and the Earth.* Edited by Susan Hopkins and Jeffry Winters, Concerned Educators for a Safe Environment. New Society Publishers: Philadelphia, Penn., Santa Cruz, Calif., and Gabriola Island, BC; 800-333-9093. Reprinted with permission.

World Foods: Activity Chart

Children need roots and identity.	Spices come from all over the world and change taste and smell.	People eat bread in many different forms.
Make a bread basket with white playdough by weaving designs over bread pan —bake.	Make a "spice circle." Children each share spice from home and glue on circle.	
Taste many different kinds of breads from many ethnic sources.	Smell spice jars marked with pictures that represent home country (curry–India; chili–South America).	Observe and compare making yeast and unleavened breads.
Play "Stir Fry." Large "tape" circle on floor is "pan." Children hop in pan as they call out what food they are.		
	Push cloves into oranges to make pomander balls.	Stir, sift, knead, chop, etc.
		Act out adding ingredients for bread. Add yeast and everyone rises.
Discuss kinds of food children eat at home—traditions from grandparents, etc.	Children share information about spice brought from home, how it is used in food, family traditions.	Learn bread names and associate with countries of origin.
Have a "Festival of Breads." Parents bake bread and share culture and traditions.		Make various types of bread.

- Are your holiday celebrations inclusive? Do they honor the cultural needs of all the families? Do they take into account that not everyone of the same ethnic background celebrates holidays in the same way?

- What if some parents object to holiday celebrations? What kind of satisfactory alternatives will you provide for their children?

- If you are including historical or cultural education in your celebration, have you checked to be sure that your information is accurate and does not promote stereotypes or perpetuate historical myths?

- Will you explain to the children the differences between holidays and everyday life within cultures? If they will be seeing people dressed in festival costumes doing special dances and eating special holiday foods, will you also explain how this is different from the day-to-day life of the people?

"Elaborateness"

- How elaborate do you expect the celebration to be?

- Can you find creative alternatives to the bombardment of commercialism that surrounds the major holidays celebrated in the United States?

- Are your plans simple enough so that the children won't feel overwhelmed?

- Do your plans take the economic means of the children into account? If you plan to ask children to bring food or gifts, do you know that this won't create a hardship for anyone?

- Do you have enough help? If not, who can you recruit to help you? Can you collaborate on a celebration with another child care program?

Health and Safety

- Are you planning a healthful menu? Have you and the parents reached an agreement about an appropriate amount of sweets or other foods of questionable nutritional value?

- Are materials used for decorations or in activities non-hazardous?

- Are you using the same caution (regarding supervision and household safety) that you would on a day-to-day basis?

Note: Remember that you can choose whether or not to celebrate holidays. Other options could be to celebrate seasonal changes, birthdays, or special milestones for each child, such as learning a new skill. Feel free to create your own special traditions and celebrations with and for the children that are meaningful, developmentally appropriate, healthy, and fun.

Where Does Food Come From?

Children who live on a farm may learn through their daily life experience about where their food comes from. For other children it will take a variety of experiences for them to realize that food doesn't magically appear on their plate or even in the grocery store. Here are some suggestions of things to do to help children learn that many people work hard in the long, step-by-step process that eventually brings the food to their table.

- Plan field trips to places where food is grown, processed, sold, and cooked: a farmer's market, plant nursery, orchard, farm, food-processing factory, supermarket, corner grocery store, commercial kitchen, restaurant; or go on a guided tour of the kitchen in your own child care center or family day care home.

- Display posters representing the workers who participated along the path that our food takes: farmers, factory workers, truck drivers, grocery store clerks, cooks, etc. Provide magazine pictures for making collages showing the people who help to bring us our food. Select posters that do not perpetuate racial or sexual stereotypes.

- Invite parents who work in food-related jobs to come as visitors and talk about what they do.

Let's Play Grocery Store, Truck Driver, Farm, Restaurant

After children have been on field trips to food production or distribution facilities, or after they've read books about the people who work to make food available for them, they often enjoy pretending that they are involved in these roles. It's a lot of fun to set up role-playing environments for children, and you will find that much of the equipment can be obtained quite inexpensively by asking friends or the children's parents for usable items, or by combing through thrift shops and flea markets.

Grocery Store

Activities: Buying, taking home, storing, cooking, eating food

Materials: Food boxes, cans, etc.
                  Shopping cart or baskets, grocery bags, "money"
                  Cash register
                  Shelves, table, refrigerator, stove, sink

Truck Drivers

Activities: Loading and unloading boxes of food
                  Driving trucks

Materials: Truck drivers' uniforms
Clipboards
"Trucks"
Boxes or blocks

Farmers

Activities: Spading, planting, watering, hoeing, harvesting, caring for animals

Materials: Play area (preferably with dirt!)
Buckets or watering cans
Shovel, trowel, hoe
Empty seed packets
Fruit and vegetable models, baskets
"Farm animals"

Restaurant

Activities: Preparing food for "customers," providing service to customers, ordering from menus, settling bills

Materials: Trays
Tableware, placemats, tablecloths
Cash register and play money
Order pads and pencils
Aprons, hats
Menus (you can make these by laminating pictures of food onto lightweight cardboard, or have the children make them up using pictures or words)
Play food
Food preparation equipment (play stove, sink, pots and pans, etc.)

Helping Children Become Smart Consumers

The food industry in this country spends billions of dollars a year influencing children through advertising. Parents, especially those who are tired and overworked, are particularly vulnerable to being influenced by persistent offspring to purchase foods that have less than ideal nutritional value. When children learn to be discriminating consumers themselves, parents will be less likely to face these power struggles. Here are some suggestions as to how you might educate children to become smart consumers:

- Plan a food shopping trip with school-age children, in which they are included in the entire process—meal planning, list making, selection of brands, label reading, shopping cart pushing, and unpacking and putting the food away. This will offer opportunities for discussion about checking expiration dates on labels, comparing prices, careful storage of foods which need to be frozen and refrigerated (they need to be put away as soon as you get home), selecting products that are packaged with ecology in mind, the comparisons between canned, frozen, and fresh foods, and on and on. Encourage younger children to help you in any way that is appropriate, and talk aloud as you compare prices and read labels. They will be learning a lot just by listening to you.

- Have the children tally the number of commercials during an hour of Saturday morning television. Ask the following questions:
  - How many were for food items?
  - How many were for nutritious food items? How do you know?
  - Why do you think they were shown during children's programs?
  - Do you think that everything the ads said was true? If not, why not?
  - If not, does that bother you?

- At the grocery store, compare sizes and prices of a particular product, such as frozen corn. Are all sizes and brands the same price? How do they vary? How can you determine which is the best bargain? Compare packaged mixes to fresh foods. Read some labels. Are there some unfamiliar words? How do they decide in what order to list the ingredients? When packages say "natural," "lite," etc., what does that mean—if anything? How can you find out? Compare the calories, fat, or sugar content in three of your favorite snack foods. Compare packaging of different brands of the same type of food. Which company used the most wasteful packaging? Which used the least?

Consumer Reports has a website designed to help children (8–14 years) become wise consumers:

> *Zillions: Consumer Reports for Kids.* Online: www.zillions.org

Where Do the Leftovers Go?

Does our garbage just disappear? If not, what happens to it? Here are some activities that will help the children learn the answers.

- Save food scraps (other than meat products) and use them to make compost. See page 244 for instructions on making your compost pile.

- Do a "planting" experiment to find out what biodegradable means. Bury a variety of items in the soil—an apple core, a glass bottle, a styrofoam cup, some fallen leaves, etc. Dig them up every week or so for a month to see which ones change and which ones do not. Discuss the results.

- Go on field trips to a garbage dump and a recycling center.

- Do a cleanup at the park and see how much food packaging litter you find.

- Do a one-day study of household garbage with older children. Sort it by type and weigh and measure it at the end of the day. How much is recyclable? How much isn't? How much came from packaging? How much can go in the compost pile? Make a chart to record results. Compare one day to another. See how much you can reduce a day's garbage with some planning.

- Do a study of leftover food garbage only. After a meal, collect, sort, and evaluate the leftover food. How much of each item was uneaten? Not all waste is the result of people's carelessness. Food waste studies can open dialogue between adults and children to find out why certain foods are not being eaten. The results may be surprising—children may be uncomfortable in their eating environment, they may be in a hurry to get to recess, or they may just not like the meatloaf recipe!

Here are some books about what happens to garbage:

Where Does the Garbage Go? by Paul Showers and Randy Chewning, Harper Trophy, 1994. Ages 4–8.

Recycle! A Handbook for Kids by Gail Gibbons, Little, Brown, 1998. Ages 4–8.

Additional Nutrition Activities for Kids

Classic Children's Books About Food

There are, of course, thousands of wonderful books for children. Some, however, are more useful than others for conveying positive nutrition messages. The list below is by no means exhaustive, but we have found these books to be both appropriate in content and readily available.

Primarily Picture Books . . .

Bread • Bread • Bread. Ann Morris. New York: Lothrop, Lee, and Shepard Books, 1989. Beautiful pictures of people and the breads they eat, all around the world.

Families the World Over series. Minneapolis: Lerner Publications. Everyday life, including family mealtimes, in many cultures.

Eating the Alphabet: Fruits and Vegetables from A to Z. Lois Ehlert. San Diego: Harcourt Brace Jovanovich, 1989.

Growing Vegetable Soup. Louis Ehlert. San Diego: Harcourt Brace Jovanovich, 1987.

What's on My Plate. Ruth Belov Gross. Illustrations by Isadore Seltzer. New York: Macmillan Publishing Company, 1990. Food orgins are presented in this beautifully illustrated book.

Strawberry. Jennifer Coldroy and George Bernard. Englewood Cliffs, N.J.: Silver Burdett Press, 1988. (Also: *Bean & Plant, Chicken & Egg, Mushroom, Potato*). These books trace the lifecycles of a variety of foodstuffs.

My Five Senses. Aliki. New York: Harper & Row, Publishers, 1989.

The Carrot Seed. Ruth Krauss. New York: Harper & Row, Publishers, 1945.

The Very Hungry Caterpillar. Eric Carle. Philomel Books, 1987.

The Pigs' Alphabet. Leah Palmer Preiss. Boston: David R. Godine, Publisher, 1990. Two pigs eat their way through a menu from A to Z, with predictable results.

More Challenging Reading . . .

Winnie-the-Pooh: A Tight Squeeze. A.A. Milne. Wisconsin: Golden Press, 1976. What happens when a bear eats too much!

Bread and Jam for Frances. Russell Hoban. New York: Harper & Row, Publishers, 1964. Frances announces that she will only eat bread and jam, and she gets an opportunity to try just that!

The Berenstain Bears and Too Much Junk Food. Stan and Jan Berenstain. New York: Random House, 1985.

The Berenstain Bears Forget Their Manners. Stan and Jan Berenstain. New York: Random House, 1985.

A Medieval Feast. Aliki. New York: Harper & Row, Publishers, 1983. This exquisitely illustrated book describes preparations for a kingly feast during the Middle Ages.

Pancakes for Breakfast. Tomie dePaola. San Diego: Harcourt Brace Jovanovich, 1978.

Stone Soup. Marcia Brown. New York: Macmillan Publishing Company, 1986. Cooperative soup-making.

Chicken Soup with Rice. Maurice Sendak. New York: Scholastic Book Service, 1962.

Green Eggs and Ham. Dr. Seuss. New York: Beginners Books, 1960.

Gregory, the Terrible Eater. M. Sharmat. New York: Scholastic Book Service, 1980.

How My Parents Learned to Eat. Ina R. Friedman. Boston: Houghton Mifflin, Publishers, 1984. A bi-cultural look at eating customs.

Manners. Aliki. New York: Greenwillow Books, 1990. A humorous look at good manners.

Reach for the Riddles

Children love guessing games. You can use riddles, either read aloud or on flash cards, to communicate nutrition concepts or help young children learn to identify foods. Clues can be given that:

* Describe a food by color, size, shape, or taste.

* Ask for rhyming words.

* Ask for words that begin with certain letters.

We'll give you a few examples and let you make up your own riddles. You can also have the children make up riddles for each other!

I'm orange and long
I rhyme with "parrot."
I grow in the ground.
I'm a _____, (carrot)

I have four legs.
And I say "moo."
I eat grass and make milk for you.
What am I? (a cow)

Now it's your turn!

_____   _____

_____   _____

_____   _____

_____   _____

_____   _____

_____   _____

_____   _____

_____   _____

_____   _____

Some Simple Silly Songs to Sing

Here are some simple songs about the topics in this book that we have composed to sing with preschool children. We put them to the tunes of familiar songs and nursery rhymes so that you would be able to learn them easily. You and the children can have great fun adding original verses or composing your own songs. Use familiar melodies or make them up.

The Vegetable Song (to the tune of *Twinkle, Twinkle, Little Star*)

Carrots, peas, and broccoli,
Vegetables are good for me.
For my snack and in my lunch,
Veggie sticks are great to munch.
Carrots, peas, and broccoli,
Vegetables are good for me.

Brush, Brush, Brush Your Teeth (to the tune of *Row, Row, Row Your Boat*)

Brush, Brush, Brush Your Teeth,
'Til they're shiny bright,
They'll be healthy, they'll be strong,
If you treat them right.

A Recycling Song (to the tune of *Frere Jacques*)

Save your bottles, save your bottles,
Save your cans, Save your cans.
Bundle up your papers,
Bundle up your papers,
That's the plan.
That's the plan.

The Good Food Song (to the tune of *Old MacDonald Had a Farm*)

Vegetables are good for me,
EE I EE I O
And so I eat them happily,
EE I EE I O
(Children take turns naming vegetables they like)
With a carrot, carrot here
And a carrot, carrot there,
Here a carrot, there a carrot,
Everywhere a carrot carrot.
Vegetables are good for me,
EE I EE I O.

Fruits are very good for me,
EE I EE I O.
And so I eat them happily,
EE I EE I O
(Children take turns naming fruits they like)
With an apple, apple here
And an apple, apple there,
Here an apple, there an apple,
Everywhere an apple, apple.
Fruits are very good for me,
EE I EE I O.

Use your own creativity to add other categories. Some possibilities: grains, breads, proteins, cheese, soups, etc.

Oh, Before I Eat My Meals (to the tune of *If You're Happy and You Know It, Clap Your Hands; pantomime the actions*)

Oh, before I eat my meals I wash my hands
    (scrub, scrub)
Oh, before I eat my meals I wash my hands,
    (scrub, scrub)
Oh it's very smart, I think,
Sends those germs right down the sink.
Oh, before I eat my meals I wash my hands,
    (scrub, scrub)
Oh, before I eat my meals I set my place
    (set, set)
Oh, before I eat my meals I set my place
    (set, set)
I set everything I need,
I feel very proud indeed.
Oh, before I eat my meals I set my place,
    (set, set)
Oh, before I eat my meals I pass the food,
    (pass the plate)
Oh, before I eat my meals I pass the food,
    (pass the plate)
'Cause we know it's only fair
For us all to have our share
Oh, before I eat my meals I pass the food
    (pass the plate)

A Planting Song (to the tune of *Mary Had A Little Lamb;* when you are doing a planting activity, use the names of the children in the group in the place of "Mary.")

[Mary] had a little seed,
Little seed, little seed.
[Mary] had a little seed,
And hoped that it would grow.

She watered it and pulled the weeds,
Pulled the weeds, pulled the weeds.
She watered it and pulled the weeds,
With sprinkling can and hoe.

And every day the sun would shine,
Sun would shine, sun would shine.
And every day the sun would shine,
And warm it for a while.

And soon a little sprout came out,
Sprout came out, sprout came out.
And soon a little sprout came out,
It made dear [Mary] smile.

A lettuce plant began to grow,
Began to grow, began to grow.
A lettuce plant began to grow,
So fresh and crisp and green.

Then carefully she picked some leaves,
Picked some leaves, picked some leaves.
Then carefully she picked some leaves,
And rinsed them nice and clean.

Now homegrown salad she will eat,
She will eat, she will eat.
Now homegrown salad she will eat,
She grew a healthy treat.

When We Eat Together (to the tune of *Here We Go 'Round the Mulberry Bush;* (pantomime the actions)

This is the way we pass the plate,
Pass the plate, pass the plate,
This is the way we pass the plate,
When we eat together.

And this is the way we use our fork,
Use our fork, use our fork,
This is the way we use our fork,
When we eat together.

And this is the way we pour our milk,
Pour our juice, pour our milk,
This is the way we pour our milk,
When we eat together.

This is the way we cut our food,
Cut our food, cut our food,
This is the way we cut our food,
When we eat together.

This is the way we clear our place,
Clear our place, clear our place,
This is the way we clear our place,
When we eat together.

(Make up and add your own verses or have the children make up their own.)

The More That We Recycle (to the tune of *Did You Ever See a Lassie Go this Way and That?*)

Oh, the more that we recycle, recycle, recycle,
Oh, the more that we recycle,
The happier we'll be.
'Cause your earth is my earth
And my earth is your earth,
So the more that we recycle,
The happier we'll be.

One Small Planet (Written by Jon Fromer; Used with permission.)

We've got to keep the waters pure,
We've got to keep the mountains high,
And make sure the birds keep flying
In the clear blue sky.
'Cause we've got . . . chorus

There's only so much water,
There's only so much land,
There's only so much air to breathe,
Let's keep it clean while we can,
'Cause we've got . . . chorus

Chorus:

One small planet
With a lot of people
It's all we've got so let's take
care.
One small world for us to live
in,
It's all we have, so we've got
to share.

Appendix A

· ·

Special Topics

Allergies to Foods

It is now estimated that 4% to 6% of young children have food allergies, and for reasons that aren't clearly understood, that number is increasing over time. In a true food allergy, the body's immune system reacts to contact with an offending substance (allergen) by making antibodies. The next time the person eats that food, the body releases a flood of chemicals that cause the symptoms of allergy, affecting the respiratory system, gastrointestinal tract, skin, or cardiovascular system. In some case, food allergies are only minor inconveniences. They can, however, produce chronic health complaints and in extreme cases, life-threatening reactions.

There is no cure for food allergies at this time; the only way to prevent a reaction is to avoid the offending food. Some research indicates that allergies may be prevented in infants at high risk for developing allergies (such as those whose parents both have a history of food allergy). Accordingly, the American Academy of Pediatrics recommends that these infants be exclusively breastfed for 4 to 6 months, that they receive solid foods no sooner than at 6 months of age, and that cow's milk not be introduced until 12 months of age, eggs until 24 months of age, and peanuts, tree nuts, and fish until the child is 3.

Symptoms of food allergies may include:

- Hives

- Nausea and vomiting

- Eczema

- Diarrhea

- Anaphylactic shock

- Sleep disturbances

- Drop in blood pressure

- Abdominal cramps

- Coughing

- Swelling of the throat and tongue

- Nasal congestion

- Sneezing

- Conjunctivitis

- Asthma

A reaction can take from a few minutes to 2 hours to occur. The severity of the reaction can depend upon:

- How much of the allergen was eaten

- How often the food was eaten

- Physical or emotional stress

The foods most likely to cause allergies in children are: cow's milk, soy, peanut, wheat, and eggs. Adults are more likely to be allergic to shellfish, fish, eggs, peanuts, and tree nuts. While children often outgrow their allergies to egg, milk, soy, and wheat, allergies to peanuts, tree nuts, fish, and shrimp are usually lifelong.

Children can also have **sensitivities** or **intolerances** to foods, which are often confused with allergies; for example, lactose intolerance, which is the inability to digest the sugars in milk, and sensitivities to food colorings and MSG.

A child should have a professional evaluation when food allergies or intolerances are suspected. It's a shame when a child suffers unnecessarily from allergy-related symptoms. It's also a shame when a child is forced to avoid enjoyable foods that may not even be a problem for her. And there have been cases of growth failure in children when their parents "diagnosed" food allergies and restricted their diets without guidance.

Be aware that allergies are not to be taken lightly and can result in some troublesome feeding situations:

- Children can develop aversions to eating when they've been scared by severe allergic reactions or when restrictions make mealtimes unpleasant.

- Highly restrictive diets can be boring; they can also lead to serious nutrient deficiencies if they aren't well planned.

- Children may use eating "forbidden" foods, or not eating at all, to manipulate their parents or caregivers.

Guidelines for Managing Food Allergies in Child Care

- Establish a written policy on parent/caregiver responsibilities in allergic conditions.

- Have a physician's statement on file that describes the allergy and recommended substitutions.

- Find out if the child's allergy is so severe that she cannot even inhale cooking fumes, and take the necessary precautions.

- Make sure a list of children's names with their allergies and "forbidden" foods is readily available for any adult who might be involved in preparing food or serving it to the children.

- If a child is subject to life-threatening reactions from foods, obtain authorization to administer the appropriate medications and the necessary training to do so safely.

> **Anaphylactic shock can be fatal! Its warning signs are:**
>
> - Itching and flushing of the skin
>
> - Severe nausea or diarrhea
>
> - Swelling of the respiratory passages

- Children with multiple food allergies, or allergies to foods that are primary sources of nutrients (as milk is in the United States), should be monitored by a physician or dietitian. Parents and caregivers may wish to receive counseling together regarding appropriate food choices.

- Be matter-of-fact about a child's food restrictions. Let the child take increasing responsibility for his food selections, as his awareness of what must be avoided grows. Tell other children in the group why the restrictions are necessary; hopefully they'll be supportive of their peer.

- Remember that children generally hate being singled out. Become adept at planning menus that everyone can eat, and when you find that you must make substitutions for a child, be sure that what she gets is as nice as what everyone else is getting. Don't make it too spectacular, though, or you'll have everyone else clamoring for that special treatment! (We recall one preschool classroom that was disrupted every lunch hour for weeks when a child's mother brought him fast-food chicken nuggets as his "allergy-free" lunch. Needless to say, none of the other children were interested in the standard menu.)

- Become thoroughly familiar with foods that potentially contain the allergens you're avoiding. Read labels like crazy. Beware of "hidden" allergens in foods.

- Make every effort to replace the nutrients that will be missing when a child must avoid major foods and food groups. For example, apple juice is not a substitute for milk. Sure, they're both beverages, but apple juice has virtually none of milk's protein, calcium, riboflavin, vitamin A, or vitamin D.

Check Appendix D for allergy cookbooks and suppliers of specialty foods.

Avoiding allergens in foods has just gotten easier since the implementation of the Food Allergen Labeling and Consumer Protection Act of 2004. Beginning January 1, 2006, all food labels must declare the common name of any of the 8 most common food allergens: egg, wheat, soy, milk, peanuts, tree nuts, fish, and crustaceans (shellfish). This can be found in a "contains" statement next to the ingredient statement or in parentheses in the ingredient list. Spices, flavorings, colorings, or incidental additives that contain one of these major food allergens must also be avoided. You still must carefully read labels for common or alternative names of allergens that aren't in the "top eight," and not all foods will have nutrition labels, for example, food in restaurants.

Milk Allergies

Some foods or ingredients to avoid:

- Milk

- Cheese

- Cottage cheese

- Yogurt

- Butter
- Margarine with milk solids
- Milk chocolate
- Creamed foods
- Custards and puddings
- Lactate solids
- Casein
- Caseinate
- Whey
- Lactalbumin
- Sodium caseinate
- Lactose
- Cream
- Calcium caseinate
- Nonfat milk solids

Substitutes for dairy foods:

Fortified soy milk

Soy formulas

Tofu

Fortified rice milk

Nut milks

Juices, in baked goods

Broth, in sauces or soups

Oat milk

Alternative food sources of important nutrients

Protein: Meats, poultry, fish, eggs, dried beans, peanut butter, tofu

Calcium: Spinach, collards, kale, turnip greens, broccoli, bok choy, soybeans, tofu (made with calcium sulfate), mustard greens, canned salmon with bones (they're soft!), sardines, corn tortillas (made with lime), blackstrap molasses, calcium-fortified orange juice, fortified soy or rice milk

Riboflavin: Mushrooms, beet greens, spinach, broccoli, romaine lettuce, bok choy, asparagus, dried peaches, bean sprouts, fortified cereals

Egg Allergies

Some foods or ingredients to avoid:

- Eggs
- Egg whites
- Egg yolks
- Some egg substitutes
- Mayonnaise
- Some salad dressings
- Egg noodles
- Most fresh pasta
- Custards, tapioca, pudding
- Meringues

- Many baked goods

- Many breaded/batter-fried items

- Albumin

- Globulin

- Livetin

- Ovomucin

- Ovomucoid

- Vitellin

Substitutes for eggs in recipes

Ener-G Egg Replacer®

Extra ½ teaspoon baking powder for each egg missing

Arrowroot powder as a binder

Tofu for pudding-like texture; can be "scrambled," too

Most dried pasta

Alternative food sources of important nutrients

Protein: Meats, poultry, fish, dairy products, dried beans, nut butters

Vitamin A: Fortified milk and margarine, yellow/orange and green leafy
fruits and vegetables

Citrus Allergies

Alternative sources of vitamin C

Cantaloupe	Papaya	Strawberries
Green peppers	Broccoli	Cabbage
Chiles	Tomatoes	Potatoes

Wheat Allergies

Some foods or ingredients to avoid:

- Wheat

- Wheat germ

- Wheat bran

- Modified food starch

- Graham flour

- Farina

- Semolina

- Gluten

- Vegetable starch

- Vegetable gum

- Enriched flour

- Hydrolyzed vegetable protein

- Some yeast (Fleischman's is wheat-free)

- Postum, malted milk

- Most baked goods

- Most crackers

- Macaroni, spaghetti

- Noodles

- Gravies, cream sauces

- Fried food coating

- Most baking mixes

- Soy sauce (read label)

- Some hot dogs, sausages

- Some salad dressings

- MSG

Substitutes for wheat in recipes

Cornstarch, tapioca, rice flour as thickeners

Wheat-free breads, crackers

Rice cakes

Corn tortillas

Oatmeal

Polenta

Cream of rice

Wheat-free pasta

Popcorn

Rice flour

Potato flour

Oat bran

Rice bran

Wheat-free cereal crumbs

Baking mix: 1 cup cornstarch, 2 cups rice flour, 2 cups soy flour, 3 cups potato flour (bake at lower temperature for a longer time, and you may want to cut down on the added fat in the recipe)

Alternative food sources of important nutrients

Complex carbohydrates, B vitamins, fiber: Other whole grains (corn, millet, rice, oats), potatoes, dried beans

Soy Allergies

Some foods or ingredients to avoid

- Soybeans

- Soy flour

- Soybean oil

- Soy protein isolate

- Texturized vegetable protein (TVP)

- Vegetable starch

- Vegetable gum

- Tofu

- Hydrolyzed vegetable protein

- Soy sauce

- Teriyaki sauce

- Worcestershire sauce

- Soy milk

- Soy infant formulas

- Some margarines

- Soy nuts

- Tempeh

- Miso

- Vegetable protein concentrate

Corn Allergies

Some foods or ingredients to avoid

- Cornmeal

- Cornstarch

- Masa harina

- Corn oil

- Corn syrup

- Corn sweetener

- Vegetable starch

- Vegetable gum
- Modified food starch
- Some baked goods
- Some baking powder
- Corn tortillas
- Corn chips
- Some cold cereals
- Pancake syrups
- Many candies
- Corn solids

Substitutes for corn in recipes

Other flours

Potato starch, rice flour, arrowroot, tapioca as thickeners

Beet or cane sugar

Pure maple syrup

Baking soda and cream of tartar for leavening

Honey

Wheat flour tortillas

Anemia and Iron Deficiency

Normally oxygen is carried to the body's tissues as part of a molecule called hemoglobin in the red blood cells. When there's not enough hemoglobin around, a condition called anemia is the result. Most anemia is caused by **iron deficiency**. Iron-deficiency anemia is a common nutritional problem in the United States, affecting primarily children 12 to 36 months old, teenage boys, and women of childbearing age. Iron-deficiency anemia is found among children of all income levels, although it is more common in children from poorer families.

Unfortunately, at a critical time in infancy, iron-deficiency anemia may cause irreversible abnormalities in brain growth and development. Iron deficiency may also make a child more susceptible to lead poisoning, which can cause growth stunting and neurological problems. Even before outright anemia appears, iron deficits can have serious effects on the body's functioning. Infants with iron deficiency appear fearful, tense, unresponsive to examiners, and generally "unhappy." Older children with mild iron deficiency have exhibited:

- A shortened attention span

- Irritability

- Fatigue

- Inability to concentrate on tasks

- Poor performance on vocabulary, reading, math, problem-solving, and psychological tests

- Lowered resistance to infection

How heartbreaking that children may do poorly in school or be labeled "lazy" or "unmanageable," when in fact they are suffering from a preventable nutritional problem!

Iron deficiency can have several causes: a diet that's lacking in good sources of iron; poor absorption of iron in the intestines; increased requirements for iron, particularly during periods of rapid growth; heavy or persistent losses of blood; and some infections. When young children become iron-deficient, it's often because they didn't get enough iron during their first year of life or because they've been consuming too much milk and not enough iron-rich foods.

What you can do to prevent iron deficiency

- Give infants **breast milk** or **iron-fortified formula** up to the age of 1 year. Breastfeeding mothers may want to discuss iron supplementation with their pediatricians.

- When feeding cereal to infants who are between 6 months and 1 year old, use **iron-fortified infant cereals**.

- Don't feed children whole cow's milk during their first year; it can cause some gastrointestinal bleeding.

- Serve children **iron-rich foods** frequently for snacks as well as for meals. Organ meats, shellfish, and muscle meats are the richest sources of highly absorbable iron; don't feed liver more than once a week, though, or vitamin A toxicity can result. Nuts, green vegetables, whole grains, enriched breads and fortified cereals, and dried fruits are also good sources of iron.

- The iron in nonmeat foods is absorbed better when meats or **vitamin C–rich foods** are served at the same meal. Dairy products, eggs, and tea hinder the absorption of nonmeat iron.

- Don't allow children to fill up on milk and ignore other foods. A pint of milk a day is plenty for children between the ages of 1 and 8 years.

Choking on Food

Every five days, a child in the United States dies from choking on food. Young children lack the chewing skills to deal with foods that are hard or tough. And foods that are round or sticky can block their airways, which are smaller than those of adults.

Although children have been known to choke on apple pieces, peanut butter sandwiches, cookies, carrots, popcorn, beans, and even bread, four foods that have caused the most deaths are:

- Hot dogs

- Nuts

- Hard candies

- Grapes

Every adult who takes care of children should be aware of the simple precautions that can drastically reduce the risk of choking.

Choking Prevention

- *Always* supervise children while they are eating.

- Insist that children eat calmly and while they're sitting down.

- Encourage children to chew their food well.

- Infants should be fed solid foods only while they're sitting up.

- Make sure that the foods you serve the children are appropriate for their chewing and swallowing abilities. Do not give the following foods to children younger than 4 years of age, unless they are modified

Hot dogs	Popcorn
Nuts	Peanut butter
Grapes	Marshmallows
Hard candies	Chips
Hard pieces of fruits or vegetables	Pretzels

- Never use styrofoam cups and plates for young children; pieces can easily break off.

- Don't allow children to eat in the car or bus; if a child started choking, it might be hard to get the vehicle to the side of the road safely in order to help her.

- Review the instructions on pages 320 and 321 for how to deal with choking emergencies when a person is conscious or unconscious.

Calcium and Osteoporosis

Calcium is the most abundant mineral in our bodies. Ninety-nine percent of it is stored in our bones; the rest is found in fluids inside and outside of the body cells, where it performs crucial roles in the movement of nerve impulses, contraction of muscles, movement of materials across cell membranes, and clotting of blood. The calcium concentrations in these fluids are so important that the body will dissolve bone if necessary to make the mineral available to them. In this way, the bones act as a form of "calcium bank account." As people age, they start to lose more calcium from their bones (osteoporosis) and may suffer fractures on very little impact. Women have this problem more than men, and heredity, exercise, and many other factors play a role. Prevention of osteoporosis involves building up as hefty a bank account of calcium as possible during the years when bone-building can occur and minimizing the loss of bone in later years.

Scientists are working very hard to determine when the critical times of life for building bone mass happen, how much calcium we need to ingest

Choking (When Conscious)

HAVE SOMEONE CALL EMS #911 IMMEDIATELY!

Infant (Birth to 1 Year)

1. Supporting infant's head and neck, straddle over forearm, with head lower than trunk, and administer 4 back blows, high, between the shoulder blades (Figure 1).

Figure 1

2. Supporting infant's head and neck, turn on back and give four chest thrusts with 2–3 fingers ½ inch deep, at one finger-width below the nipples (midsternal region) (Figure 2).

3. Repeat steps 1 and 2 until obstruction clears.

Figure 2

Child (Older Than 1 Year) and Adults

Ask, "Are you choking?" If victim cannot speak, cough, or breathe, take the following action (Heimlich maneuver):

1. Kneel behind the child (stand behind a taller child or adult) (Figure 3).

2. Wrap your arms around the child's waist.

Figure 3

3. Make a fist with one hand. Place your fist (thumbside) against the child's stomach in the midline just above the navel and well below the rib cage.

4. Grasp your fist with your other hand.

5. Press inward and upward into stomach with a quick thrust (Figure 4).

6. Repeat thrust until obstruction is cleared.

Figure 4

Abdominal thrusts (Heimlich maneuver) should NOT
be done on an infant.

Source: *Childhood Emergencies—What to Do: A Quick Reference Guide,* by Marin Child Care Council (formerly Project Care for Children). Palo Alto: Bull Publishing Company, 1989.

Choking (When Unconscious)

CALL EMS #911. If necessary, you can leave the phone off the hook and shout information into the phone while attending to the child.

Infant (Birth to 1 Year)

An infant who has become unconscious should be placed in a supine (lying on back) position.

1. Perform jaw tongue lift (Figure 5) and sweep mouth only for visible objects. *Do not use "blind" finger sweeps of mouth*, as the object can be pushed back, causing further obstruction.

Figure 5

2. Attempt to ventilate (Figure 6). If airway remains blocked, proceed to step 3.

3. Perform 1 set of 4 back blows, then 4 chest thrusts (see Figures 1 and 2 on page 320).

Figure 6

4. Repeat steps 1, 2, and 3 until airway is clear or medical help arrives.

Important: If child is coughing, do not interfere! If child cannot cough, speak, or cry and/or is turning blue, use these techniques immediately!

Child (Older Than 1 Year) and Adults

A child who has become unconscious should be placed in a supine (lying on back) position.

1. Perform jaw tongue lift (Figure 7) and sweep the mouth only for visible objects. *Do not use "blind" finger sweeps of the mouth,* as the object can be pushed back, causing further obstruction.

Figure 7

2. Attempt to ventilate. If airway remains blocked, proceed to step 3.

3. Deliver compressions by kneeling at the child's feet or straddling the child's legs, pressing the heel of one hand on the midline of the abdomen, slightly above the navel, pressing the free hand over the positioned hand and locking your elbows, and giving 6–10 rapid upward abdominal thrusts (Figure 8).

Figure 8

4. Repeat steps 1, 2, and 3 until airway is clear.

during these times, and what other dietary factors may be involved. It does appear that childhood is a window of opportunity for preventing osteoporosis and that getting enough calcium even at a very young age could help. The extent to which eating too many animal-protein foods, drinking a lot of phosphoric-acid-containing soda drinks (primarily colas), and eating too much salt affect our bones is still under investigation. The Institute of Medicine made these recommendations for calcium intake for children:

- Children ages 1 through 3 years: 500 mg per day

- Children ages 4 through 8 years: 800 mg per day

- Children ages 9 through 18 years: 1,300 mg per day

What do these recommendations mean in practical terms? For infants who are breastfed or receiving infant formula, you needn't worry; they'll get the calcium they need. For older children, you can usually figure that they'll get about 200 mg of calcium in their usual consumption of various foods. The other 600 to 1,100 mg is usually supplied by milk and dairy products such as yogurt or cheese. One cup of low-fat milk contains about 300 mg of calcium. So, a child up through age 8 can get the calcium she needs from 2 cups of milk, an older child from 3 cups of milk. A study of child care sites found that children don't drink as much milk when juice is also on the table, so if you're wondering how to get the children to drink more milk, this is something you might want to consider. Most children under the age of 9 years are getting enough calcium in their diets, but if a child can't or won't drink milk, some care is needed in planning for adequate calcium intake, although the fortification of some common foods is making this easier.

Constipation and Fiber

Some people think that constipation means not having a bowel movement every day. Actually, the number of days between bowel movements isn't really the issue. Constipation is defined as having bowel movements that are hard and passed with pain or difficulty. An occasional hard stool need not cause special concern, but if a child has persistent constipation and her abdomen is swollen, her physician should examine her to make sure there isn't an underlying disease.

True constipation is rare in infants. There is a wide variation in the normal number of bowel movements a baby may have in a day, or even in a week; it isn't necessary to have one daily. It's also normal for infants to strain and turn red in the face while having a normal bowel movement, alarming as this may be to an adult bystander. Parents often change formulas hoping to solve this "problem," but generally it isn't necessary.

Toddlers sometimes develop constipation after they've had painful bowel movements. They hold them in, trying to avoid the discomfort. But what happens is that when they hold their bowel movements in, the intestines draw the water out of them, which makes them harder and of course more painful. You can see the potential for a vicious cycle here. In these situations, physicians will often temporarily prescribe a stool softener. Hopefully, the child will get the idea that it doesn't always hurt to go to the bathroom, and he'll be more willing to "answer nature's call."

When older children are constipated, it is often because they can't use the bathroom when they need to, like when they're running on tight schedules or have to wait for recess at school. Also, some kids don't want to use school bathrooms, if they aren't given the privacy they want.

Maybe you're wondering at this point if we're ever going to talk about the role of nutrition in constipation. We're getting to that; but you should know that constipation can have other causes, too. So if you look at what a child's been eating, and there doesn't seem to be a problem with it, consider the factors already mentioned.

Okay, now for the nutrition part. You know that dietary fiber contributes to regular bowel function. Fiber is the part of our food (usually plant matter) that we can't digest. It attracts water into the intestines, which makes the stool softer and bulkier. Most children—and most adults, for that matter—don't get enough fiber in their diets. That's too bad, because in addition to helping maintain normal bowel function, fiber may help reduce the risk of cardiovascular disease, some cancers, and adult-onset diabetes.

The American Health Foundation offers a guideline for fiber intake for children 3 years and older that's easy to remember: **age plus 5** (grams of fiber). For example, a 6-year-old should get 11 grams of fiber daily. A diet with sufficient calories and plenty of unprocessed foods and fresh produce will pretty much ensure adequate fiber intake. But you need to practice moderation. Children can be deprived of needed nutrients when they're restricted to high-fiber, low-calorie foods. We generally don't recommend fiber supplements (like bran concentrates), either.

Constipation Prevention Plan

- Offer children fiber-rich foods often. Whole grains, fresh fruits and vegetables, dried fruits, dried beans, nuts, and popcorn are good sources of fiber.

- Make sure children drink water when they're thirsty. It helps fiber do its job.

- Encourage children to use the bathroom when they feel the urge to go, and allow them enough time to take care of their business. Make sure the bathroom is a pleasant enough place to be!

- Encourage plenty of physical activity. Exercise is thought to be beneficial in maintaining bowel regularity.

Dental Health

Nutrition affects the health of teeth in two ways. First, adequate amounts of certain nutrients are necessary for the formation of teeth. Second, the foods that go into the mouth can cause tooth decay.

All of the primary ("baby") teeth and some permanent teeth are already forming in a baby's jaw before he is born. The teeth depend on nutrients for development until the last permanent tooth erupts. Sufficient amounts of protein, calcium, phosphorus, magnesium, and the vitamins A, C, and D must be present if healthy teeth are to develop. The minerals fluoride, iron, and zinc help make the teeth resistant to decay.

Most people don't realize that tooth decay is actually the result of infection passed on to children by parents or caregivers (babies aren't born with the bacteria that cause tooth decay). We don't tell you this to keep you from kissing your children! But the fact is that children tend to have fewer cavities when their parents practice good oral hygiene. So pay close attention . . . this is important for everyone.

The bacteria that cause tooth decay use the carbohydrates in foods we eat, both for energy and for making plaque that helps them stick to the teeth. The bacteria also produce acids that dissolve tooth enamel and form cavities.

You're familiar with the sugars that feed these bacteria—table sugar, brown sugar, honey, maple syrup, molasses, and corn syrup are the principal ones. In addition, bacteria can produce sugar by breaking down the starches in foods such as potatoes and bread, if these foods stay in the mouth long enough. That means a dry, unsweetened cracker stuck to the teeth might be more harmful than a can of soda!

So, if a tooth is to end up with a cavity, three things are necessary:

- **Bacteria** . . . to produce the acids that dissolve the tooth's enamel

- **Carbohydrates** . . . to feed the bacteria and glue them to the tooth

- **Time** . . . for the bacteria to do their work

When we talk about preventing cavities, we're generally trying to make sure at least one of these factors is missing. For example, brushing teeth removes food particles, as well as some of the bacteria in the plaque.

To Keep Tooth Decay Away

- Serve a well-balanced diet, being careful to include good sources of calcium and phosphorus.

- Cut down on foods that are high in sugar, such as soda pop, candy, cookies, pastries, jams, syrups, and presweetened breakfast cereals.

- Avoid foods that stick to the teeth. Raisins, other dried fruits, fruit rolls, and gummy-style fruit candies fall into this category.

- Serve raw vegetables often. They scrub the teeth and stimulate the flow of saliva, which can help protect the teeth.

- Limit the number of snacks you serve. Each time we eat sugars and starches, the teeth are attacked by acids for 20 minutes.

- If you are going to serve a sweet food, do it at mealtime, not as an ongoing snack. This will cut down on the amount of time the teeth are exposed to the sugar.

- Encourage children to brush their teeth after meals. If that's not possible, they should at least floss and brush their teeth twice a day. Be sure children brush their teeth after eating sticky foods.

- Children should be drinking fluoridated water. Find out whether your water supply has fluoride. Bottled waters have differing levels.

- Never send a child to bed with a bottle, unless it has plain water in it.

20 Non-Candy Items That Children Love . . .

They will feel perfectly at home in trick-or-treat bags, Christmas stockings, piñatas, Easter baskets, or as holiday gifts and favors.

Stickers	Playing cards
Pencils and pens	Coins
Erasers	Stamps for collecting
Tiny farm animals	Colorful socks
Pocket-size cars	Movie passes
Small books	Crayons
Music tapes	Notepads
Small bouncing balls	Dimestore jewelry
Jacks	Hair ornaments
Tangerines or other small fruits	Individual packets of sunflower seeds or nuts

Diarrhea

Diarrhea has been defined as the passage of frequent, watery stools. There are some children who have bowel movements that are normal for them but look like diarrhea, just as some children have bowel movements so infrequently that their parents think they're constipated. Parents and caregivers have to determine what is normal for a particular child. In addition to being a bother, to say the least, diarrhea can affect a child's nutritional status. And what a child is eating can sometimes be a cause of diarrhea.

Acute Diarrhea

Usually caused by a viral or bacterial infection called enteritis, acute diarrhea may be accompanied by fever and vomiting. It can be a serious problem for infants or very young children because they can become dehydrated. Consequently, many parents use glucose-electrolyte maintenance beverages such as Pedialyte® to replace fluids lost from vomiting, diarrhea, and fever. These beverages are readily available in supermarkets and drug stores, but *they should be used only as advised by a physician. They are not meant to be substitutes for feeding.* Parents and caregivers often make the mistake of waiting too long to resume feeding a child who has had a bout with enteritis. While eating may cause more stool volume, the child actually does gain some value from the food.

Here's what the Centers for Disease Control recommends:

- Don't feed the child if he is vomiting a lot, has significant dehydration, or his abdomen is swollen (call the doctor!).

- When there is no vomiting or dehydration, resume feeding the child.
  - Infants tolerate breast milk well and should continue nursing on demand.
  - On rare occasions, infants need to drink lactose-free formula for a few days, but most will do fine with their regular formula.
  - The child should be offered a normal diet, though foods high in sugar are best avoided.
  - Keep the child's fluid intake high.

Chronic Nonspecific Diarrhea

Also called "toddler diarrhea," this condition can occur any time between 6 months and 5 years of age. The child will have 4 or 5 stools a day, 4 or 5 days out of a month, yet have no specific diseases and exhibit normal growth and development. Chronic nonspecific diarrhea isn't particularly dangerous, but it is messy, and in some cases dietary changes can help solve the problem. After the child's physician has ruled out parasites or infections that need treatment, it may be worth experimenting with diet rather than waiting for the child to outgrow the condition.

- Susceptible children can get diarrhea when fat is restricted too severely in their diets. Fat slows down the digestive process, so adding some fat to the diets of these children may alleviate the diarrhea.

- Children may also develop diarrhea when they're allowed to drink excessive amounts of juice or sweetened liquids. Some children seem to have a sensitivity to the sugars in juices and will get diarrhea when they drink even modest amounts. Apple, pear, and grape juice have all been found to cause sugar malabsorption in some children.

- It's a good idea to avoid serving foods with artificial sweeteners to children because these may contribute to diarrhea.

It is usually not necessary to restrict dairy products, eggs, or wheat in the diets of children with chronic diarrhea; in fact, children risk nutrient deficiencies when such restrictions are applied without careful planning.

Diabetes and Other Chronic Diseases

The purpose of this section is not to give you specific instructions about caring for children with diabetes or other diseases. Rather, we're going to bring up some nutritional issues related to diabetes and suggest ways to handle them.

Parents and caregivers are usually very concerned about doing the right thing for a child with a chronic health condition, as they should be. Things go better, however, when they are neither intimidated nor overprotective. It's important to follow a medical treatment plan while allowing the child to take increasing responsibility for himself and enjoy being as much like other children as possible.

While chronic health conditions vary, common nutritional issues are bound to come up when caring for children who have them:

- It can be difficult to follow a prescribed dietary plan without interfering with a child's decisions about the kinds and amounts of foods to eat.

- Children generally detest being treated differently from other children, and they will probably resent having to eat special foods.

- Children with chronic diseases need to learn self-care skills; this includes making appropriate food choices in unsupervised situations.

- These children may eat forbidden foods—or not eat at all—in an attempt to manipulate their parents' and caregivers' behavior.

Diabetes

About one in every 400 to 500 children develops diabetes, usually the "insulin-dependent" form of the disease. Most people produce the hormone insulin, which moves glucose (sugar) from the blood into the cells of the body, where it can be used for energy. People with diabetes either don't produce insulin, or the insulin they do produce isn't effective. So the glucose stays in the bloodstream, while the cells are starved for fuel. High blood sugars can have serious short- and long-term consequences.

Treatment of insulin-dependent diabetes generally involves (1) injections of insulin to make up for what's lacking in the body, (2) a food plan formulated to avoid very high or very low blood sugars and to provide the nutrients for normal growth and development, and (3) a program of exercise, which helps stabilize blood sugars and maintain normal weight.

In order to care for a child with diabetes, you will need to know:

- The symptoms of **hypoglycemia** (low blood sugar) and **ketoacidosis** (the result of high blood sugars), and what to do about them

- How to plan meals and snacks—the types of food offered, the amounts, and the timing. The diabetic diet is basically the same healthy diet we recommend for everyone!

- When necessary, how to help the child test blood sugars and inject insulin

- How to help the child manage her exercise regime

- How and when to contact the child's health care provider

Cystic Fibrosis

Cystic fibrosis is an inherited glandular disease. It affects digestion and absorption, causes the loss of vital minerals in perspiration, and can lead to chronic lung infections. Treatment may include pancreatic enzyme replacement for better digestion and antibiotics to fight infections.

Children with cystic fibrosis don't always get the nourishment from food they need to grow well. They may require extra calories, specially formulated fats that they can absorb, extra salt when they've been sweating a lot, and vitamin and mineral supplements.

Inborn Errors of Metabolism

Some children are born without the enzymes needed to handle particular food elements such as sugars and amino acids. Toxic levels of these elements can build up in the blood, causing damage to the nervous system and hindering growth. Phenylketonuria (PKU), galactosemia, and fructose intolerance are examples of inborn errors of metabolism that call for strict dietary modifications. Often special formulas and food products are necessary.

Acquired Immune Deficiency Syndrome (AIDS)

Children with AIDS may have a number of medical problems that make it difficult for them to eat enough and for their bodies to make use of what they do eat. They need high-calorie, high-protein foods. Often, their foods must be modified to reduce irritation; for example, nonacidic foods are necessary when a child has sores in her mouth. Food safety is always important in child care, but it takes on a new dimension when caring for someone who is so highly susceptible to food poisoning. We recommend that you call on a registered dietitian who specializes in AIDS if you will be caring for a child with the condition.

Children with Chronic Diseases . . . Nutrition Guidelines

- When it is possible to arrange it, parents and child care providers can benefit from receiving training *together* in the care of children with chronic health conditions. That way there can be a better understanding and coordination of efforts.

- Avoid making a big deal out of serving special foods. Try to plan meals and snacks that *everyone* can eat. When you must enforce restrictions, be matter-of-fact about it and serve an enjoyable substitute.

- Allow the child as much control in the feeding situation as you can. Even when their range of options is limited, children still like to make decisions about what they're going to eat. Teach the child to recognize foods that contain "forbidden" ingredients. Allow the child to participate in planning menus.

- Enlist the other children as "buddies" who can alert you to signs of low blood sugar in their friend or who can help the child stick to her regimen.

Eating Disorders

Lots of parents consider their children to be problem eaters. It's normal for children to go through periods of lagging appetites, pickiness, and preferring candy bars to vegetables. But occasionally a child's eating problem is serious enough to be called an **eating disorder**. It may manifest itself as failure to thrive, obesity, excessive pickiness, or monumental struggles between the child and the parent or caregiver about eating. (What we usually think of as eating disorders—anorexia nervosa and bulimia—don't show up until adolescence or later.)

Child feeding expert Ellyn Satter stresses that an eating disorder consists of a severe disturbance in eating or feeding accompanied by an emotional problem. There are lots of circumstances in which eating disorders can develop, from too much pressure to eat more or less food, to problems in the parents' marital relationship. When adults begin to exercise an inappropriate amount of control over a child's eating, when the situation is highly charged emotionally, and when no one is willing to change, it's time to see a therapist. The underlying emotional issues need to be resolved before eating can return to normal.

Helping to Prevent Eating Disorders

- It's important for a family to be functioning well and for the individual family members to be emotionally healthy.

- Adults should be role models for healthy attitudes toward eating and body image.

- The child should be supported in following his own internal sense of food regulation. Parents and caregivers should neither withhold food from a child nor force a child to eat.

- Teach the child to feel good about herself, no matter what body size and shape she has acquired.

Food-Drug Interactions

Rare is the child who at some time doesn't receive medication for an illness. She may need antibiotics for a short time for an infection, or she may require long-term drug therapy for asthma or seizures. Many people are unaware that foods and medications can interact to produce unwanted effects. This is especially important for children, because they may suffer longer from their illnesses or experience poor growth and nutrient deficiencies if the food-drug interactions aren't taken into account.

Foods can alter the effectiveness of a drug by:

- Reducing or increasing the amount of the drug absorbed

- Changing the way the drug is used in the body

- Causing more or less of the drug to be excreted in the urine

Drugs can affect a child's nutritional state by:

- Changing the way foods taste and smell

- Increasing or reducing appetite

- Causing nausea, vomiting, or diarrhea

- Changing the amounts of nutrients that are absorbed

- Altering the way nutrients are used in the body

- Causing more or less of a nutrient to be excreted in the urine

When you must administer medications to a child, ask:

- Whether the drug should be taken with food or on an empty stomach

- If any foods should be *avoided*

- If any nutrients should be *emphasized*

Call a pharmacist if you have any questions about food-drug interactions.

Junk Food

We try not to label foods as "good" or "bad." Instead, we look for "good eating habits" and "bad eating habits." Good eating habits provide the necessary nutrients in appropriate amounts to maintain well-being. Bad eating habits do not.

It's hard to think of any foods that would actually be harmful for most children to eat *once in a while*. But it's easy to name dozens of foods that have little nutritional value and could lead to health problems if consumed *frequently*. These are what concerned adults call "junk foods," and they are characteristically high in sugar, salt, or fat. Candy, cookies, sodas, and snack chips are examples.

Parents and caregivers have valid concerns regarding the following:

- Frequent consumption of sugary foods can cause tooth decay.

- Eating a lot of junk foods can give a child less appetite for the truly nutritious foods he needs for growth.

- It's easy to take in too many calories when eating foods high in fat and sugar.

The problem is, children don't look at the situation this way. They don't worry about developing nutrient deficiencies; they just know they like to eat foods that taste good.

The sweetness or saltiness of junk foods makes them particularly appealing. Babies are born with a preference for sweet flavors, and children can acquire a taste for salt, even cravings for it, when they've habitually eaten salty foods. Children also want to eat what the other kids are eating.

Adults and children can get into some major battles over junk foods. Parents and caregivers who are sincerely trying to provide good nutrition for kids may prohibit them from eating these foods. What usually happens next isn't too surprising: the forbidden foods become *very* attractive. Have you noticed how children whose parents never allow them to eat foods with sugar go absolutely wild over sweets at parties and at their grandparents' houses?

Yes, it's true that we don't *need* junk foods. Most of us are better off without them, especially as we grow older and more sedentary and as our caloric needs go down. But because it is unlikely that sweet, fatty, and salty foods are going to disappear anytime soon, and because many people find them enjoyable, the reasonable thing to do is teach children how to work them into an otherwise healthful way of eating.

As we said earlier, eating a piece of candy every now and then is not likely to do harm; it's when candy is providing a significant portion of a child's calories that nutritional problems will occur. You can maintain your commitment to good nutrition *and* allow children to experience an occasional cupcake or handful of snack chips.

- The best way to teach children how to manage junk foods is to serve them occasionally without any more fuss than you would for carrot sticks or cheese slices. If the children ask why they can't have these foods more often, just let them know that they aren't as good for them as other foods, but they're okay once in a while.

- Minimize the damage by making your own nutritious versions of junk foods. You can make cookies with less sugar, muffins instead of frosted cupcakes, or baked potato sticks rather than french fries. Think about the attributes of junk foods when you're concocting substitutes for them; most junk foods are at least one of the following: sweet, salty, crunchy, bubbly, eaten with the fingers, or served in individual portions in some kind of cute packaging. Fight back! Use your imagination!

- Emphasize the other celebratory aspects of holidays and birthdays besides eating. Plan lots of games, songs, storytelling, and similar activities. Give prizes and party favors that aren't candy (see page 327).

- *Never* use food as a reward for good behavior or as consolation for upsets and injuries.

- Be careful about the amount of time children spend watching television. It's hard for kids *not* to be interested in nutritionally questionable foods when confronted with dazzling advertising.

Lactose Intolerance

Lactose is a form of sugar found in almost all animal milks, including human milk. If a person doesn't have the enzymes in the small intestine to digest lactose (which is the case for most adults in the world), it goes into the large intestine, where bacteria cause it to ferment. This fermentation process results in acids and gases that can cause abdominal cramps, flatulence, and diarrhea.

Children can generally handle the lactose in dairy products until they're about 5 or 6 years old. After that, their tolerance to lactose will depend upon heredity. (Scientists tell us that northern Europeans, Hungarians, members of the Fulani and Tussi tribes in Africa, the Punjabi from India, and perhaps Mongolians are able to digest lactose as adults. The rest of the world's peoples cannot, unless they can count some of these "lactose digesters" among their ancestors.)

A physician can test for lactose tolerance. If a child is lactose intolerant, you will need to change what you're feeding him:

- Many people with lactose intolerance can digest fermented dairy products: yogurt, hard cheese, cottage cheese, and acidophilus milk.

- Enzyme preparations such as Lactaid® can be added to milk; they "predigest" the lactose.

- Some children can tolerate regular milk if they simply drink smaller portions more frequently.

- If a child is unable to tolerate *any* dairy products, be sure to offer him foods rich in the nutrients he'll be missing, such as calcium.

Low-Fat Diets and Children

Several health organizations have made dietary recommendations aimed at reducing our risks of heart disease, cancer, and stroke. Common to all of them is the advice to limit fat intake to no more than 35% of calories, to cut the saturated fat in our diets to 10% of calories or less, and to eat an average of no more than 300 mg cholesterol daily. Many adults are taking these recommendations seriously—eating less red meat, taking the skin off their chicken, and switching from whole milk to low-fat or nonfat milk. And they're wondering if it's okay to do the same for their children.

There's been a lot of research into the relationship between lifestyle factors (including diet) and heart disease. Some of the findings have led experts to recommend low-fat diets for children:

- In countries where adults have high rates of heart disease, both children and adults have higher blood cholesterol levels than in countries where the incidence of heart disease is low.

- People from countries where heart disease rates and blood cholesterol levels are lower tend to eat less saturated fat and cholesterol than people from countries with higher heart disease rates.

- Children develop fatty streaks in their blood vessels, which *may* develop into the lesions of atherosclerosis, at an early age. Autopsies show that children with lesions have higher levels of LDL (low density lipoprotein—"bad") cholesterol and VLDL (very low density lipoprotein—also "bad") cholesterol in their blood.

- Children with high fat intakes are more likely to have serum cholesterol levels in the middle or high range.

Health experts disagree, sometimes heatedly, on the implications of these findings. Questions that need to be settled are: Does what children eat (or does having high blood cholesterol) affect their chance of getting chronic diseases like atherosclerosis when they're adults? Will making the recommended changes in diet actually lower blood cholesterol levels enough to affect the risk of disease? And will restricting fat in their diet lead to poor growth or nutrient deficiencies?

In some cases, fears about children on low-fat diets have been justified. There have been reports of children who suffered growth failure because their parents limited the fats in their diets too severely. With professional nutritional guidance, children on low-fat diets can thrive. But without guidance, children usually replace the lost fat calories with sugar calories. Even when they get enough calories for growth, they may lack the essential fatty acids, vitamins, and minerals that are essential for health and development.

No doubt the controversy will continue; meanwhile, the best argument for providing low-fat foods to children is that eating patterns and preferences are formed in childhood. It isn't necessary to count every gram of fat a child takes in; what's important is that he learns while he's young to enjoy eating poultry, seafood, low-fat dairy products, whole grains, fruits, and vegetables. It will be much harder to change his eating habits when he's an adult.

This book contains many suggestions for reducing fat and saturated fat in the foods you serve. You'll find that many changes are easy to make. Keep in mind that there are other risk factors for heart disease that are important to work on during childhood—and adolescence, too—such as obesity, lack of physical fitness, and cigarette smoking.

- *Never* restrict fat in the diet of a child younger than 2 years old.

- Don't restrict fat in the diet of a child who is underweight and a fussy eater.

- Avoid getting too involved in what children are eating. Offer healthful choices, but don't hover over them, monitoring every pat of butter or slice of cheese.

- Emphasize the "healthy fats" in oils such as olive and canola and foods like nuts, seeds, avocado, and fish.

- Children may need to eat more often, because foods low in fat aren't satisfying for long, and because they may not be able to eat enough at regular mealtimes to get the calories they require.

- Be a good role model for a healthy lifestyle, conscientious without being fanatic. You've heard the old saying: Too much worrying about your health can be bad for your health.

Sodium

Sodium is an essential mineral for the functioning of our bodies. However, the amount we need is actually very small compared to the amount many of us consume. The sodium in our food is primarily in the form of **sodium chloride**, or table salt; a teaspoon of salt contains about 2,300 milligrams of sodium. Some sodium is also contributed by additives like sodium bicarbonate (baking soda) and monosodium glutamate (MSG). Only about 10% of the sodium in our foods is naturally present; the rest is added during cooking and at the table (15% of our total intake) and during food manufacturing (75% of intake). Cereals and baked goods, processed meats, and dairy products are the major sources of sodium in the American diet.

Many consumers have been trying to cut down on salt consumption because of evidence that connects sodium with high blood pressure. In truth, most people don't develop high blood pressure from eating a lot of salt. But it's impossible to predict who will and who won't, so health authorities recommend moderation in sodium intake for everyone, and increased potassium intake, which may lower blood pressure.

It has not been proven that children get high blood pressure from eating a lot of salt, but it is clear that a preference for salty foods can be cultivated by eating them frequently. This could lead to problems later on, if these children grow up to be some of the adults who *do* develop hypertension as the result of salt sensitivity. It makes sense, then, to exercise moderation in the use of salt and foods high in sodium when feeding children. They should learn to enjoy the natural taste of foods.

We've provided suggestions for reducing salt during your food preparation earlier in this book (page 87). And many tasty reduced-sodium versions of favorite foods have appeared on supermarket shelves in response to consumer demand! The sodium content in foods that children commonly eat is listed on page 342.

Although specific guidelines for children's sodium intake aren't yet available, the Dietary Guidelines for Americans 2005 advise that we all keep our daily sodium intake below about 2,300 milligrams, and eat lots of potassium-rich foods like fruits and vegetables.

Special Needs and Feeding

Children with developmental or physical disabilities are prone to the same nutritional problems that affect their peers: obesity, iron-deficiency anemia, underweight, and tooth decay. Their risks of nutrient deficiencies and excesses are greater, however, because they may have trouble eating or have altered nutrient requirements. And it can be more difficult for a child with disabilities to develop the self-esteem that comes, among other things, from successfully managing eating.

Nutrition-related concerns that may arise when a child has developmental delays or physical disabilities include:

- An increased requirement for calories, due to medications, diseases, or central nervous system damage

Sodium Content of Foods
Children Commonly Eat

Food	Serving	Sodium (mg)
Corn flake cereal	1 oz.	351
Shredded wheat biscuits	1 oz.	3
Tomato soup	8 oz.	700-1,260
Tomato juice	8 oz.	340-1,040
Milk	8 oz.	130
Orange juice	8 oz.	2
Low-fat cottage cheese	½ cup	435
Processed American cheese	1 oz.	238
Cheddar cheese	1 oz.	190
Plain low-fat yogurt	1 cup	159
Beef hot dog	1	425
Bologna	2 slices	450
Tuna, water-packed	2 oz.	312
Chicken breast, roasted	2 oz.	42
Peanut butter	2 T.	167
Canned baked beans	1 cup	810
Canned spaghetti and meatballs	7.5 oz.	1,000
Pizza	1 slice	500–1,000
Fast-food deluxe hamburger	1	1,510
Cheese goldfish crackers	10	117
Pretzels	1 oz.	290-560
Butter-flavored crackers	3	97
Tortilla chips	1 oz.	105-160
Dill pickle	2 oz.	700
Mustard	1 T.	212
Ketchup	1 T.	154
Mayonnaise	1 T.	80
Salad dressing	2 T.	110-505

Sources: *Sodium Scoreboard,* Center for Science in the Public Interest, 1501 16th St., NW, Washington, DC 20036; "Wrap-Up Sodium," University of California, Berkeley, *Wellness Letter* 2:4, 1986; Dietary Guidelines for Americans 2005 (USDA/HHS).

- A decreased requirement for calories, due to inactivity, slow metabolism, or medications; this can lead to obesity

- Drug-nutrient interactions, which may change vitamin needs

- Lack of sensation of hunger or satiety in some children with central nervous system damage

- Feeding difficulties, which include
  - Limited sucking ability (infants)
  - Inability to sit up and balance the head
  - Lack of strength or control in the arms and wrists
  - Difficulty coordinating biting, chewing, and swallowing without choking or drooling
  - Difficulty grasping utensils or removing food from them
  - Excessive gagging and vomiting
  - Extreme sensitivity to food temperatures

- Constipation, resulting from slowed bowel action, inactivity, lack of fiber in the diet, or inadequate fluids

It can be quite a challenge to manage your feeding relationship with a child who has a disability. She will go through the same developmental sequence of eating skills and behaviors that you would expect of any child, but she will probably do it more slowly. It may be very tempting to feed her only the foods that she can eat very easily, or not to let her feed herself because she makes such a mess. It might also be tempting to try to make her eat more or eat less when you are concerned about how she's growing.

Children with disabilities are entitled to, and need, the benefits of good nutrition as much as any other children. They are also entitled to progress as far as possible in their development, to have as much control over their lives as they can, and to be treated respectfully, with consideration for their feelings and comfort. It is outside of the scope of this book to teach you the specifics of feeding children with special needs, but we will give you some general guidelines:

- Allow the child to eat foods of progressively more challenging textures as he appears able.

  - Avoid prolonged use of bottle feeding.

  - Be alert for cues (they may be subtle) that the child is ready for solid foods and coarser textures.

- Help the child to develop self-feeding skills.

  - Don't feed a child if he is at all capable of feeding himself.

  - Make sure the child is comfortable; supports for his head, arms, trunk, or feet may be necessary so that he can sit upright.

  - He may need adaptive feeding equipment.

  - Take it step by step, allowing the child to experience success before moving on to more difficult skills.

- Respect the child's preferences regarding types and amounts of food eaten (from what *you* offer, of course), pace of eating, and even whether he will eat.

- Avoid overindulgence with sweet foods and unlimited snacking. Children with special needs need limits, too.

- Find out if any of the child's medications interact with nutrients.

- When you would like training or you're having problems feeding a child with special needs, seek out professionals in your community who can help: occupational therapists, physical therapists, speech therapists, dietitians, and behavior modification specialists. See Appendix D for more information.

Sugar, Food Additives, and Children's Behavior

Parents exchange knowing looks when a mother describes how her darling child turned into a monster during the days following Halloween. And teachers fear that birthday-party cupcakes will send an entire class into a hyperkinetic frenzy. Don't blame it on the sugar . . . all kids get "wild" sometimes!

Between 3% and 7% of children develop ADHD, or Attention Deficit-Hyperactivity Disorder. This disorder is characterized by restlessness, distractibility, impulsive behavior, and a low tolerance for frustration. No one really knows what causes it. But desperate, exhausted parents sometimes wonder if there might be something to all this talk about sugar and food additives, especially food colorings. There are other dietary programs for ADHD that presently are out of the mainstream, but we won't address them here.

It has been very hard for scientists to prove a link between dietary components such as sugar and hyperactivity. When a child's diet is changed, his behavior may improve because his parents expect it to. Or there might be changes in family dynamics. Maybe the child feels better because he's eating a more nourishing diet than he was before.

The majority of research trials in which neither the parents, the child, nor the observers knew whether the child received sugar (or an additive) or a placebo have failed to find a connection between those dietary components and behavior. Some studies have even indicated that sugar has a calming effect on children! In fairness, we must say that a few research studies have found that a *very* small number of children do respond to sugar or additives, especially food colorings, with behavior changes. The results of one study, albeit a small one, suggest that children's hormones may respond differently from adults' to large doses of sugar on an empty stomach.

Most health experts believe that there are other reasons why children get "hyper" after they've eaten sugar, such as the general excitement or fatigue that accompanies celebrations. Maybe they become super-excited about being able to indulge in otherwise "forbidden" treats.

It's a good idea to consult a physician before imposing an unnecessarily restrictive diet on a child. Diets completely free of sugar and food additives can be a lot of work for the adults and traumatic for the child. At the same time, there are good reasons for limiting the amounts of sugar and additives in the foods you serve. Frequent sugar intake causes tooth decay. Eating lots of sugary foods can displace other more nutritious foods in the diet, leading to borderline nutrition. And while some food additives seem to be safe, there are questions about the safety of others, including some coloring agents, nitrates, nitrites, and saccharin. Many additives, especially colorings, can be easily avoided.

There are other aspects of children's food patterns that can have effects on their behavior. They are:

- **Nutrient deficiencies.** Deficiencies of most nutrients will affect behavior. The most common deficiency in the United States is iron deficiency. The brain is very sensitive to a lack of iron, and this can have profound effects: fatigue, distractibility, irritability, reduced tolerance for challenging tasks, and headaches.

- **Skipping meals.** Children need to eat at least every 4 to 6 hours to supply their brains with needed glucose. Children who skip breakfast or other meals tend to be irritable and unable to concentrate on the tasks at hand. That's why midmorning snacks are a good idea, and why kids should eat their breakfast!

- **Caffeine.** Caffeine is often overlooked as a source of "wild" behavior in children. But for a child's size, a 12-ounce can of cola can contain the caffeine equivalent to 3 or 4 cups of coffee for an adult.

- **Food allergies.** Although most allergists don't believe that food allergies themselves can cause behavior problems, a child who feels miserable because of allergy symptoms is likely to be difficult to manage.

This sounds like the same old-fashioned advice we heard when we were children, but there really is no substitute for regular, well-balanced meals and snacks, regular sleep, and regular exercise. It's a good idea to monitor television viewing, too; many of the shows children enjoy are violent and overstimulating. Sometimes the simplest interventions are the last ones we consider. Consider them first!

A Common-Sense Approach to Dealing with Children and Sugar

- Never use sweet foods as a reward for eating other parts of a meal or for "good" behavior.

- When serving sugary foods, make them part of a meal or snack containing protein (milk with a cookie, for example).

- Sweet foods should also have some nutritional value, that is, contain some protein, fiber, vitamins, and/or minerals.

- Serve snacks other than sweets most of the time.

- Reduce sugar intake when possible.

- Have children brush their teeth after eating sweet foods.

Television

The average child in the United States spends more time watching television than in any other activity except sleeping. Children today spend an average of 5½ hours every day with screen media—television, videos, video games, and computers. How all of this television viewing affects a child will depend upon what she sees and for how long she sees it. Television can have a huge impact on children's nutrition, as you will see.

Here's what nutritionists don't like about television:

- It's a sedentary activity.

- Children see about 40,000 commercials a year, of which most promote foods of low nutritional value. Younger children are particularly inclined to believe claims that the products being advertised are *good* for them.

- It encourages children to manipulate their parents' purchasing decisions at the grocery store. Why do you think advertisers pay all that money for television ads?

- It is conducive to mindless snacking.

- It can hinder social interaction at mealtimes.

- It has been associated with obesity, high blood cholesterol levels, low levels of physical fitness, and lowered metabolic rate. (Note: "association" doesn't necessarily mean "proof of cause.")

Television does have its good features, however:

- It can be a source of useful information presented in a way that is very attractive to children.

- It can be a trigger for talking about nutrition and health behaviors.

Watching television may not be an option in your home or child care center. If it is, there are ways you can emphasize its positive aspects and downplay the negative ones.

Guidelines for Children's Television and Screen Media

- Limit daily viewing time to no more than 1 or 2 hours of quality programs or videos that you have chosen. Children under 2 should not watch television at all.

- Be selective about what the children are watching. Some networks make more of an effort to be nutrition-friendly than others.

- Watch television *with* the children and talk about the eating and health behaviors portrayed on the programs. Discuss the ways that consumers can be misled by advertising.

- Balance passive activities like television and video games with lots of physical activity.

- *Don't allow children to eat while they watch television.*

Underweight Children

Some children are destined to be small. Others have the potential to grow larger or grow more quickly, but for some reason they don't. Sometimes in our weight-conscious society we get very concerned about a child who is overweight, yet fail to notice when a child isn't growing as well as she could. Faltering growth can be a serious problem, with many causes:

- Some children require more calories for their size than others, due to heredity or activity, and caregivers may underestimate their food needs.

- Children may eat poorly because they are exceedingly finicky, can't handle sitting at the table for long, are resistant to what they perceive as pressure to eat, or suffer from anxiety or depression.

- Children can exhibit poor growth when their parents severely restrict fat or calories in their diets.

- Children may have limited self-feeding skills or difficulty chewing and swallowing the food that is offered.

- Certain disease processes can interfere with growth.

A child who is lagging in her growth should be evaluated by a physician, of course, and treatments vary. You as a parent or caregiver can do much to help the underweight child:

- Make sure that you provide a supportive and attractive environment for eating.

- Provide regular meals and snacks, including foods the child enjoys, *with no pressure* on the child to eat.

- Check to make sure there's enough fat in the child's diet.

- Observe whether the child has any problems with chewing or swallowing the foods you offer; you may be offering foods too advanced for the child, or she may need professional help.

- Be alert to signs that the child is anxious, withdrawn, or depressed; therapy may be in order.

- Accept the child's body, no matter how she turns out.

Vegetarianism

People may choose not to eat meat, or any foods of animal origin, for religious, health, ethical, or political reasons. Much of the world's population is vegetarian for economic reasons. Some vegetarians eat no meat, poultry, or fish but do eat eggs and dairy products (**lacto-ovo-vegetarians**); some avoid eggs as well (**lacto-vegetarians**); and some eat no animal products whatsoever (**vegans**).

A vegetarian diet can't guarantee good health, just as eating meat doesn't guarantee poor health. But vegetarians do seem to enjoy some health benefits, including lower blood cholesterol levels, lower blood pressure, and less risk of osteoporosis, gallstones, and diabetes. In the past, many child-health experts expressed concern as to whether vegetarian diets were beneficial for children, but now most agree that a well-planned lacto-ovo- or lacto-vegetarian diet is compatible with normal growth and development.

Vegan diets are viewed with more concern. Researchers have found that vegan children tend to be shorter and lighter than other vegetarians or children who eat meat, though they fall within the normal range of growth. By the age of 10 years, vegan children tend to catch up in height, but remain lighter than children on mixed diets. There have been a few horror stories of rickets, vitamin B_{12} deficiencies, and outright malnutrition among vegan children, but usually their parents were using misguided feeding practices or the breastfeeding mothers had dietary deficiencies.

Vegan diets are typically high in fiber and low in calories; it can be difficult for a small child to eat enough to satisfy her calorie requirements. Fiber can hinder the absorption of iron, calcium, and zinc. The transition from breast milk or formula to solid foods is an especially vulnerable time for vegan children. Inadequate protein, calcium, essential fatty acids, riboflavin, iron, zinc, vitamin D, or vitamin B_{12} are potentially matters of concern in a vegan diet, especially if the child is a picky eater and rejects good sources of these nutrients.

It's quite simple to work out an adequate diet for a child who eats dairy products and eggs. Planning to meet the needs of the vegan child requires considerably more effort.

Meal Planning for Vegan Children

- Use soy or rice milk or formula fortified with vitamins D and B_{12}.

- Use cooked dried beans, nuts and nut butters, and seeds as meat alternatives (high in protein).

- Tofu can be a good source of calcium, but only if it is made with calcium sulfate—check the label. Corn tortillas (made with lime) and greens such as kale, bok choy, and collards are also high in calcium. Calcium-fortified orange juice or soy or rice milk is another option.

- Serve foods rich in vitamin C at meals to enhance iron absorption.

- Children may require more frequent meals and snacks because vegan meals tend to be filling but low in calories.

- Consider serving eggs and dairy products to very young children or children who are picky eaters and not growing well (with parental approval, of course).

For excellent discussions of vegetarian meal planning and delicious recipes, we highly recommend *The New Laurel's Kitchen*, by Laurel Robertson, Carol Flinders, and Brian Ruppenthal, published by Ten Speed Press, Berkeley, California.

Vitamin and Mineral Supplements

More than half of preschool- and school-age children receive multivitamin/mineral supplements. Often these children aren't the ones who could really benefit from them.

Parents usually give vitamin and mineral supplements to their children because they feel the need for insurance against the ups and downs of their children's appetites. Some use supplements as alternatives to conventional medical therapy for a variety of health problems. For some children supplements may be helpful, for others they are harmless but a waste of money, and for others they can cause significant problems. It's important to know this about vitamin and mineral supplements:

- It isn't necessarily true that if a little of a nutrient is good, more is better; some nutrients are toxic at high doses, and they may interfere with the body's ability to use other nutrients. Children who are on megavitamin or megamineral therapy need close monitoring by their health care providers.

- Vitamin and mineral supplements can give parents a false sense of security about their children's diets. Supplements contain only a fraction of the many nutrients needed for health.

- Children can get the message that pills, not nutritious foods, are necessary for growing into healthy adulthood.

- Children have mistaken vitamin or mineral tablets for candy and have suffered fatal overdoses.

The American Academy of Pediatrics has determined that most children don't need vitamin or mineral supplements. Those who probably do are:

- Children whose diet is significantly limited because of severe allergies, developmental delays, feeding problems, or poor appetite

- Children living in neglectful or abusive situations
- Children who follow a vegan diet
- Pregnant teenagers

Having said all this, we know that despite our best efforts, many children still don't eat enough fruits and vegetables, and a basic multivitamin/mineral tablet may take some pressure off the feeding situation. Parents who decide to give their children vitamin or mineral supplements should treat them as medications and keep them out of the reach of young children. Keep offering fruits and vegetables. And unless instructed otherwise by a physician, it's best to avoid giving a supplement that contains more than 100% of the DRI for any nutrient.

APPENDIX B

· ·

Nutrition Basics

- **Nutrition** is the science concerned with food and how it is used by the body. It is also the combination of processes by which a person eats, digests, absorbs, utilizes, and excretes food substances.

- Nutrition is a young science—the first vitamin was discovered only about 80 years ago, and we assume that more nutrients will be discovered in years to come. There are over 40 known nutrients, and no one food contains them all.

- **Nutrients** are the substances found in food that work together to provide energy, promote growth, and regulate body processes. The six major classes of nutrients are:

Carbohydrates	Vitamins
Proteins	Minerals
Fats	Water

Proteins, fats, and carbohydrates provide *calories*, which are small units of energy your body can use to do its work or stay warm.

The tables on pages 358–360 describe briefly the functions and good food sources of the major nutrients.

353

- Everyone has different nutritional needs, which depend on age, sex, body size, heredity, activity levels, state of health, and even climate! Although more information is becoming available, we still don't know for certain what all of those needs are.

- Some nutrients are needed in large quantities and some in small ones. In the United States, nutrient requirements have been, up to now, expressed as *Recommended Dietary Allowances*, or RDAs. A new and expanded system of guidance called the Dietary Reference Intakes (DRIs) is being developed. Some nutrients will continue to have RDAs, others will have Adequate Intakes (AIs), and acceptable upper limits for nutrient intakes will be given as Tolerable Upper Intake Levels (ULs). These DRIs are based on the best available scientific research, and they will have a far-reaching impact on consumer education, fortification of food products, and planning dietary standards for nutrition programs.

  It is important to remember that DRIs have their limitations when we use them to measure the quality of an individual's diet. For one thing, although they are expressed as daily requirements, they are actually daily intakes averaged over a week or more. Thus, falling short of a nutritional requirement one day is unlikely to cause any harm; it's what's eaten over a longer term that's important. In addition, the DRIs are meant to be used as goals but not applied rigidly, because individual nutritional needs vary. For example, suppose that someone habitually ingested just 50% of his RDA for vitamin C. We couldn't necessarily assume he is suffering from a vitamin deficiency! Maybe his body needs only 25% of the RDA. But then again, he might need 95% of the RDA (unfortunately, human beings aren't born with owner's manuals, so we don't really know how much of each nutrient will make each person's body work best). It would be fair to say that if this fellow habitually got about 50% of the RDA for vitamin C, he would have a greater *risk* of a deficiency than someone who took in 100% of the RDA. For this reason, it's a good idea to aim for food patterns that supply nutrients in quantities close to the DRIs.

- Although it is true that some people in the United States don't get enough of certain nutrients, it is far more common for us to get too much of others, namely, fat, sugars, and sodium. Excessive intakes of these substances, along with a lack of fiber, are related to the "diseases of affluence" that kill millions and millions of Americans: heart disease, high blood pressure, diabetes, and cancer.

- Getting the recommended number of servings from MyPyramid helps ensure dietary intakes consistent with guidelines for disease prevention and optimum growth and development (see page 78).

- In the field of nutrition right now, exciting research is being conducted on substances in plant foods called *phytochemicals*. These substances, produced by plants to protect themselves from invading viruses, bacteria, and fungi, aren't considered nutrients, but they may help prevent some cancers, heart disease, and other chronic health problems. Carotenoids, flavinoids, indoles, isoflavones, capsaicin, and protease inhibitors are among the phytochemicals being studied. Avoid running to the store to buy supplements containing one or several of these substances, and follow Mom's advice to eat lots of fruits and vegetables instead (a bit of tea and chocolate now and then probably won't hurt either!). And stay tuned. . . .

A User-Friendly Guide
to Some Major Nutrients

Nutrients	Primary Functions	Rich Food Sources
Energy Nutrients (supply calories)		
Proteins	Supply amino acids to be used for growth and maintenance of the body	Meat, poultry, fish, eggs, milk, cheese, dried beans, tofu, peanut butter, seeds, nuts
Carbohydrates	Primary source of energy for the body's activities	*Complex carbohydrates:* Breads, cereals, rice, pasta, tortillas, potatoes, vegetables *Sugars:* Sugar, honey, jelly, molasses, candy, milk, fruits

Fiber is also a carbohydrate, but it can't be digested by humans, so it provides bulk or "roughage" and no calories. Good sources are whole grains, fresh fruits and vegetables, dried fruits, and dried beans.

Nutrients	Primary Functions	Rich Food Sources
Fats	Provide energy, cushion vital organs, and supply essential fatty acids that maintain skin and membranes	Oils, butter, margarine, meat, lard, cream, olives, coconut, avocados, nuts

Fat Facts

Fats are made up of different combinations of fatty acids. These fatty acids may be saturated (solid at room temperature) or mono- or polyunsaturated (liquid at room temperature). Saturated fats are the ones that raise blood cholesterol. They are *usually* found in animal foods, like meat or milk (palm oil and coconut oil are two vegetable oils that are highly saturated, however).

Cholesterol is found only in foods of animal origin. It is possible for a food to have no cholesterol in it but still be very high in fat (and calories!). Corn oil, for example, is cholesterol free but 100% fat.

A User-Friendly Guide
to Some Major Nutrients (continued)

Nutrients	Primary Functions	Rich Food Sources
Water-Soluble Vitamins		
Thiamin (B_1)	Helps the body use carbohydrates for energy; important for health of nervous system	Pork, organ meats, yeast, eggs, green leafy vegetables, whole or enriched grains, dried beans
Riboflavin (B_2)	Helps the body get energy from carbohydrates, fats, and proteins; important for healthy mucous membranes	Milk, organ meats, yeast, cheese, eggs, green leafy vegetables, whole or enriched grains
Niacin	Helps the body release energy from foods; promotes healthy skin, digestive tract, and nervous system	Liver, yeast, whole or enriched grains, beef, pork, peanuts
Vitamin B_6	Helps the body use proteins and fats; keeps nervous system healthy	Yeast, whole grains, fish, poultry, meats, bananas, green leafy vegetables
Folic acid (folate/folacin)	Helps make new body cells through its role in making RNA and DNA; helps make red blood cells	Leafy vegetables, some fruits, dried beans, liver, wheat germ, fortified cereals, most enriched grain products
Vitamin B_{12}	Helps the body make its genetic material; vital for health of nerve tissue	Meat, poultry, fish, eggs, milk products, a few specially fortified plant foods
Vitamin C	Helps form collagen; keeps bones, teeth, and blood vessels healthy; antioxidant	Citrus fruits, tomatoes, peppers, potatoes, cantaloupe, strawberries, cabbage

A User-Friendly Guide
to Some Major Nutrients (continued)

Nutrients	Primary Functions	Rich Food Sources
Fat-Soluble Vitamins		
Vitamin A	Helps in growth and maintenance of skin and membranes; needed for healthy eyes and night vision	Liver, cream, egg yolk, butter, fortified dairy products; green, orange, and yellow vegetables and fruits
Vitamin D	Helps form and maintain bones and teeth; aids in calcium absorption	Fatty fish, liver, eggs, butter, fortified dairy foods
Vitamin E	Helps form red blood cells and other tissues; protects fatty acids and vitamin A	Vegetable oils, wheat germ, whole grains, liver, green leafy vegetables
Vitamin K	Needed for normal blood clotting	Cabbage, cauliflower, liver, vegetable oils, green leafy vegetables
Minerals		
Calcium	Builds and maintains bones and teeth; needed for blood clotting and muscle contraction	Milk products, fish eaten with bones, dried beans, broccoli, bok choy, collards, kale, blackstrap molasses
Iron	Forms components of blood that carry oxygen to cells	Liver, meat, dried beans, dried fruits, fortified cereal
Fluoride	Keeps bones and teeth strong	Fluoridated water, tea, sardines
Iodine	Part of thyroid hormones	Seafood, iodized salt, seaweed
Water (the most important nutrient)	An essential component of the body's structure; a solvent, transports nutrients and wastes, regulates body temperature	Beverages and most solid foods

How Can You Tell Whether a Child Is Getting Proper Nutrition?

A physician or registered dietitian is in the best position to judge whether a child is truly well nourished, but in general, you can feel reasonably assured that a child is getting the nutrition she needs if she is growing well, is vigorous, and seems to have good resistance to illness (of course, most children will have occasional colds or bouts with flu). There are other indicators of good nutrition as well. A child who is well nourished will have:

- Erect posture and straight arms and legs (excepting infants)

- Good muscle tone

- Smooth skin, slightly moist, and with good color

- Good attention span, normal reflexes, psychologically stable

- Good appetite, normal elimination

- Normal heart rate and rhythm, normal blood pressure

- Normal sleeping habits

- Shiny hair, firmly rooted, and healthy scalp

- Smooth, moist lips

- Smooth, red tongue, not swollen

- Gums with a good pink color, no swelling or bleeding

- Teeth that are clean and free of cavities, well-shaped jaw

- Bright, clear eyes with healthy pink membranes

- Firm nails with pink nailbeds

We do not recommend that you take it upon yourself to get into the medical diagnosis business, but you can alert families to signs that professional evaluation and treatment might be in order. Obviously, not all of these criteria are appropriate to use in the case of some children with physical disabilities.

Appendix C

....

References

Chapter One:
What You Should Know About Feeding Children

American Academy of Pediatrics, Committee on Nutrition: Policy Statement: Prevention of pediatric overweight and obesity. *Pediatrics* 112(2): 424-430, 2003.

American Academy of Pediatrics, Committee on Nutrition: The use and misuse of fruit juice in pediatrics. *Pediatrics* 107 (5): 1210-1213, 2001.

American Dietetic Association: Position of the American Dietetic Association: Benchmarks for nutrition programs in child care settings. *JADA* 105(6): 979-986, 2005.

American Dietetic Association, Committee on Prevention of Obesity in Children and Youth: Preventing childhood obesity: health in the balance: executive summary. *JADA* 105 (1): 131-138, 2005.

Birch, L.L., Johnson, S.L., and Fisher, J.A.: Children's eating: the development of food acceptance patterns. *Young Children* Jan: 71, 1995.

Centers for Disease Control, National Center for Chronic Disease Prevention and Health Promotion: *Overweight and Obesity Health Consequences.* www.cdc.gov/nccdphp/dnpa/obesity/index.htm

The Center for Health and Health Care in Schools (The George Washington University Medical Center): *Childhood overweight: what the research tells us.* March 2005. www.healthinschools.org/sh/obesityfs.asp.

Crawford, P, Mitchell, R., and Ikeda, J.: *Childhood overweight: A fact sheet for professionals.* University of California, Berkeley, Cooperative Extension.

Fisher, J.O. and Birch, L.L.: Parents' restrictive feeding practices are associated with young girls' negative self-evaluation of eating. *JADA* 100: 1341-1346, 2000.

Fisher, J.O. and Birch, L.L.: Restricting access to foods and children's eating. *Appetite* 32: 405-419, 1999.

Healthwise: Long-term health problems related to being overweight as a child.

Institute of Medicine of the National Academies: *Childhood Obesity in the United States: Facts and Figures*. Fact Sheet, September 2004.

Narayan, K.M.V., Boyle, J.P., Thompson, T.J., Sorenson, S.W., and Williamson, D.F.: Lifetime risk for diabetes mellitus in the United States. *JAMA* 290: 1884-1890, 2003.

National Education Association. *The Relationship Between Nutrition & Learning. A School Employee's Guide to Information and Action.* Washington, D.C.: National Education Association of the United States, 1989.

Ogden, C.l., Carroll, M.D., Curtin, L.R., McDowell, M.A., Tabak, C.J., and Flegal, K.M.: Prevalence of overweight and obesity in the United States, 1999-2004. *JAMA* 295: 1549-1555, 2006.

Satter, E.: Helping all you can to keep your child from being fat. *How to Get Your Kid to Eat...But Not Too Much.* Palo Alto: Bull Publishing Company, 1987.

Satter, E.: Internal regulation and the evolution of normal growth as the basis for prevention of obesity in children. *JADA* 96: 860, 1996.

Sombke, L.: How our meals have changed. *USA Weekend*, November 11-13, 1988.

Story, M. and Brown, J.E.: Do children instinctively know what to eat? The studies of Clara Davis revisited. *New England Journal of Medicine* 316: 103, 1987.

U.S. Department of Health and Human Services and U.S. Department of Agriculture. *Dietary Guidelines for Americans, 2005.* 6th edition, Washington, DC: U.S. Government Printing Office, January 2005. www.healthierus.gov/dietaryguidelines.

Chapter Two: Feeding and Growth

American Academy of Pediatrics: Policy Statement. Breastfeeding and the use of human milk. *Pediatrics* 115: 496-506, 2005.

American Academy of Pediatrics. *Pediatric Nutrition Handbook*. Elk Grove Village, IL: American Academy of Pediatrics, 1993.

American Academy of Pediatrics, American Public Health Association, and National Resource Center for Health and Safety in Child Care: *Stepping Stones to Using Caring for Our Children: National Health and Safety Performance Standards*, 2nd ed. 2003.

American Dietetic Association and Gerber Foods: *Start Healthy^{TM} Stay Healthy Feeding Guidelines*, 2005. www.gerber.com.

Beal, V.: The preschool years (one to six). In *Nutrition in the Life Span*. New York: John Wiley & Sons, 1980.

Birch,L.L. and Fisher, J.O.: Development of eating behaviors among children and adolescents. *Pediatrics* 101: 539-549, 1998.

Caring for Our Children: National health and Safety Performance Standards: Guidelines for Out-of-Home Child Care Programs, 2nd edition. Elk Grove Village, IL: American Academy of Pediatrics and Washington, DC: American Public Health Association. Available at: http://nrc.uchsc.edu.

Centers for Disease Control and Prevention: *Breastfeeding: Recommendations: Proper Handling and Storage of Human Milk*. Accessed at: www.cdc.gov/breastfeeding/recommendations/handling_breastmilk.htm

Committee on Nutrition, American Academy of Pediatrics: The use of whole cow's milk in infancy. *Pediatrics* 89: 1105, 1992.

Committee on Nutrition, American Academy of Pediatrics: Follow-up or weaning formulas. *Pediatrics* 83: 1067, 1989.

DeBruyne, L.K. and Rolfes, S.R.: Infants: a nurtured beginning. *Life Cycle Nutrition. Conception Through Adolescence*. St.Paul: West Publishing Company, 1989.

DeBruyne, L.K. and Rolfes, S.R.: Focal point 3: dental health. *Life Cycle Nutrition. Conception Through Adolescence*. St.Paul: West Publishing Company, 1989.

Fomon, S.J.: Reflections on infant feeding in the 1970s and 1980s. *American Journal of Clinical Nutrition* 46: 171, 1987.

FDA/CFSAN: *Food Safety for Moms-to-Be: Once Baby Arrives*. September 2005. www.cfsan.fda.gov/~pregnant/once.html.

Food and Nutrition Service. *Feeding Infants. A Guide for Use in the Child Care Food Program*. Washington, D.C.: U.S. Department of Agriculture, 1988.

Gortmaker, S.L., Dietz, W.H., and Cheung, L.W.Y.: Inactivity, diet, and the fattening of America. *JADA* 90: 1247, 1990.

Hagan, J.: Out of the jar or homemade: what's best for baby and when? *Environmental Nutrition* 13: 1, 6-7, 1990.

Keating, J.P.: Schears, G.J., and Dodge, P.R.: Oral water intoxication in infants. An American epidemic. *American Journal of Diseases of Children* 145: 985, 1991.

Leach, P. *Your Baby and Child from Birth to Age Five*, 2nd Edition. Alfred Knopf, 1995.

Morgan, K.J. and Zabik, M.E.: Amount and food sources of total sugar intake by children ages 5 to 12 years. *American Journal of Clinical Nutrition* 34: 404, 1981.

Nelms, B.C. and Mullins, R.G. *Growth and Development. A Primary Health Care Approach.* Englewood Cliffs, N.J.: Prentice-Hall, Inc., 1982.

Pipes, P.L.: Infant feeding and nutrition. *Nutrition in Infancy and Childhood*, Fifth Edition. St. Louis: Times Mirror/Mosby College Publishing, 1993.

Pipes, P.L. and Trahms, C.M.: Nutrition: growth and development. *Nutrition in Infancy and Childhood*, Fifth Edition. St. Louis: Times Mirror/Mosby College Publishing, 1993.

Pipes, P.L.and Trahms, C.M.: The preschool-age child. *Nutrition in Infancy and Childhood,* Fifth Edition. St. Louis: Times Mirror/Mosby College Publishing, 1993.

Radbill, S.X.: Infant feeding through the ages. *Clinical Pediatrics* 20: 613, 1981.

Redel, C.A. and Shulman, R.J.: Controversies in the composition of infant formulas. *Pediatric Clinics of North America* 41(5): 909, 1994.

Satter, E. *Child of Mine. Feeding with Love and Good Sense.* Boulder: Bull Publishing Co., 2000.

Satter, E. *How to Get Your Kid to Eat...But Not Too Much.* Boulder: Bull Publishing Company, 1987.

U.S. Department of Health and Human Services and U.S. Department of Agriculture. *Dietary Guidelines for Americans, 2005.* 6th edition, Washington, DC: U.S. Government Printing Office, January 2005. www.healthierus.gov/dietaryguidelines.

————: *Exchange Lists for Meal Planning.* The American Diabetes Association, Inc. and The American Dietetic Association.1986.

Chapter Three: Planning How and What to Feed Children

American Academy of Pediatrics, Committee on Nutrition: Calcium requirements of infants, children, and adolescents. *Pediatrics* 104: 1152-1157, 1999.

Asami, K.A., Hong, Y., Barrett, D.M., and Mitchell, A.E.: Comparison of the total phenolic and ascorbic acid content of freeze-dried and air-dried marionberry, strawberry, and corn grown using conventional, organic, and sustainable agricultural practices. *J.Agric.Food Chem.* 51(5): 1237-1241, 2003.

Bedinghaus, J.B. and Doughten, S.: Childhood nutrition: from breastmilk to burgers. *Primary Care* 21: 655, 1994.

California Academy of Sciences Seafood Guide, updated November 2004. www.calacademy.org.

Caring for Our Children: National health and Safety Performance Standards: Guidelines for Out-of-Home Child Care Programs, 2nd edition. Elk Grove Village, IL: American Academy of Pediatrics and Washington, DC: American Public Health Association. Available at: http://nrc.uchsc.edu.

Curl, C., Fenske, R., and Elgethun, K.: Organophosphorous pesticide exposure of urban and suburban pre-school children with organic and conventional diets. *Environmental Health Perspectives* 111: 377-382, 2003.

Deutsch, R.M. and Morrill, J.S. *Realities of Nutrition.* Palo Alto: Bull Publishing Company, 1993.

Environmental Working Group: *Shopper's Guide to Pesticides in Produce.* www.ewg.org.

Environmental Working Group: *Summary—PCBs in farmed salmon.* www.ewg.org.

The Essential Eating Well Seafood Guide. *Eating Well*, Spring 2004.

Goldman, L.R., Shannon, M.W., and the Committee on Environmental Health: Technical Report: Mercury in the environment: Implications for pediatricians. *Pediatrics* 108: 197-205, 2001.

Harvard School of Public Health, Department of Nutrition: Calcium and milk. www.hsph.harvard.edu/nutritionsource/

Harvard School of Public Health, Department of Nutrition: Fats & cholesterol. www.hsph.harvard.edu/nutritionsource/

Margen, S. and the Editors of the UC Berkeley Wellness Letter: *Wellness Foods A to Z.* New York: Rebus, Inc. 2002.

MyPyramid. www.mypyramid.gov

National Research Council, National Academy of Sciences. *Pesticides in the Diets of Infants and Children.* Washington, DC: National Academy Press, 1993.

National Research Council's Board on Agriculture and Natural Resources, National Academy of Sciences: *Report in Brief: Safety of Genetically Engineered Foods: Approaches to Assessing Unintended Health Effects*. July 2004.

Natural Resources Defense Council: *Mercury contamination in fish: A guide to staying healthy and fighting back*. www.nrdc.org/health/effects/mercury/tuna.asp

Nestle, Marion. *Safe Food: Bacteria, Biotechnology, and Bioterrorism*. Berkeley: University of California Press, 2003.

Nutrition Division, Calgary Health Services. *Day Care Nutrition and Food Service Manual*. Calgary, Alberta: Calgary Health Services, 1988.

Pipes, P.L.: Infant feeding and nutrition. *Nutrition in Infancy and Childhood, Fifth Edition*. St. Louis: Times Mirror/Mosby College Publishing, 1993.

Resnicow, K.: The relationship between breakfast habits and plasma cholesterol levels in schoolchildren. *Journal of School Health* 61: 81, 1991.

Satter, E: The feeding relationship. *Child of Mine. Feeding with Love and Good Sense*. Boulder: Bull Publishing Co., 2000.

U.S. Department of Agriculture, Food and Nutrition Service. *Food Buying Guide for Child Nutrition Programs*, 2001.

U.S. Department of Health and Human Services and U.S. Department of Agriculture. *Dietary Guidelines for Americans, 2005*. 6th edition, Washington, DC: U.S. Government Printing Office, January 2005. www.healthierus.gov/dietaryguidelines.

Wellness Letter, University of California, Berkeley: Salmon: down on the farm, April 2004.

Zhao, Y. and Weaver, C.: Calcium bioavailability of soyfoods, dairy explained. *The Soyfood Connection*, Fall 2005.

Chapter Four: The Recipes

Consumer Reports: A better butter? New research shows peanut butter is good for you. (Don't tell the kids.). www.consumerreports.org.

Margen, S. and the Editors of the UC Berkeley Wellness Letter: *Wellness Foods A to Z*. New York: Rebus, Inc. 2002.

MyPyramid. www.mypyramid.gov

U.S. Department of Agriculture, Food and Nutrition Service. *Food Buying Guide for Child Nutrition Programs*, 2001.

U.S. Department of Health and Human Services and U.S. Department of Agriculture. *Dietary Guidelines for Americans, 2005*. 6th edition, Washington, DC: U.S. Government Printing Office, January 2005. www.healthierus.gov/ dietaryguidelines.

Chapter Six: Running a Ship-Shape Kitchen

Bailey, J. *Keeping Food Fresh*. New York: Harper & Row, Publishers, 1989.

Blume, E.: Germ wars. Cleaning up our food. *Nutrition Action Healthletter* 13 (6): 1, 1986.

Blumenthal, D.: An unwanted souvenir...lead in ceramic ware. *FDA Consumer*, December 1989-January 1990.

Caring for Our Children: National health and Safety Performance Standards: Guidelines for Out-of-Home Child Care Programs, 2nd edition. Elk Grove Village, IL: American Academy of Pediatrics and Washington, DC: American Public Health Association. Available at: http://nrc.uchsc.edu.

Duyff, R. L.: *American Dietetic Association Complete Food and Nutrition Resource Guide*, 2nd edition. New Jersey: John Wiley & Sons, Inc. 2002.

Farley, D.: Keeping up with the microwave revolution. *FDA Consumer*, March 1990.

Food Safety and Inspection Service, United States Department of Agriculture: *"Is it done yet?"* April 2006. www.IsItDoneYet.gov.

Hillman, H. *Kitchen Science*. Revised Edition. Boston: Houghton Mifflin Company, 1989.

Kurtzwell, P.: Labeling rules for young children's food. *FDA Consumer* Mar: 14, 1995.

Lefferts, L.Y. and Schmidt, S.: Microwaves: the heat is on. *Nutrition Action Healthletter* 17:1, 1990.

Miller, R.: Mother Nature's regulations on food safety. *FDA Consumer*, April 1988.

Satter, E.: Diarrhea. *Child of Mine. Feeding with Love and Good Sense*. Palo Alto: Bull Publishing Co., 2000.

Shugart, Grace and Molt, Mary. *Food for Fifty*, 9th ed. New York: Macmillan Publishing Company, 1993.

U.S. Department of Agriculture, Human Nutrition Information Service. *Shopping for Food & Making Meals in Minutes Using the Dietary Guidelines*. Washington, D.C.: U.S. Government Printing Office, 1989.

U.S. Food and Drug Administration/Center for Food Safety and Applied Nutrition: *Advice to Consumers: Food Allergen Labeling and Consumer Protection Act of 2004 Questions and Answers*, December 12, 2005. www.cfsan.fda.gov/~dms/alrgqa. html.

U.S. Food and Drug Administration/Center for Food Safety and Applied Nutrition: *How to Understand and Use the Nutrition Facts Label*, June 2000, updated July 2003 and November 2004. Available at: http://vm.cfsan.fda.gov/~dms/foodlab.html.

————: How safe is the microwave for kids? *American Health*, September 1990.

————: Large microwave ovens. *Consumer Reports*, November 1990.

————: Microwave heating of infant formula and breast milk. *Child Health Alert*, July 1990.

————. *Sunset Microwave Cookbook*. Menlo Park, CA.: Lane Publishing, 1981.

Chapter Seven: Environmental Concerns

Dadd, D.L. *The Nontoxic Home*. Los Angeles: Jeremy Tarcher, Inc., 1986.

Dadd, D.L. *Nontoxic and Natural: How to Avoid Dangerous Everyday Products and Buy or Make Safe Ones*. Los Angeles: Jeremy Tarcher, Inc., 1984.

Earthworks Group. *50 Simple Things Kids Can Do to Save the Earth*. Kansas City: Andrews and McMeel, 1990.

Earthworks Group. *The Recycler's Handbook: Simple Things You Can Do*. Berkeley: Earthworks Press, 1990.

Earthworks Group and Pacific Gas and Electric. *30 Simple Energy Things You Can Do to Save the Earth*. 1990.

Elkington, J., Hailes, J., Hill, D., and Makower, J. *Going Green: A Kid's Handbook to Saving the Planet*. New York: The Penguin Group, 1990.

Hadingham, E. and J. *Garbage! Where It Comes From, Where It Goes*. New York: Simon and Schuster, Inc., 1990.

Heloise. Heloise: *Hints for a Healthy Planet.* New York: The Putnam Publishing Group, 1990.

Kimbrell, A.C.: *Environmental house cleaning. The Green Lifestyle Handbook: 1001 Ways You Can Heal the Earth.*

Lamb, M. *2 Minutes a Day for a Greener Planet: Quick and Simple Things Americans Can Do to Save the Earth.* New York: Harper & Row, Publishers, Inc., 1990.

Logan, Karen. *Clean House, Clean Planet.* New York: Pocket Books, 1997.

MacEachern, D. *Save Our Planet: 750 Everyday Ways You Can Help Clean Up the Earth.* New York: Dell Publishing, 1990.

Morris, D.: A materials policy from the ground up. *The Green Lifestyle Handbook: 1001 Ways You Can Heal the Earth.* New York: Henry Holt & Co., 1990.

Smith, K.: Home economics. *The Green Lifestyle Handbook: 1001 Ways You Can Heal the Earth.* New York: Henry Holt & Co., 1990.

Chapter Eight: A Basic Scheme for Nutrition Education

Barnett, Kathy: Hunger: In *Discovering the World: Empowering Children to Value Themselves, Others, and the Earth.* Philadelphia: New Society Publishers, 1990.

Choose Well, Be Well: A Curriculum Guide for Preschool and Kindergarten. California State Department of Education, 1982.

Derman-Sparks, Louise, and the A.B.C. Task Force: *Anti-Bias Curriculum: Tools for Empowering Young Children.* Washington, DC: National Association for the Education of Young Children, 1989.

Earthworks Group. *50 Simple Things Kids Can Do to Save the Earth.* Kansas City: Andrews and McMeel, 1990.

Elkington, J., Hailes, J. Hill, D., and Makower, J. *Going Green: A Kid's Handbook to Saving the Planet.* New York: The Penguin Group, 1990.

Feeney, Lisa. *Learning Through Play: COOKING, A Practical Guide for Teaching Young Children.* New York: Scholastic Inc, 1992.

Hadingham, Evan and Janet. *Garbage! Where It Comes From, Where It Goes.* New York: Siman and Schuster, Inc., 1990.

Hertzler, A.: Preschoolers' food handling skills—motor development. *Journal of Nutrition Education* 21: 100B, 1989.

Hopkins, Susan. Families. In *Discovering the World: Empowering Children to Value Themselves, Others, and the Earth.* Philadelphia: New Society Publishers, 1990.

Olmstead, Kathy: World Foods. In *Discovering the World: Empowering Children to Value Themselves, Others, and the Earth.* Philadelphia: New Society Publishers, 1990.

Rubin, Laurie. *Food First Curriculum: An Integrated Curriculum Guide for Grade 6.* San Francisco: Institute for Food and Development Policy, 1984.

Schwab, M.G.: Participatory research with children: a new approach to nutrition education. *Journal of Nutrition Education* 21: 184B, 1989.

Appendix A—Special Topics

Allergies to Foods

The American Academy of Allergy, Asthma, and Immunology: *Food Allergies and Reactions.* www.aaaai.org.

Bock, S.A.: Prospective appraisal of complaints of adverse reactions to foods in children during the first 3 years of life. *Pediatrics* 79: 683, 1987.

Bock, S.A. and Sampson, H.A.: Food allergy in infancy. *Pediatric Clinics of North America* 41: 1047, 1994.

Cant, A.J.: Food allergy in childhood. *Human Nutrition: Applied Nutrition* 39A: 277, 1985.

FDA/CFSAN: *Advice to Consumers: Food Allergen Labeling and Consumer Protection Act of 2004 Questions and Answers,* December 12, 2005. www.cfsan.fda.gov/~dms/alrgqa.html.

Pipes, P.: Special concerns of dietary intake during infancy and childhood. *Nutrition in Infancy and Childhood,* Fourth Edition. St. Louis: Times Mirror/Mosby College Publishing, 1989.

Roesler, T.A., Barry, P.C., Bock, S.A.: Factitious food allergy and failure to thrive. *Archives of Pediatric and Adolescent Medicine* 148, 1159, 1994.

Roesler, T.A., Bock, S.A., and Leung, D.Y.M.: Management of the child presenting with allergy to multiple foods. *Clinical Pediatrics* Nov: 608, 1995.

Sicherer, S.H., Muñoz-Furlong, A., Murphy, R., Wood, R.A., and Sampson, H.A.: Symposium: Pediatric food allergy. *Pediatrics* 111: 1591-1594, 2005.

Zeigner, R.S. Food allergen avoidance in the prevention of food allergy in infants and children. *Pediatrics* 111:1662-1671, 2005.

Anemia and Iron Deficiency

Florentino, R.F. and Guirriec, R.M.: Prevalence of nutritional anemia in infancy and childhood with emphasis on developing countries. *Iron Nutrition in Infancy and Childhood.* New York: Nestle, Vevey/Raven Press, 1984.

Fomon, S.J.: Reflections on infant feeding in the 1970s and 1980s. *American Journal of Clinical Nutrition* 46:171, 1987.

Kline, N.: A practical approach to the child with anemia. *Journal of Pediatric Health Care* 10: 99, 1996.

Oski, F.A.: Iron deficiency in infancy and childhood. *New England Journal of Medicine* 329: 190, 1993.

Oski, F.A.: Iron deficiency—facts and fallacies. *Pediatric Clinics of North America* 32: 493, 1985.

Satter, E.: Feeding the toddler. *Child of Mine. Feeding with Love and Good Sense.* Boulder: Bull Publishing Co., 2000.

———. *The Relationship Between Nutrition and Learning. A School Employee's Guide to Information and Action.* Washington, D.C.: National Education Association, 1989.

Calcium and Osteoporosis

Abrams, B. and Berman, C,: Women, nutrition, and health. *Current Problems in Obstetric, Gynecology, and Fertility* XVI: 1, 1993.

Fassler, A.L.C. and Bonjour, J.P.: Osteoporosis as a pediatric problem. *Pediatric Clinics of North America* 42: 811, 1995.

Harvard School of Public Health, Department of Nutrition: Calcium and milk. www.hsph.harvard.edu/nutritionsource/

Meyer, M. and Larson, E.: Osteoporosis, and the vegetarian diet. *Vegetarian Journal* Nov/Dec: 8, 1995.

NIH Consensus Statement. Optimal Calcium Intake. *Nutrition* 11(5): 409, 1995.

Norris, J.M., Beaty, B., Klingensmith, G., Yu, L., Chase, H.P., Erlich, H.A., Hamman, R.F., Eisenbarth, G.S., and Rewers, M.: Lack of association between early exposure to cow's milk protein and b-cell autoimmunity. Diabetes Autoimmunity Study for the Young (DAISY). *JAMA* 276: 609, 1996.

Thomas, L.F., Keim, K.S., Long, E.M., and Zaske, J.M.: Factors related to low milk intake of 3- to 5-year-old children in child care settings. *JADA* 96: 911, 1996.

U.S. Department of Health and Human Services and U.S. Department of Agriculture. *Dietary Guidelines for Americans, 2005.* 6th edition, Washington, DC: U.S. Government Printing Office, January 2005. www.healthierus.gov/dietaryguidelines.

Wyshak, G. and Frisch, R.E.: Carbonated beverages, dietary calcium, the dietary calcium/phosphorus ratio, and bone fractures in girls and boys. *Journal of Adolescent Health* 15: 210, 1994.

Choking on Food

Caring for Our Children: National health and Safety Performance Standards: Guidelines for Out-of-Home Child Care Programs, 2nd edition. Elk Grove Village, IL: American Academy of Pediatrics and Washington, DC: American Public Health Association. Available at: http://nrc.uchsc.edu.

Food and Nutrition Service. *Feeding Infants. A Guide for Use in the Child Care Food Program.* Washington, D.C.: U.S. Department of Agriculture, 1988.

Harris, C.S., Baker, S.P., Smith, G.A., and Harris, R.M.: Childhood asphyxiation by food. A national analysis and overview. *JAMA* 251: 2231, 1984.

Pipes, P.L.and Trahms, C.M.: The preschool-age child. *Nutrition in Infancy and Childhood*, Fifth Edition. St. Louis: Times Mirror/Mosby College Publishing, 1993.

Project Care for Children: *Childhood Emergencies. What to Do.* Boulder: Bull Publishing Company, 1987.

Constipation

Conference on Dietary Fiber in Childhood, New York, May 24, 1994: A summary of conference recommendations on dietary fiber in childhood. *Pediatrics* 96(5): 1023, 1995.

Dwyer, J.T.: Dietary fiber for children: how much? *Pediatrics* 96(5): 1019, 1995.

Hillemeier, C: An overview of the effects of dietary fiber on gastrointestinal transit. *Pediatrics* 96(5): 997, 1995.

McClung, H.J., Boyne, L., and Heitlinger, L.: Constipation and dietary fiber intake in children. *Pediatrics* 96(5): 999, 1995.

Rappaport, L.A. and Levine, M.D.: The prevention of constipation and encopresis: a developmental model and approach. *Pediatric Clinics of North America* 33:859, 1986.

Saldanha, L: Fiber in the diet of U.S. children: results of national surveys. *Pediatrics* 96(5): 994, 1995.

Williams, C.L. and Bollella, M.: Is a high-fiber diet safe for children? *Pediatrics* 96(5): 1014, 1995.

Williams, C.L., Bollella, M., and Wynder, E.L.: A new recommendation for dietary fiber in childhood. *Pediatrics* 96(5): 985, 1995.

Dental Health

DeBruyne, L.K. and Rolfes, S.R.: Focal point 3: dental health. *Life Cycle Nutrition. Conception Through Adolescence.* St. Paul: West Publishing Company, 1989.

Diabetes and Other Chronic Diseases

Pipes, P. and Glass, R.:Developmental disabilities and other health care needs. *Nutrition in Infancy and Childhood*, Fifth Edition. St. Louis: Times Mirror/Mosby College Publishing, 1993.

Satter, E.: Feeding the child with special needs. *How to Get Your Kid to Eat...But Not Too Much.* Boulder: Bull Publishing Company, 1987.

Siminerio, L.M. and Betschart, J. *Children with Diabetes.* Alexandria, VA: The American Diabetes Association, Inc., 1986.

———: Diet for cystic fibrosis. *Manual of Clinical Dietetics.* Chicago: The American Dietetic Association, 1988.

———: Inborn errors of metabolism. *Manual of Clinical Dietetics.*Chicago: The American Dietetic Association, 1988.

Diarrhea

Cohen, S.A., Hendricks, K.M., Eastham, E.J., Mathis, R.K., and Walker, W.A.: Chronic nonspecific diarrhea, a complication of dietary fat restriction. *American Journal of Diseases in Childhood* 133: 490, 1979.

Green, H.L. and Ghishan, F.K.: Excessive fluid intake as a cause of chronic diarrhea in young children. *Journal of Pediatrics* 102: 836, 1983.

Hyams, J.S., Etienne, N.L., Leichtner, A.M., and Theuer, R.C.: Carbohydrate malabsorption following fruit juice ingestion in young children. *Pediatrics* 82: 64, 1988.

Hyams, J.S. and Leichtner, A.M.: Apple juice: an unappreciated cause of chronic diarrhea. *American Journal of Diseases in Childhood* 139: 503, 1985.

Kneepkens, C.M.F. and Hoekstra, J.H.: Chronic nonspecific diarrhea of childhood. Pathophysiology and management. *Pediatric Clinics of North America* 43: 375, 1996.

Lloyd-Still, J.D.: Chronic diarrhea of childhood and the misuse of elimination diets. *Journal of Pediatrics* 95: 10, 1979.

Managing acute gastroenteritis among children: Oral rehydration, maintenance, and nutritional therapy. *MMWR* 52: 1-16, November 21, 2003.

Satter, E.: Diarrhea. *Child of Mine. Feeding with Love and Good Sense*. Boulder: Bull Publishing Co., 2000.

Eating Disorders

Satter, E.: Eating disorders. *Child of Mine. Feeding with Love and Good Sense*. Boulder: Bull Publishing Co., 2000.

Satter, E.: Eating disorders. *How to Get Your Kid to Eat...But Not Too Much*. Boulder: Bull Publishing Company, 1987.

Food-Drug Interactions

Powers, D.E. and Moore, A.O. *Food Medication Interactions*. Phoenix: F-M I Publishing, 1986.

"Junk Food"

Satter, E.: Nutritional tactics for preventing food fights. *How to Get Your Kid to Eat...But Not Too Much.* Boulder: Bull Publishing Company, 1987.

Shapiro, L.R., Crawford, P.B., Clark, M.J., Pearson, D.J., Ray, J., and Huenemann, R.L.: Obesity prognosis: a longitudinal study of children from the age of 6 months to 9 years. *American Journal of Public Health* 74: 968, 1984.

————: Accounting for taste. University of California, Berkeley, *Wellness Letter* 7: 7, 1990.

Lactose Intolerance

Committee on Nutrition, American Academy of Pediatrics: Practical significance of lactose intolerance in children: supplement. *Pediatrics* 86: 643, 1990.

Low-Fat Diets and Children

American Academy of Pediatrics: Endorsed Policy Statement: Dietary recommendations for children and adolescents: A guide for practitioners. *Pediatrics* 117(2): 544-559, 2006.

Committee on Nutrition, American Academy of Pediatrics: Statement on cholesterol. *Pediatrics* 90: 469, 1992.

Gaull, G.E., Giombetti, T., and Yeaton Woo, R.W.: Pediatric dietary lipid guidelines: a policy analysis. *Journal of the American College of Nutrition* 14: 411, 1995.

Gidding, S.S., Deckelbaum, R.J., Strong, W., and Moller, J.H.: Improving children's heart health: a report from the American Heart Association's Children's Heart Health Conference. *Journal of School Health* 65: 129, 1995.

Lifshitz, F. and Moses, N.: Growth failure. A complication of dietary treatment of hypercholesterolemia. *American Journal of Diseases in Childhood* 143: 537, 1989.

National Cholesterol Education Program: Report of the expert panel on blood cholesterol levels in children and adolescents. *Pediatrics* 89 (suppl): 525, 1992.

Newman, W., Freedman, D.S. and Voors, A.W.: Relation of serum lipoprotein levels and systolic blood pressure to early atherosclerosis. *New England Journal of Medicine* 314: 138, 1986.

Nicklas, T.A., Webber, L.S., Koshak, M., and Berenson, G.S.: Nutrient adequacy of low fat intakes for children: the Bogalusa Heart Study. *Pediatrics* 89: 221, 1992.

Nicklas, T.A., Webber, L.S., Johnson, C.C., Srinivasan, S.R., and Berenson, G.S.: Foundations for health promotion with youth: a review of observations from the Bogalusa Heart Study. *Journal of Health Education* 26 (suppl): S18, 1995.

Pugliese, M.T., Weyman-Daum, M., Moses, N., and Lifshitz, F.: Parental health beliefs as a cause of nonorganic failure to thrive. *Pediatrics* 80: 175, 1987.

Tershakovec, A.M., Shamiz, R., Van Horn, L., and Shannon, B: Dietary recommendations for children. *American Journal of Clinical Nutrition* 62: 443, 1995.

U.S. Department of Health and Human Services and U.S. Department of Agriculture. *Dietary Guidelines for Americans, 2005.* 6th edition, Washington, DC: U.S. Government Printing Office, January 2005. www.healthierus.gov/dietaryguidelines.

Sodium

Sodium Scoreboard. Washington, D.C.: Center for Science in the Public Interest.

U.S. Department of Health and Human Services and U.S. Department of Agriculture. *Dietary Guidelines for Americans, 2005.* 6th edition, Washington, DC: U.S. Government Printing Office, January 2005. www.healthierus.gov/dietaryguidelines.

Wrap-up: sodium. University of California, Berkeley *Wellness Letter* 2:4, 1986.

Special Needs and Feeding

Pipes, P. and Glass, R. Developmental disabilities and other health care needs. *Nutrition in Infancy and Childhood*, Fifth Edition. St. Louis: Times Mirror/Mosby College Publishing, 1993.

Satter, Ellyn. *How to Get Your Kid to Eat...But Not Too Much.* Boulder: Bull Publishing Company, 1987.

Sugar, Food Additives, and Children's Behavior

Bachorowski, J., Newman, J.P., Nichols, S.L., Gans, D.A., Harper, A.E., and Taylor, S.L.: Sucrose and delinquency: behavioral assessment. *Pediatrics* 86: 244, 1990.

Kaplan, B.J., McNichol, J., Conte, R.A., and Moghadam, H.K.: Dietary replacement in preschool-aged hyperactive boys. *Pediatrics* 83: 7, 1989.

Rowe, K.S., and Rowe, K.J.: Synthetic food coloring and behavior: a dose response effect in a double-blind, placebo-controlled, repeated-measures study. *Journal of Pediatrics* 125: 691, 1994.

Whitney, E.N., Cataldo, C.B., and Rolfes, S.R.: *Nutrition and behavior. Understanding Normal and Clinical Nutrition.* St. Paul: West Publishing Company, 1988.

Wolraich, M.L., Lindgren, S.D., Stumbo, P.J., Stegink, L.D., Appelbaum, M.I., and Kiritsy, M.C.: Effects of diets high in sucrose or aspartame on the behavior and cognitive performance of children. *New England Journal of Medicine* 330: 301, 1994.

Wolraich, M.L., Wilson, D.B., and White, J.W. : The effect of sugar on behavior or cognition in children. A meta-analysis. *JAMA* 274: 1617, 1995.

———: Sugar may jolt adrenaline in kids. *Environmental Nutrition* 13(7): 3, 1990.

Television

American Academy of Pediatrics, Committee on Public Education: Children, adolescents, and television. *Pediatrics* 107: 423-426, 2001.

Committee on Communications, American Academy of Pediatrics: The commercialization of children's television. *Pediatrics* 89: 343, 1992.

DuRant, R.H., Baranowski, T., Johnson, M., and Thompson, W.O.: The relationship among television watching, physical activity, and body composition of young children. *Pediatrics* 94: 449, 1994.

Kaiser Family Foundation: *Issue Brief: The role of media in childhood obesity.* February 2004. www.kff.org.

Klesges, R.C., Shelton, M.L., and Klesges, L.M.: Effects of television on metabolic rate: potential implications for childhood obesity. *Pediatrics* 91, 281, 1993.

Schmidt, S.: Hawking food to kids. *Nutrition Action Healthletter* 16: 1, 1989.

Sylvester, G.P., Achterberg, C., and Williams, J.: Children's television and nutrition: friends or foes? *Nutrition Today* 30, 6, 1995.

Taras, H.L. and Gage, M.: Advertised foods on children's television. Archives of *Pediatric and Adolescent Medicine* 149: 649, 1993.

Trahms, C.: Factors that shape food patterns in young children. *Nutrition in Infancy and Childhood*, Fifth Edition. St. Louis: Times Mirror/Mosby College Publishing, 1993.

———. *Promoting Nutritional Health During the Preschool Years*. Canadian Guidelines. Network of the Federal/ Provincial/ Territorial Group on Nutrition and National Institute of Nutrition, 1989.

Underweight Children

Satter, E.: The child who grows poorly. *How to Get Your Kid to Eat...But Not Too Much*. Boulder: Bull Publishing Company, 1987.

Vegetarianism

O'Connell, J.M., Dibley, M.J., Sierra, J., Wallace, B., Marks, J.S., and Yip, R.: Growth of vegetarian children: the Farm study. *Pediatrics* 84: 475, 1989.

Saunders, T.A.B.: Vegetarian diets and children. *Pediatric Clinics of North America* 42, 955, 1995.

Trahms, C.: Vegetarian diets for children. *Nutrition in Infancy and Childhood, Fifth Edition*. St. Louis: Times Mirror/Mosby College Publishing, 1993.

Vitamin and Mineral Supplements

American Academy of Pediatrics, Committee on Nutrition: Vitamin and mineral supplement needs of normal children in the United States. *Pediatrics* 66: 1015, 1980.

Appendix B: Nutrition Basics

Christakis, G. (ed). *Nutritional Assessment in Health Programs*. Washington, DC: American Public Health Association, 1973.

Duyff, R. L.: *American Dietetic Association Complete Food and Nutrition Resource Guide*, 2nd edition. New Jersey: John Wiley & Sons, Inc. 2002.

Food and Nutrition Board, National Academy of Sciences. Dietary Reference Intakes (DRI) and Recommended Dietary Allowances (RDA). Accessed at: www.nal.usda.gov/fnic/etext/000105.html

Margen, S. and the Editors of the UC Berkeley Wellness Letter: *Wellness Foods A to Z*. New York: Rebus, Inc. 2002.

MyPyramid. www.mypyramid.gov

U.S. Department of Health and Human Services and U.S. Department of Agriculture. *Dietary Guidelines for Americans, 2005*. 6th edition, Washington, DC: U.S. Government Printing Office, January 2005. www.healthierus.gov/dietaryguidelines.

Appendix D

. . . .

Resources

General Nutrition

The American Dietetic Association Complete Food and Nutrition Resource Guide, 2nd edition by Roberta Larson Duyff. New Jersey: John Wiley & Sons, Inc. 2002.

Federal Citizen Information Center
(Booklets and free downloads on a variety of consumer topics)
Dept. WWW
Pueblo, CO 81009
(888) 8PUEBLO
www.pueblo.gsa.gov

MyPyramid website
www.mypyramid.gov

Nutrition Action Healthletter
Center for Science in the Public Interest (CSPI)
1875 Connecticut Ave. NW
Suite 300
Washington, DC 20009-5728
(202) 332-9110
www.cspinet.org

The Nutrition Source: Knowledge for Healthy Eating
Department of Nutrition
Harvard School of Public Health
www.hsph.harvard.edu/nutritionsource/

Tufts University Health and Nutrition Letter
P.O. Box 420233
Palm Coast, FL 32142-0235
(800) 274-7581
http://healthletter.tufts.edu/

U.S. Department of Health and Human Services and U.S. Department of Agriculture. *Dietary Guidelines for Americans, 2005.* 6th edition, Washington, DC: U.S. Government Printing Office, January 2005.
www.healthierus.gov/dietaryguidelines.

U.S. National Library of Medicine and National Institutes of Health
(Links to a variety of nutrition resources)
www.nlm.nih.gov/medlineplus/nutrition.html

University of California at Berkeley Wellness Letter
P.O. Box 420148
Palm Coast, FL 32142
(800) 829-9170
www.wellnessletter.com

Wellness Foods A to Z by Sheldon Margen and the Editors of the UC Berkeley Wellness Letter. New York: Rebus, Inc. 2002.

What to Eat by Marion Nestle. New York: North Point Press. 2006.

Child Health and Nutrition

Administration for Children & Families
U.S. Department of Health and Human Services
Fit Source links to food and activity resources for child care
http://www2.nccic.org/fitsource/

American Dietetic Association and Gerber Foods: *Start Healthy*™ *Stay Healthy Feeding Guidelines*, 2005. www.gerber.com.

Baylor College of Medicine
USDA Children's Nutrition Research Center
www.kidsnutrition.org

Caring for Our Children: National health and Safety Performance Standards: Guidelines for Out-of-Home Child Care Programs, 2nd edition. Elk Grove Village, IL: American Academy of Pediatrics and Washington, DC: American Public Health Association. *and:* American Academy of Pediatrics, American Public Health Association, and National Resource Center for Health and Safety in Child Care: *Stepping Stones to Using Caring for Our Children: National Health and Safety Performance Standards, 2nd ed.* 2003. Available at: http://nrc.uchsc.edu

Child of Mine: Feeding with Love and Good Sense by Ellyn Satter. Boulder: Bull Publishing Company, 2000. www.bullpub.com

Dairy Council of California
www.mealsmatter.org

Healthy Child Care America
American Academy of Pediatrics
www.healthychildcare.org

Healthy Kids Challenge
www.healthykidschallenge.com
Healthy eating and physical activity resources.

How to Get Your Kid to Eat...But Not Too Much by Ellyn Satter. Boulder: Bull Publishing Company, 1987. www.bullpub.com

Kids in Action: Fitness for Children Birth to Age Five
www.fitness.gov/funfit/kidsinaction.html

Kidnetic
www.kidnetic.com
Healthy eating and active living website targeting kids age 9-12.

Mealtime Memos for Child Care (in English and Spanish).
National Food Service Management Institute (NFSMI)
www.nfsmi.org/Information/Newsletters/index.html

Tiny Tummies
P.O. Box 5756
Napa, CA 94581
(707) 251-0550
www.tinytummies.com
Written by a registered dietitian, this monthly newsletter offers nutrition information for parents and children.

Breastfeeding Support

Breastfed Babies Welcome Here. Toolkit from
Supplemental Food Programs
Division Food and Nutrition Service—USDA
3101 Park Center Drive
Alexandria, VA 22302
(703) 305-2746

La Leche League
www.lalecheleague.org

The National Women's Health Information center
www.4woman.gov/breastfeeding

Food Allergies

Dealing with Food Allergies: A Practical Guide to Detecting Culprit Foods and Eating a Healthy, Enjoyable Diet by Janice Vickerstaff Joneja. Boulder: Bull Publishing Company, 2003. www.bullpub.com

The Food Allergy and Anaphylaxis Network
11781 Lee Jackson Hwy, Suite 160
Fairfax, VA 22033
(800) 929-4040 (orders)
www.foodallergy.org
This national nonprofit organization was established to help families learn to cope with food allergies and increase public awareness about food allergies and anaphylaxis. Books, videos, some supplies, and memberships (including a newsletter) are available.

Healthy School Meals Resource System
http://schoolmeals.nal.usda.gov/Resource/specialdiets.html

Living Without Magazine
Lifestyle Guide for People with Allergies and Food Sensitivities
(847) 480-8810
www.livingwithout.com
In addition to articles, there are extensive lists of resources on the website.

Diabetes

American Diabetes Association
1701 North Beauregard Street
Alexandria, VA 22311
(800) DIABETES
www.diabetes.org

Dealing with Diabetes Mellitus—A Practical Handbook, 8th ed. by Sue K. Milchovich and Barbara Dunn-Long. Boulder: Bull Publishing Company, 2002.
www.bullpub.com

Diabetic Cooking Magazine
http://diabeticcooking.com

Exchanges for All Occasions: Meeting the Challenge of Diabetes, 4th ed. By Marion J. Franz. Minneapolis: Chronimed Publishing, 1997.
Diabetic exchange lists, recipes, and hints for managing events like travel, illness, and children's parties.

Everyone Likes to Eat. How Children Can Eat Most of the Foods They Enjoy and Still Take Care of Their Diabetes, 2nd edition, by Hugo J. Hollerorth, Ed.D., and Debra Kaplan, RD, MS. New Jersey: John Wiley & Sons, Inc., 1993.

Healthy School Meals Resource System
http://schoolmeals.nal.usda.gov/Resource/specialdiets-diabetes.htm

Prana Publications
5623 Matilija Ave.
Van Nuys, CA 91401
(818) 780-1308
Source of many self-help books for people with diabetes, including a large collection of books for children with diabetes and for their parents or caregivers.

Other Special Feeding Needs

Children's Disabilities Information
www.childrensdisabilities.info/feeding/

Healthy School Meals Resource System
http://schoolmeals.nal.usda.gov/Resource/specialdiets-other.htm

National Food Service Management Institute
NSFMI Special Needs Fact Sheets for Child Nutrition Professionals
www.nfsmi.org/Information/Newsletters/Special_index.html

Gluten Intolerance Group
15110 10 Ave. SW, Suite A
Seattle, WA 98166-1820
(206) 246-6652
www.gluten.net

Celiac Disease Foundation
13251 Ventura Blvd., Suite 1
Studio City, CA 91604-1838
(818) 990-2354
www.celiac.org

Children's P.K.U. Network (CPN)
(858) 509-0767
PKUnetwork@aol.com

National PKU News
http://web47.radiant.net/~pkunews/index.htm

Nutritionists in state and local health departments

Pediatric nutritionists, occupational therapists, and physical therapists in programs serving children with special needs; for example, genetics treatment centers, diagnostic evaluation centers, and teaching hospitals.

Vegetarian Children

The New Laurel's Kitchen by Laurel Robertson, Carol Flinders, and Brian Ruppenthal. Berkeley: Ten Speed Press, 1986.

The Vegan Handbook, edited by Debra Wasserman and Reed Mangels, Ph.D.
The Vegetarian Resource Group
PO Box 1463, Baltimore, MD 21203
(410)366-8343
www.vrg.org

VegFamily Online Magazine
"The Magazine for Vegan Family Living"
www.vegfamily.com

Cooking and Information About Foods

Centers for Disease Control and Prevention 5-a-Day website with information about many fruits and vegetables in English and Spanish: www.cdc.gov/nccdphp/dnpa/5aDay/ and www.cdc.gov/nccdphp/dnpa/5AlDia/

Cooking Light Magazine
P.O. Box 62376
Tampa. FL 33662
www.cookinglight.com

Dole Food Company
www.dole5aday.com
Information on fruits and vegetables, recipes, and interactive learning for kids

Eating Well Magazine
823A Ferry Rd.
P.O. Box 52919

Charlotte, VT 05445
(802) 425-5700
www.eatingwell.com

www.epicurious.com
(extensive free recipe database)

Five A Day the Color Way
Produce for Better Health Foundation
www.5aday.org

www.harvestofthemonth.com
(fruit and vegetable information, activities, and parent handouts in English and Spanish)

www.molliekatzen.com
(food tidbits and recipes from a popular cookbook author)

The World's Healthiest Foods
George Mateljan Foundation
www.whfoods.org

Food Safety

FDA Food Information Line (toll-free)
(888) SAFEFOOD

Gateway to Government Food Safety Information
www.foodsafety.gov

Healthy School Meals Resource System
http://schoolmeals.nal.usda.gov/Safety/FNSFoodSafety.htm

National Food Service Management Institute (NFSMI)
Free food safety posters and training materials
www.nfsmi.org/Information/postindx.htm

National Lead Information Center
(800) 424-LEAD
www.epa.gov/lead/

National Restaurant Association Educational Foundation
(800)765-2122
www.nraef.org/
Offers a variety of handbooks and complete training packages about food safety.

USDA Meat and Poultry Hotline
(800) 535-4555
In Washington, DC: (202) 720-333
TTY: (800) 256-7072

U.S. Food and Drug Administration
Center for Food Safety and Applied Nutrition
www.cfsan.fda.gov

Earth-Friendly Cleaning and Home Supplies

Clean and Green. The Complete Guide to Nontoxic and Environmentally Safe Housekeeping by Annie-Berthold-Bond. Woodstock, NY: Ceres Press, 1994.

Clean House, Clean Planet by Karen Logan. New York: Pocket Books, 1997.

Planet Natural
(800) 289-6656
www.planetnatural.com

Real Goods/Gaiam
(800) 919-2400
www.realgoods.com

Social and Environmental Concerns

Center for Ecoliteracy
2528 San Pablo Avenue
Berkeley, CA 94702
www.ecoliteracy.org
We can't recommend this site enough for thoughtful essays on food topics and sustainable living and useful guides to and school gardens and reforming school lunch programs.

The Center for Food Safety
660 Pennsylvania Ave. SE, #302
Washington, DC 20003
(202) 547-9359
www.centerforfoodsafety.org
Promotion of organic/sustainable agriculture.

Children's Health Environmental Coalition
12300 Wilshire Blvd., Suite 410
Los Angeles, CA 90025
(310) 820-2030
www.checnet.org/
Education about environmental toxins and their effects on children.

Consumers Union Guide to Environmental labels
www.eco-labels.org

Environmental Working Group
www.ewg.org
Lots of information on the relationship between health and the environment.

Farmers Market Information
www.ams.usda.gov/farmersmarkets/map.htm

50 Simple Things Kids Can Do to Recycle by The EarthWorks Group. Berkeley: EarthWorks Press, 1994.
This book is full of recycling projects for children, offers clear explanations of recycling concepts, and has an extensive listing of resources for books, pamphlets, videos, and recycling curricula.

National Resources Defense Council
www.nrdc.org

Oldways Preservation and Exchange Trust
266 Beacon Street
Boston, MA 02116
(617) 421-5500
www.oldwayspt.org/
The "food issues think tank" has lots of interesting information, including food pyramids from different cultures.

Organic Consumers Association
www.organicconsumers.org

Redefining Progress and Earthday Network
www.myfootprint.org
Interactive website that lets you discover your own "ecological footprint."

TV-Turnoff Network
1200 29th Street NW, LL#1
Washington, DC 20007
(202) 333-9220
www.tvturnoff.org

Gardening with Children

California Foundation for Agriculture in the Classroom
www.cfaitc.org/

Gardening Wizardry for Kids by L. Patricia Kite. New York: Barron's, 1995.
This book contains a huge array of activities and interesting information about plant foods.

Lifelab Science Program
www.lifelab.org
Curricula and activity guides for garden-based education.
Including:

The Growing Classroom...Garden-Based Science by Roberta Jaffe and Gary Appel. Menlo Park: Addison-Wesley Publishing Company, 1990. A comprehensive garden-based curriculum for schools.

Getting Started: A Guide for Creating School Gardens as Outdoor Classrooms by the Center for Ecoliteracy and Lifelab Science program, 2006.

National Agriculture in the Classroom Office
Stop 2251
U.S. Department of Agriculture
1400 Independence Ave. NW
Washington, DC 20250-2251
www.agclassroom.org

National Gardening Association
www.kidsgardening.com

Roots, Shoots, Buckets, and Boots by Sharon Lovejoy. New York: Workman Publishing Company, 1999.

Cooking with Kids

Cook and Learn: Pictorial Single Portion Recipes by Beverly Veitch and Thelma Harms. Menlo Park: Addison-Wesley Publishing Company, 1981.

The Cooking Book: Fostering Young Children's Learning and Delight by Laura J. Colker. Washington, DC: National Association for the Education of Young Children, 2005.

The Healthy Start Kids' Cookbook: Fun and Healthy Recipes that Kids Can Make Themselves by Sandra K. Nissenbuerg, MS,RD. New Jersey: John Wiley & Sons, Inc., 1994.

Honest Pretzels and 64 Other Amazing Recipes for Cooks Ages 8 & Up by Mollie Katzen. Berkeley: Tricycle Press, 1999.

Learning Through Play: COOKING, A Practical Guide for Teaching Young Children by Lisa Feeney. New York: Scholastic Inc, 1992.
This book is a must-have for anyone cooking with groups of children. It offers thorough coverage of kitchen setup and safety, including a section on cooking with children who have special needs, developmental considerations, and activity plans for cooking experiences that use healthful ingredients.

Pretend Soup and Other Real Recipes: A Cookbook for Preschoolers & Up by Molly Katzen and Ann Henderson. Berkeley: Tricycle Press, 1994.

Salad People and More Real Recipes: A New Cookbook for Preschoolers & Up by Mollie Katzen. Berkeley and Toronto: Tricycle Press, 2005.

The Travel-the-World Cookbook by Pamela Marx. Glenview, IL: GoodYearBooks, 1996.

Other Nutrition Education

How to Teach Nutrition to Kids by Connie Liakos Evers. 24 Carrot Press, 2006. Activities for kids ages 6-12. The website has a free newsletter, recipes, and more. www.nutritionforkids.com

More Than Mud Pies, 4th ed. From the National Food Service Management Institute. Fifty-nine lessons for preschoolers on how foods grow, how to prepare them, and nutrition (Free). (800) 623-7266 www.nfsmi.org/Information/mudpies.html

Nutrition Activities for Preschoolers by Debby Cryer, Thelma Harms, and Adele Richardson Ray. Pearson Learning, 1996.

Sesame Street Healthy Habits for Life
www.sesameworkshop.org/healthyhabits

Smartmouth (Center for Science in the Public Interest)
www.cspinet.org/smartmouth
Fun interactive website for kids.

Miscellaneous Resources

The American Dietetic Association
216 W. Jackson Boulevard
Chicago, IL 60606-6995
(800)877-1600, ext 5000
www.eatright.org
Offers a variety of educational materials for an adult audience.

DINE Systems, Inc.
163 Brunswick Electric Road
Whiteville, NC 28472
(800) 688-1848
www.dinesystems.com
Nutrition education/diet analysis software.

Foodplay Productions
221 Pine Street
Florence, MA 01062
(800) FOODPLAY
Nutrition videos and guidebooks.

Laptop Lunches (Obentec, Inc.)
849 Almar Ave., Suite C-323
Santa Cruz, CA 95060
(831) 457-0301
www.laptoplunches.com
Earth-friendly lunch boxes, recipes, and a free newsletter

NASCO educational materials
(800) 558-9595
www.enasco.com

National School Products
101 East Broadway
Maryville, TN 37804-2498
(800) 627-9393 (ask for the nutrition catalog)
www.nationalschoolproducts.com
Stickers, videos, food replicas, computer software, and many other educational products.

NCES (Nutrition Counseling Education Services)
1904 East 123rd Street
Olathe, KS 66061-5886
(800) 623-7266
www.ncescatalog.com
Books, videos, games, and other teaching aids.

Neat Solutions, Inc.
(888) 577-6328
www.neatsolutions.com
Huge variety of nutrition resources

Noteworthy Creations, Inc.
P.O. Box 335
Delphi, IN 46923
(800) 305-4167
www.funwithfood.com
Nutrition education materials for children.

Produce for Better Health Foundation
5 A Day The Color Way—5 A Day Catalog
(888) 391-2100
www.shop5aday.com

Scholastic, Inc.
(800) 724-6527
www.scholastic.com
Books, videos, and professional resources.

Yummy Designs
(888) 74YUMMY
Puppets, books, games, and audiotapes
www.yummydesigns.com

Index